Profiting from the Bank
and
Savings & Loan Crisis

ALSO BY STEPHEN PIZZO AND PAUL MUOLO

Inside Job (with Mary Fricker)

Profiting from the Bank
and
Savings & Loan Crisis

....

How Anyone Can Find Bargains
at America's Greatest Garage Sale

....

Stephen Pizzo and Paul Muolo

HarperBusiness
A Division of HarperCollins*Publishers*

Designed by Irving Perkins Associates

The Library of Congress has catalogued the hardcover edition as follows:

Pizzo, Stephen.
Profiting from the bank and savings & loan crisis : how anyone can find
bargains at America's greatest garage sale / Stephen Pizzo and
Paul Muolo. — 1st ed.
p.   cm.
Includes index.
ISBN 0-88730-596-2
1. Real estate investment—United States.   2. Government sale of
real property—United States.   3. Savings and Loan Bailout, 1989–
4. Resolution Trust Corporation (U.S.)—Information services.
5. Federal Deposit Insurance Corporation—Information services.
I. Muolo, Paul.   II. Title.
HD1382.5.P585   1993
332.67′24′0973—dc20   92-53369

ISBN 0-88730-665-9 (pbk.)
94 95 96 97 98 PS/**CW** 10 9 8 7 6 5 4 3 2 1

For the nation's taxpayers

Contents

Introduction to the Paperback Edition

A great deal has changed since this book was published in hardcover back in February 1993. For starters, the Resolution Trust Corporation and the Federal Deposit Insurance Corporation—the two government agencies responsible for liquidating failed S&Ls and banks—have made great progress in auctioning off billions of dollars' worth of real estate and loans.

Three years ago the two agencies had an asset inventory of $400 billion. Today that inventory is down to about $100 billion. For the investor, that means less to choose from.

But don't despair. While the RTC and the FDIC are starting to run low on inventory, the private sector—mostly "healthy" banks and insurance companies—has copied their sales techniques right down to the tee.

In short, the RTC and FDIC have been trailblazers when it comes to auctioning real estate and loans. For the investor—whether you are a "little guy" or a "wheeler-dealer"—that means there will be plenty to choose from during the next few years.

Great Western Bank FSB, Beverly Hills, for example, has been auctioning repossessed homes in southern California, using the same sales techniques as the RTC. Citibank in New York has been selling repossessed apartments, condos, and cooperatives as well. Ditto for many of the nation's insurance companies, including the Travelers Corp., Hartford, Connecticut, and Prudential, Newark, New Jersey.

Every week the *Wall Street Journal* and the *New York Times* carry advertisements in their Friday editions announcing real estate auctions of all types—for example, condos in New York and New Jersey that have beginning bid prices of $25,000 or less. It sounds crazy, but it's true.

The techniques outlined in this book, which originally applied to the RTC and FDIC, can be used by investors to buy homes, real estate, and loans from any bank or insurance company in the nation.

These techniques also can be used to buy property from the Department of Housing and Urban Development (HUD) and the General Services Administration (GSA). HUD administers foreclosed loans made by the Federal Housing Administration and the Veterans Administration. GSA has been given the task of overseeing the enormous liquidation of billions of dollars' worth of real estate belonging to the armed services. Remember all the press reports about downsizing the military? Well, the time has come. Think about it: entire air force and army installations and the housing on those bases—all will be sold to the highest bidder.

Keep in mind that other government agencies, including the U.S. Marshals Service, also auction real estate and other assets that once belonged to convicted felons. (Why pay premium when you can buy it cheap from the government?)

Yes, the RTC and FDIC are downsizing. The RTC has just six offices left—Atlanta, Dallas, Denver, Kansas City, Newport Beach, and Valley Forge—compared to more than twenty three years ago. The FDIC hopes to reduce its field offices to seven by 1996, compared to twenty-two in 1993. What happened? Low interest rates and "fire sales" by both agencies helped reduce their enormous caseload. Many investors made out like bandits, while others sat on the sidelines.

These agencies still have plenty to sell but the pickings will get slimmer. Still, as we've noted, look to the private sector for the real bargains, but don't discount the RTC and FDIC. As Yogi Berra once said: "It ain't over until it's over."

STEPHEN PIZZO AND PAUL MUOLO
December 1993

Introduction

● ●

Anybody who buys from the Resolution Trust Corporation is going to make a profit.

—ALBERT CASEY,
former RTC chief executive officer

During the past decade the gap between rich and poor widened to an unbridgeable chasm. The traditional bridge over that gap—the American middle class—shrank while the number of millionaires doubled. Some of the luckier ones made it across the middle-class bridge into the "Promised Land" of the 1980s, but many more were left behind to worry about how they were going to afford housing, medical care, food, and education for their children. Economists are now concerned that this polarity between rich and poor could become permanent and upset the delicate social chemistry that sustained a once robust American economy—an economy predicated on the promise of upward mobility.

But for those who despair that this bleak prediction might be true, and for those who missed the 1980s gravy train, we have some very good news. The train is back. But don't miss it again, because it very well might be the last good ride for a very long time. This gravy train isn't operated by savings and loan high flyers or Wall Street insider traders. This is a government-controlled railroad called the RTC & FDIC. The

RTC (Resolution Trust Corporation) sells assets of failed savings and loans. The FDIC (Federal Deposit Insurance Corporation) sells the assets of failed banks. And both agencies have billions of dollars worth of real estate, loans, and other assets to sell.

The financial meltdown of America's savings and loans, as well as its banks, has been catastrophic for our society. Together, the two debacles will sap much-needed taxpayer resources well into the twenty-first century. But for investors who know how to use the system, this cloud has a $100 billion silver lining: dirt-cheap homes, apartment buildings, timeshares, office buildings, raw land, automobiles, office equipment—all of which can be purchased without limit by just about anyone. In the pages ahead we will tell you how to tap into this gold mine.

So if you were among those left behind in the 1980s and don't have a lot of money to invest, or if you have money and want terrific investment bargains, this book is for you.

Come On In, the Water's Fine

John Lewis, a renter all of his life, knew exactly which house he wanted to buy. It was the one he was already renting with his wife, Lula, and their three children in suburban Pensacola, Florida. The three-bedroom home was owned by Citizens and Builders Savings Association, a local S&L that had taken title to the house after its previous owner stopped making mortgage payments. The Lewises rented the house from Citizens for $300 a month and even made a bid to buy it in 1989, offering $22,000 for the home, which had been listed at $35,000. The thrift[1] rejected their bid.

In early 1991 Citizens and Builders Savings was shut down by federal S&L regulators and the Lewises' home was taken over by the Resolution Trust Corporation (RTC), the government agency created in 1989 to clean up and sell the nation's insolvent S&Ls.

In late 1991 the Lewises learned that the RTC would sell their home at public auction to the highest bidder. The family was there the day the bids were taken, and when the auctioneer's gavel fell the home had

---

[1] "Thrift" is a synonym for S&L—as in it used to be "thrifty" to save so people placed their money in a savings institution or "thrift."

new owners—the Lewises. And much to their delight, they paid just $11,500 for it, about a third of what it was worth.

To sweeten the deal further, the RTC even loaned the couple the money to buy the home. The Lewises only had to put down $500 in cash, and the rest was financed by the government. Today their monthly mortgage payment is just $125 a month—less than half their rent.

Frederick E. Miles of Marblehead, Massachusetts, was shopping for a bargain. Mr. Miles had heard that the government was chin-deep in assets from failed S&Ls and banks. For months he and his wife, Jean, had shopped for just the right deal by attending public real estate auctions held by the Resolution Trust Corporation (RTC) and the Federal Deposit Insurance Corporation (FDIC). Serious investors, at one point in their search the two almost bought a Sheraton Hotel in Cypress Gardens, Florida, that was once listed for $8 million. By the time they decided to make a bid the Sheraton had already sold—for $948,000, about an eighth of its original asking price.

But the couple's perseverance finally paid off in December of 1991 when they paid the FDIC $625,000 for the Chamberlain Resorts Hotel, a 20-room hotel with two-bedroom suites located near Bethel, Maine, in the heart of prime ski area. Not only did they acquire a "turn key" spanking-new resort complex, but along with the package came 215 acres of riverfront property, a heated outdoor pool, and a picture-postcard view of the Longfellow Mountains ski area. The hotel had been the property of the failed First Mutual Bank of Boston in Massachusetts, which had lent a developer $2.09 million to build the resort in 1989. When the developer failed to make his loan payments, the bank foreclosed. The bank itself fell on hard times and was "foreclosed" on by the FDIC, the government agency that regulates and insures the nation's banks. The FDIC paid off the bank's insured depositors and acquired title to all its real estate holdings.

Local real estate agents in nearby Hanover, Newry, and Bethel were shocked at how little the Mileses paid for the resort hotel. The township had just reassessed the property at $1.3 million. Even with the regional recession, the local ski economy remained strong and was

anticipating 600,000 ski visits to the area for the 1992 season—
meaning the hotel would probably do a brisk business.

The FDIC had hoped to get as much as $750,000 for the Chamber-
lain. But when only eight bidders showed up for the auction the FDIC
quickly had to decide just how much it wanted to be in the ski resort
business. The answer was: We're the government; we don't want to
be in the ski business. So the FDIC accepted the Miles's bid, which
was the highest.

Miles, a retired auto dealer, put $161,000 down and financed the
balance of the purchase price through the FDIC with a seven-year loan
at 8.8 percent.

When Joseph and Millie Smith of Sacramento, California, heard that
S&Ls were dropping like flies in Texas they decided to investigate
what sounded like a real opportunity. The couple had been investing in
real estate on a small scale for years, building a portfolio of low- to
moderate-income rental units near their home in Sacramento.

The couple discovered that for about $150 they could buy an RTC
catalog of available S&L assets. The evening the catalog arrived they
pulled their chairs up to the fireplace and began thumbing through it.
The sheer number of properties available was numbing. They decided
to narrow their search and started "clipping" catalog listings for any
homes that cost $10,000 or less. By the time they reached the end of
the catalog Millie had gone through five boxes of paper clips.

The couple telephoned the real estate brokers the RTC had hired to
sell the properties and began making offers. A few months later the
Smiths had purchased at least 50 properties from bankrupt S&Ls
controlled by the RTC and from shaky S&Ls.[2]

Because of tax breaks offered by the federal government, wealthy

---

[2] Revlon is known for its manufacture of cosmetics and hair and skin care
products for women. Perelman, the chairman of Revlon, used his investment company, MacAndrews & Forbes, to buy a handful of Texas S&Ls
from the government in 1988. The amalgam of thrifts he acquired is known
today as First Gibraltar Bank, FSB, Dallas, Texas. The U.S. Government
granted Perelman $1.8 billion in federal tax breaks and gave him $9.5

S&L investors, such as Revlon chairman Ronald Perelman, were allowed to sell foreclosed homes and other assets at steep discounts. Why? Desperate to unload these bankrupt S&Ls, the federal government promised these investors that no matter what price they sold a piece of real estate for, the government would make up the difference on the loss! (Generous with our money, aren't they?) Therefore, Perelman and others could sell their S&L assets to anyone they wanted and Uncle Sam would pick up the cost.

The months that followed were good to the Smiths. They were in constant contact with Texas realtors with RTC properties, and the deals began to pour in. The Smiths were getting first crack at houses selling for $500, $800, and $1,200. They couldn't believe their good fortune. "In real estate, generally, you make a low-ball offer with the anticipation that it will be rejected and then a counteroffer will be given so you have grounds for negotiation," said Millie Smith. "And when they [the RTC] just accepted our opening bids we were really amazed. We thought they might accept 1 or 2 of them but not all 32."

By early 1992 the Smiths had purchased more than 300 properties from the RTC, FDIC, or directly from ailing banks and thrifts that were anxious to unload their foreclosed properties at any cost. They fixed some of the homes up, selling them quickly for two, three, or four times what they paid for them. A house they bought in Fort Worth, Texas for $1,750, they sold a week later for $7,500 simply by nailing up a hand-painted "For Sale by Owner" sign. They hadn't done a thing to the house—not even cut the lawn.

---

billion (yes, billion) in federal assistance over 10 years to take these problem S&Ls off its hands. Since he took control, First Gibraltar has been profitable—thanks to all the billions of dollars in assistance from the government. As an incentive to get MacAndrews & Forbes to buy these bankrupt S&Ls, the government allowed them to use "past" losses of the S&L to shelter future earnings. In other words, if the "old" First Gibraltar had lost $1 billion over five years, then the new First Gibraltar would not have to pay any income tax on its first $1 billion in earnings. What's so amazing about all this is that these tax losses could be used to shelter earnings by Revlon.

*   *   *

What these investors have in common is that they each quickly recognized the enormous opportunity created by the meltdown of this nation's banking and savings and loan industries. What most Americans saw as a national disaster, these people saw as a once-in-a-lifetime opportunity to buy real estate cheaply.

These are just selected examples of the kind of real estate opportunities available from the RTC and FDIC, the two government agencies responsible for liquidating and selling the nation's insolvent savings and loans and banks. We could fill a book with just such success stories.

CLOSE, BUT NO FREE LUNCH

But we want to stop right here and make the following point—this is *not* a "get rich quick" book. The only easy way to make money is to inherit it or win the lottery. The only completely safe way to double your money is to fold it in half and put it back in your pocket. All other routes to riches, including those in this book, involve work, commitment, patience, and risk. This book is designed to guide you to the greatest investment opportunity in decades—the government's enormous portfolio of properties inherited from some 2,000 failed banks and savings and loans across America. Once we get you there and show you the ropes, the rest is up to you. If you play your cards right you will be able to parlay your modest savings into a highly profitable investment, as the three examples above prove. But in the process you will also experience your share of frustration and will invest as much "sweat equity" as real money.

A BOOK FOR THE PRO AND NOVICE ALIKE

We have structured this book to be a useful tool for experienced investors as well as for those who have never attended an auction or purchased a piece of real estate. For beginners we delve into details professionals will find obvious. For the professional the most important sections of this book are those dealing with how the RTC and FDIC are structured, who to call for specific types of assets, inside information from the RTC's own policy manuals on how it appraises and values properties, and how the RTC and FDIC analyze bids. We also offer information on how to buy homes from a third government agency, the Department of Housing and Urban Development, which sells about 70,000 homes each year.

THE RTC AND FDIC: OPPORTUNITIES OF A LIFETIME

Thanks to the meltdown of the savings and loan and banking industries, opportunity isn't just knocking right now, it's pounding on your door. Two elements have coincided to create this extraordinary window of opportunity:

1) A slow economy combined with a temporary oversupply of real estate has created the softest real estate sales market since World War II. As sellers, the RTC and FDIC are anxious—and on occasion, desperate. The two agencies are accepting offers far lower than they ever would have considered previously, further driving the cost of real estate down for the first time in decades. It's an aberration, and it won't last. Keep in mind that each year government agencies—including the RTC and FDIC—sell 200,000 units of housing, everything from single-family homes to apartment buildings. Those who buy now will reap the benefits of renewed inflation when the market turns around.

2) As if that weren't enough, bank and thrift regulators have been ordered by Congress to sell repossessed bank and savings and loan properties—*$100 billion worth*—into this already soft market. Doing so creates a vicious cycle. First, the government has to accept lower prices because of the already soft market. Second, dumping more properties on that market softens it further because it creates an even greater oversupply, depressing prices.

It's a terrible time to be a seller, but a marvelous time to be a buyer.

THE SYSTEM WORKS—SO WORK IT

Since 1989 the authors have been investigating and reporting on the RTC and FDIC, and we've discovered something remarkable—the government liquidation system is now working. These two agencies still have flaws, but despite what you may have read, they're actively selling real estate every day of the week and buyers are getting terrific deals.

In late 1991, plagued by complaints that the RTC was an unmanageable bureaucracy (and it was!), Congress radically reorganized the agency, stripping away layer after layer of inefficient management. By the fall the RTC was a lean machine and finally began functioning as Congress had originally intended. Private-sector professionals were brought into the management loop as properties for sale were listed with real estate brokers rather than handled by bureaucrats in Washington. Also, both the RTC and FDIC began to computerize, putting their asset inventory "on-line." The only thing you need today to tap into this inventory is a telephone and a personal computer. We'll explain how later. With the touch of a button you have access to thousands of pages of listings of homes, apartment buildings, motels, and other types of available properties, all across the nation.

When it comes to computerized listings of properties, the RTC is particularly well organized. By early 1992 the agency had installed banks of toll-free 800 lines and hired private telemarketing companies that you can call to request asset-specific searches—for a single-family house, a two-family rental unit, an apartment building—for whatever you want. Both agencies also installed public-access computer data bases so prospective buyers could search for properties nationwide from the comfort of their own computer terminals.

By mid-1992 all these changes were in place, changes that finally placed within reach of the average citizen this $400 billion inventory of assets—everything from $500 homes to $100 million resorts. But, despite all the time, money, and energy spent putting these systems in place, all of this remains the best-kept secret in town to the average investor. Potential buyers continue to hold on to the misconception that they don't have a chance against the "inside the Beltway" crowd or "good ol' boy" network of professional real estate investors. Nothing, however, could be further from the truth.

Adding to this public misperception is the tendency of Congress to drag the RTC out of the closet twice a year for a public flogging. The RTC is not perfect, but it now functions more efficiently than Congress. But politicians, looking for someone besides themselves to blame for the mess they made by deregulating S&Ls and banks, use the RTC as their scapegoat. You should pay absolutely no attention to such political grand-standing. Whatever mistakes the RTC may be making have little to do with your ability to buy property from it. Let the Beltway crowd argue over policy while you get great deals.

NO SHORTAGE OF DEALS

Literally billions of dollars in assets are up for sale. In the case of the RTC, about $80 billion worth of real estate, loans, and other assets will be sold during the coming years. The FDIC, which supervises the nation's banks, will have to sell at least $20 billion in assets. HUD sells at least $3 billion worth of homes per year and will continue to do so for the next several years.

And these assets are everywhere. No longer do buyers have to relocate down south to find a good buy. In the beginning a large portion of what the government had to sell was concentrated in Colorado, Florida, Louisiana, Oklahoma, and Texas. But as the thrift crisis rolled across the country, finally reaching both coasts—and with the banks joining the S&Ls in the federal scrap heap—the inventory is now spread across all 50 states as well as Puerto Rico and Guam.

As a general rule at least half of what these two agencies have to sell is in the form of loans or mortgages. These loans and mortgages are backed by real estate and offer to the investor another way of acquiring that real estate. If you buy the loan you can foreclose on a defaulted borrower and acquire the property in that manner. We'll discuss how to do this later.

How long it takes these two agencies to sell all of its billions of dollars in assets is anyone's guess. Some experts think that if a strong economic recovery sweeps the nation the job might be finished by 1996 or 1997. Others, less sanguine about today's plodding economy, are predicting a financial mess that will last for a decade—at least. Pessimists believe the nation's financial institutions are experiencing a period of "correction" that could last well past the year 2000. Expect the RTC, FDIC, and HUD to be offering billions of dollars worth of real estate and loans at discount prices for some time to come. As the paperback edition of this book was going to press, banks, S&Ls, and insurance companies that were not owned by the government were copying the sales tactics of the RTC and FDIC. That means that billions more in real estate and loans is now available to investors.

For now and the foreseeable future the pickings being offered by these government agencies and the private sector will be plentiful. Every type of real estate asset imaginable is available for purchase: homes, hotels and motels, industrial warehouses, office buildings, raw land, strip shopping centers, even parking lots. Loans that are collateralized or backed by real estate also can be purchased. Also available at fire sale prices are airplanes, appliances, artwork, cars, calculators, computers, furniture, junk bonds, loans and mortgages, rugs, yachts— even businesses like fast food franchises, horse farms, and hot tub spas. Failed American Savings and Loan Association of Irvine, California, even had an operating bordello in Nevada that the government had to sell.

For investors with money this is an opportunity to make a lot more money. For those with little or even no money, the liquidation programs of the RTC and FDIC offer a genuine opportunity to acquire a first house, a duplex, or maybe a small apartment building.

If you are a person with low to moderate income (meaning that you make 115 percent or less than the area median income, median being the middle point where half the salaries are larger and half smaller), you can get even better bargains. Congress has mandated that those who qualify under the RTC and FDIC Affordable Housing Program must get first crack at lower-priced houses and cooperatives and condo units.

If you buy a piece of real estate from the RTC—with a few exceptions—the agency will loan you the money to acquire it. The FDIC, on the other hand, will only loan you money if the property you're buying costs $500,000 or more. However, this rule is likely to change as more banks fail and the FDIC's inventory of real estate grows. When the RTC first began selling assets its seller financing limit was also $500,000, but in 1992 it was lowered to $100,000 in order to increase the number of potential buyers. The ins and outs of real estate financing available from the RTC and FDIC will be explained at length in later chapters.

> Paul Miedens and his wife bought a two-bedroom and loft condominium in suburban Perrysburg, Ohio, from the RTC for $92,000. A few months before the Miedens bought their home, an almost identical unit in the same neighborhood sold for $111,000—22 percent more. The family had viewed six repossessed homes before buying the almost new condo. Along with two bedrooms, the Miedens got a loft, a fireplace, and two baths.

In December 1991 General Electric Capital Corp., a financial services conglomerate based in Stamford, Connecticut, bought 26 apartment buildings—20 of which were in Texas—from the RTC for $75 million. The number of rental apartments totaled 5,590. The cost per apartment unit was just $13,416. At an average rent of $400 per unit—excluding maintenance costs and taxes—GE will make its money back on the investment in less than three years. According to a study done by the Government Accounting Office, the auditing arm of Congress, the RTC is selling assets at an average cost of 60 cents on the dollar. This means that buyers are getting real estate discounts of around 40 percent. Depending on the physical condition of a property, discounts can range as high as 80 percent and 90 percent, but keep in mind you may have to put additional money into the property to make it habitable. In some cases, mostly in Texas and the Southwest, the RTC has simply *given away* homes and apartment buildings to charities and nonprofit groups that have agreed to rent them out to low-income families or fix them up while teaching job skills to unemployed and disadvantaged workers.

The nation's insolvent S&Ls and banks will cost the nation's taxpayers a whopping $300 billion (yes, billion) over the next 30 years. Taken separately or together, the S&L and banking debacles represent the greatest financial disasters in history. Never before has there been a multibillion dollar drain on the nation's economy like this. The Vietnam War, for example, in today's dollars, would cost only $160 billion. And the Marshall Plan, rebuilding all of western Europe after World War II, would cost only $60 billion today.

Not only has the S&L mess created investment opportunities in real estate, but it also has fueled job opportunities, as the government hires professionals to help manage and dispose of this enormous inventory—accountants, appraisers, auctioneers, lawyers, paralegals, real estate management specialists, security guards, and others are being hired at private-sector salaries by the government. Construction jobs are also being created as the RTC and FDIC move to repair and complete unfinished real estate projects left idle by bankrupt developers who borrowed heavily from these federally insured financial institutions. Professionals of all types can work for the FDIC and RTC as third-party contractors, or they can be hired on as staff professionals by these agencies. We'll tell you how to find and qualify for those jobs.

These real estate and employment opportunities will not last forever. As we noted earlier, the window of opportunity could start to close in 1996. This book is a wake-up call to investors and home buyers, to alert them to this terrific opportunity. It is designed to guide you through the federal government's enormous portfolio of properties inherited from some 2,000 failed banks and savings and loans across America.

Happy Hunting.

Chapter One

....

The FDIC and RTC: The Terminators

BILLIONS OF DOLLARS IN ASSETS
WITH ORDERS TO SELL IT ALL

A spot check by Congress in January 1992 showed that the Resolution Trust Corporation (RTC), created to sell assets of failed thrifts, had tens of thousands of single-family homes and apartment buildings on its shelves. The General Accounting Office's computers stopped counting at $27.3 *billion* in real estate—mostly homes, apartments, and office buildings that were available for purchase. That was *after* subtracting the $8.9 billion in homes and apartments the RTC had already sold—some 28,000 properties. And the party is just beginning.

In 1992 the RTC took over another 175 failed S&Ls. In 1993, 1994, and 1995 the RTC will inherit at least 100 more dead thrifts, each one bulging at the seams with properties and other assets that will have to be sold to the public at fire sale prices. The sheer volume of RTC assets takes on almost metaphysical proportions. A glance at the RTC at the beginning of 1992 showed the following inventory: $27 *billion* in real estate, $70 *billion* in performing mortgages, and $30 *billion* in delinquent loans, just to name a few asset categories.

As if that weren't enough, close on the RTC's heels comes the FDIC, the federal agency that sells the assets of failed banks. Between these two agencies there is something for everyone up for sale anywhere in

13

the United States at virtually any point in time. If a failed bank or S&L had an asset that could even *remotely* secure a loan, even a bad loan, the RTC and FDIC now have it in their inventory. During the go-go years of financial deregulation—which led to the S&L and banking messes—borrowers put up everything imaginable as security for loans: real estate, racehorses, rare paintings, vintage cars, hunting lodges, even casinos.

The RTC and FDIC also own all the "stuff" purchased by wild and crazy thrift and bank owners during the time they had the combination to the vault. Some of their buying habits made Imelda Marcos look like she took an oath of poverty. They bought fleets of cars, jets, yachts, expensive art, fine china, even a mechanical gorilla and a magic museum—most of which the government now has to sell.

After the RTC took over Columbia Savings and Loan in Beverly Hills it had to sell the dead thrift's brand-new headquarters building. To say it was not your run-of-the-mill S&L branch would be an understatement. Columbia's former owner, Thomas Spiegel, had been very security conscious. The building had bulletproof glass, a computer system that tracked terrorist activities worldwide, and an executive bathroom that had a bulletproof shower stall. Inside the shower were secret panels that opened to reveal a cache of assault rifles. In one of life's ironies, the RTC sold the building to the talent agency that represented "Terminator" actor Arnold Schwarzenegger.

The FDIC and RTC classify their assets into specific categories under which are subcategories. The two agencies are a lot alike, but they differ in several key ways. Let's start off with a brief look at each.

THE RTC

Since the RTC was formed by Congress in August 1989, it has taken over more than 650 S&Ls with $300 billion in assets. Most experts agree that the RTC will continue taking over sick thrifts through 1995. At that point the number of insolvent or bankrupt S&Ls will be slowing to a trickle. By the time the S&L carnage is over in 1995, about 1,500 S&Ls will still be in existence, but that number too is likely to shrink as strong and healthy institutions merge with each other and form multi-state unions in which one institution will have hundreds of branches in many different regions. Consequently, there will be billions of dollars worth of S&L assets to purchase for years to come.

When the RTC was created in 1989 it was placed under the control of the FDIC. But the arrangement proved unworkable. A gigantic bureaucracy grew around the RTC until it was immobilized. Trying to deal with the avalanche of S&L assets pouring into the RTC also put an unworkable strain on the FDIC. So in late 1991 Congress stripped away the FDIC's authority over the RTC and made it a separate agency.

Congressional passage of the Resolution Trust Corporation Refinancing, Restructuring and Improvement Act of 1991 marks the moment from which the RTC actually began to function as intended. It also created an environment in which regular taxpayers and investors—not just the rich and their well-heeled lawyers—could, for the first time, begin profiting from the S&L mess. Under the new structure the RTC functions more like a private-sector corporation than a government agency. Had this structure been chosen sooner, we might not have had the opportunity to write this book, and you might not have had so many properties to chose from.

It didn't take long for the RTC to capitalize on its newfound freedom of action. A month after the bill's passage the RTC held an auction of homes in Roswell, New Mexico, that was a smashing success—for both the RTC and home buyers. One of the projects the RTC inherited was the old, abandoned U.S. Air Force base outside Roswell. On the base were some 225 single-family homes that had once housed the base's officers and enlisted families.

The property had been neglected and the homes were quickly deteriorating in the hot desert sun. The RTC decided it wanted a quick and clean sale. About 200 people showed up to bid, and when the gavel fell for the last time that day every home had sold. Final sales prices ranged from a high price of $10,700 to a low of $1,700. First-time home buyer Rose Expinoza paid $5,500 for a three-bedroom, one-bath home. Investor Ray Sisneros purchased two homes that he planned to fix up and rent. Even in a soft real estate market he will be able to pocket a nice return on his investment by renting the property. When the market finally turns around he expects to sell the homes at a very nice profit.

But more than cheap homes are up for grabs in this giant garage sale. In fact, there is something in this grab bag for just about every size checkbook. There is definitely room here for the rich to get richer. In 1991 Denver billionaire Philip Anschutz became just a little richer when he purchased a downtown Denver skyscraper for a quarter of what it had sold for 25 years earlier. The building sold for $9 million in 1966. In 1982 it sold for $26 million. But when its owner defaulted on the loan the property joined the ranks of empty office space on the Denver market. Anschutz purchased the building from the RTC for just $2.25 million.

If it's land you want to invest in, the government has plenty. In fact, they have so much raw (undeveloped) land the RTC has said it will bend over backwards to make deals work and to speed sales. Under its streamlined land sales guidelines the RTC can sell real estate for *half* its appraised value! When was the last time anyone in America saw half-price land? And when will we ever see it again?

RTC's STRUCTURE

As we've said, the RTC is now structured much like a private corporation. It has its own board of directors that oversees its operations. Originally the RTC had two different boards, but they were combined and streamlined to cut down on bureaucratic red tape. Today the RTC board consists of the RTC chief executive, the chairman of the FDIC, the Federal Reserve chairman, the director of the OTS, and two private-sector public interest directors appointed by the President of the United States.

Headquartered in Washington, D.C., the agency further streamlined its departments in February 1992 to facilitate quicker sales and reshape policies and procedures. Four senior vice president positions were created to serve as The Four Horsemen of the S&L Apocalypse Committee. The four divisions are Legal, Planning and Corporate Relations, Operations and Sales, and Asset Management and Sales. The RTC also has an inspector general's office, which investigates internal and external matters at the agency, including third-party contractors who work for the agency. Third-party contractors include, among others, real estate managers and brokers.

Although its central nervous system is in Washington, the RTC created consolidated offices in various regions of the country whose job it is to market and sell assets directly to the general public. If you are buying real estate or loans from the RTC, 9 times out of 10 you will be dealing primarily with an RTC consolidated office—not Washington. Most likely your first contact will be a real estate broker who is a contract employee of an RTC consolidated office.

WHAT'S FOR SALE?

Because it has so many different property types to sell, the RTC sorts them into different categories. Investors looking to buy properties can choose from the following categories (see the Yellow Pages for a full listing of the RTC Consolidated Offices).

Residential Real Estate

1) Single-family homes, duplexes, triplexes, and fourplexes, condominiums, and cooperatives.
2) Individual residentially zoned lots.
3) Affordable Housing Program: Single-family homes (1 to 4 units) appraised at $67,500 or less. These homes are first offered to low- and moderate-income buyers at preferential terms.

Multifamily Income Property

1) Apartment complexes (more than four units) and condominium and townhouse developments. Generally sold on a sealed-bid basis at public auctions.
2) Affordable Housing Program: Some multifamily apartment projects are placed in the Affordable Housing Program by the RTC and offered to buyers on favorable terms but under the condition that 35 percent of the units are maintained at reduced rents for low- to moderate-income tenants for 40 years.

Commercial and Industrial

1) Office buildings
2) Shopping centers

3) Former thrift and bank branch office buildings
4) Warehouses
5) Industrial complexes
6) Business parks
7) Motels, hotels, resorts
8) Developed recreational facilities
9) Mobile home parks

(See Chapter 6.)

Land

1) Undeveloped residential subdivisions
2) Commercial or industrially zoned parcels
3) Farmland and pasture land
4) Undeveloped recreational properties

(See Chapter 6.)

Environmentally Unsound Properties

These properties are generally put up for auction in segregated groups. The properties have been found to have certain environmental problems such as asbestos contamination, underground gas tanks, contaminated soil, and so on. The value of these properties has been greatly reduced by the RTC, taking into account the cleanup costs for the next owner. Buyers of environmentally unsound properties are required to complete cleanup before title can change hands.

Special Significance Properties

1) Environmentally significant (e.g., wetlands, wilderness areas)
2) Culturally significant (e.g., old Indian burial grounds)
3) Historically significant properties (e.g., the Alamo)

Special significance properties are further divided by their "value."

NATURAL VALUE. Properties of special significance are identified as properties within or adjacent to national landmarks, national or state parks, wilderness areas, wildlife refuges, areas identified by the U.S. Fish and Wildlife Service as "critical habitats," or other special natural features that include wetlands, ocean and lake shores, caves, dunes, coastal barrier islands, and estuaries.

RECREATIONAL VALUE. Properties of recreational special significance are identified as properties that are within or adjacent to existing public recreation areas or adjacent to rivers, oceans, or lakes.

SCIENTIFIC VALUE. These properties have special scientific significance or archaeological importance.

HISTORICAL OR CULTURAL VALUE. Properties of special cultural significance, based on criteria established by the National Register of Historic Places. Properties in the historic category refer to those built before 1941 that have special significance in American history, architecture, archaeology, engineering, and culture and that have buildings, structures, and objects that possess integrity of location, design, setting, materials, workmanship, feeling, and association and that

- are associated with events that have made a significant contribution to the broad patterns of our history or
- are associated with the lives of persons significant in our past or
- embody the distinctive characteristics of a type, period, or method of construction, represent the work of a master, possess high artistic values, or represent a significant or distinguishable entity whose components may lack individual distinction or
- have yielded, or may be likely to yield, information important in prehistory or history

Buyers acquiring historical property in any one of these designations will most likely find restrictions in the deed that limit the kinds of use the property can be put to and what can be built on it. These limitations will be compensated for by a lower asking price, but if they make the property useless to you, no price can be low enough.

Non-Real Estate Assets

Besides real estate and loans, the RTC has a lot of personal property for sale as well.

FURNITURE, FIXTURES, AND EQUIPMENT (FF&E)

1) Office furniture and equipment
2) Computers
3) Phone systems
4) Cars, boats, and planes
5) Fine (and not-so-fine) art
6) Miscellaneous personal property

See Chapter 9.

LOANS

1) Performing loans (secured loans that are not delinquent or delinquent less than 90 days)
   a) Delinquent up to 30 days
   b) Delinquent 30 to 90 days
2) Nonperforming loans (loans that are more than 90 days behind in payments)

Loans are also designated by quality as good, fair, poor, and distressed. See Chapter 8.

FAILED BANKS AND THE FDIC

The U.S. has about 12,000 banks currently open and operating. This figure includes small community banks, as well as large "money center" banks such as Citicorp in New York and NationsBank in Charlotte, North Carolina.

Banks didn't begin to die off as early as thrifts. While S&Ls began dropping like flies in 1985, serious trouble didn't hit the banking industry until three years later. But when it hit, it hit with a vengeance. More than 1,000 banks have failed in recent years—the same number of failures experienced by the thrift industry—and the end appears nowhere in sight. Even banking industry leaders admit that the American banking industry will shrink by several thousand more banks before this period of "consolidation" is over. In March 1992 the Office of Management and Budget had to admit that in the coming year even some giant money center banks faced failure and predicted that a single large failure could cost the FDIC an *additional* $4 billion. Bad news for the country, but it also means more bank assets up for sale to the public for years to come.

Besides the banks that have already failed, 1,081 banks were on the FDIC's so-called problem bank list at the beginning of 1992, an increase from 1991 when 1,033 banks were on the list. Not all the listed banks will fail. Some will be able to pull their chestnuts out of the fire, but even so, new ones will go on the list to replace them. The FDIC's own economists say that, though the number of banks that fail may get smaller each year, the problem will not be completely under control until the end of the century. In the meantime the FDIC must take control of these insolvent institutions, appraise their assets, and sell them to the highest bidder as quickly as it can. That means more assets available to you, the investor or home buyer.

THE FDIC'S STRUCTURE

Like the RTC, the FDIC has its own chair and a board of directors to oversee its vast operations. Up until a few years ago the FDIC was not in the asset liquidation business. Over the years the FDIC sold bits and pieces of insolvent banks but for the most part sold them "whole" to other banks looking to expand franchise and market share. When the trickle of bank failures turned into a tidal wave, the FDIC set up a separate department inside the agency called the Division of Liquidation to sell assets (real estate and loans mostly) from failed banks.

The FDIC also has regional and consolidated offices through which it sells assets. The FDIC regional and consolidated network breaks down as follows (keep in mind, however, that the FDIC will consolidate many of these offices by 1996):

The Chicago Regional Office liquidates bank assets in Alabama, Arkansas, Delaware, District of Columbia, Florida, Georgia, Illinois, Indiana, Iowa, Kansas, Kentucky, Louisiana, Maryland, Michigan, Minnesota, Mississippi, Missouri, Nebraska, North Carolina, North Dakota,

Ohio, South Carolina, South Dakota, Tennessee, Virginia, West Virginia, and Wisconsin. The Chicago regional office has consolidated offices in

- Atlanta, Ga.
- Orlando, Fla.
- Rosemont, Ill.
- Shreveport, La.

The Dallas Regional Office liquidates bank assets in Oklahoma and Texas. The Dallas regional office has consolidated offices in

- Addison, Tx.
- Dallas
- Houston
- San Antonio

The New York Regional Office liquidates assets in Connecticut, Maine, Massachusetts, New Hampshire, New Jersey, New York, Pennsylvania, Rhode Island, Boston, Vermont, Puerto Rico, and the Virgin Islands. The New York regional office has consolidated offices in

- South Brunswick, N.J.
- Hartford, Conn.
- Franklin, Mass.
- Westboro, Mass.

The San Francisco Regional Office liquidates assets in Alaska, Arizona, California, Colorado, Guam, Hawaii, Idaho, Montana, Nevada, New Mexico, Oregon, Utah, Washington, and Wyoming. The San Francisco regional office has consolidated offices in

- Denver
- Irvine, Calif.
- San Jose, Calif.

The FDIC also has special "Owned Real Estate" (ORE) centers in Atlanta, Dallas, Denver, Franklin, Irvine, and Orlando to sell real estate assets that have been appraised at $1 million or more to investors. (For the addresses of the regional, consolidated, and sales centers, see our Yellow Pages.)

When it comes to selling assets the FDIC works much like the RTC. As with the RTC, if you want to buy a piece of real estate, you will not be dealing with Washington but with the FDIC consolidated office in charge of that asset.

The FDIC also has a computer data base called the ORE Bulletin Board (private investors and bankers use the more common REO, or Real Estate Owned, rather than ORE) where you can access all of its available assets through a personal computer. However, at this writing, unlike the RTC, the FDIC does not have a dedicated toll-free telephone number from which you can request any type of asset. The FDIC will provide you with a list of available assets, but you will have to call the consolidated office in the area in which you want to invest. We suspect that as its caseload grows it will only be a matter of time before the FDIC sets up a toll-free nationwide specific asset inquiry service like the RTC's. We cover both agencies' computer data bases later in the book.

AFFORDABLE HOUSING

One pleasant by-product of the S&L and banking debacles is the opportunity for people with low and moderate incomes to finally become homeowners. When Congress was asked to vote tens of billions of dollars to bail out depositors of failed thrifts and banks, they imposed a condition: Make some of these assets available to low- and moderate-income Americans. This was not a request, it was an order.

In response, both the FDIC and the RTC established their own separate affordable housing programs, also known as AFH programs. We believe these programs are so important and the opportunities so great that we will cover these programs in great detail later in the book. In short, the AFH programs offer the first genuine opportunity in a very long time for low- and moderate-income families and individuals to own their own homes. It's an opportunity waiting for people to act.

OTHER GOVERNMENT AGENCIES AND COMPANIES THAT SELL REAL ESTATE

HUD: THE DEPARTMENT OF HOUSING AND URBAN DEVELOPMENT

Banks and savings and loans weren't the only institutions abused during the 1980s. Republican insiders turned the Department of Housing and Urban Development (HUD) into their own personal pork barrel during the Reagan administration. Instead of building low-income housing, HUD officials handed out fat contracts to fat cat friends for upscale housing developments, recreational facilities, even an off-track betting complex—everything but housing for the economically disadvantaged.

When they did hand out a contract to build an apartment building with affordable rents, developers often pocketed the development fees and then defaulted on their obligations to HUD, and the agency got stuck with the real estate. As a result, HUD had the distinction of being the largest seller of single-family homes during the last decade as it tried to shed its growing inventory of repossessed properties.

HUD was chartered fifty years ago to promote housing affordability and to make decent housing available to lower-wage Americans who were priced out of the home market for one reason or another. The Federal Housing Authority (FHA), which is part of HUD, insures billions of dollars in single-family mortgages so lenders will make the loans. When an FHA-guaranteed loan goes into default it is HUD's job to foreclose and sell the homes.

Unfortunately for the government, HUD and FHA didn't do such a great job of underwriting home mortgages during the late 1970s and 1980s, resulting in tens of thousands of foreclosures. In 1990 HUD sold 80,179 homes, followed by 73,178 in 1991. HUD has also sold a few hundred or so apartment buildings—and there's more where these came from.

Like the RTC and FDIC, to a certain degree HUD is decentralized. You won't have to go to Washington to buy a home from the agency. HUD maintains ten regional offices that oversee eighty field offices that sell these homes. HUD regional offices are in the following cities:

- Boston
- New York
- Philadelphia
- Atlanta
- Chicago
- Ft. Worth, Tx.
- Kansas City, Mo.
- Denver
- San Francisco
- Seattle

In our section on affordable housing we will discuss buying HUD properties in greater detail.

FANNIE AND FREDDIE

The Federal Home Loan Mortgage Corporation (FHLMC), also known to investors as Freddie Mac, and the Federal National Mortgage Association (FNMA), or Fannie Mae, are two publicly traded financial institutions that buy mortgages from S&Ls, mortgage bankers, and banks. Chartered by Congress to make mortgage money more available to homeowners and to provide liquidity to the home mortgage market, these two companies have been extremely profitable during the last several years. Fannie and Freddie purchase mortgages originated by S&Ls, banks, and other lenders and package them into securities that are then sold on Wall Street. In the past few years Fannie Mae has made $1 billion per year while Freddie Mac has made about $500 million per year.

Despite their phenomenal success, they occasionally get stuck with bad loans and must foreclose. Once they foreclose they must sell the homes. In 1990, for instance, Fannie Mae seized 9,034 single-family homes and 25 apartment buildings. Once it takes control of these properties it must resell them. Besides buying from the RTC, FDIC, and HUD, investors may want to consider buying properties from these two agencies as well.

Fannie Mae has regional offices in

- Chicago
- Philadelphia
- Atlanta
- Dallas
- Pasadena

Freddie Mac has regional offices in

- Arlington, Va.
- Chicago
- Atlanta
- Sherman Oaks, Calif.

(For full listings see the Yellow Pages.)

If you want to buy a home from either agency, the place to start is the regional offices. The nice thing about dealing with Fannie Mae and Freddie Mac is that they are extremely professional and move houses at a much quicker pace than the RTC, FDIC, and HUD. Despite some defaults, their loans tend to be of a higher quality than the government's, which means the properties are likely in better physical shape. The downside is that since they are in better shape, they will cost more than government-owned real estate.

IN SUMMARY

The RTC got off to a jerky start when it was formed in 1989 to sell off S&L assets. It made a lot of mistakes and a lot of enemies during those early days. Though all that changed in 1991 after a major Congressional overhaul, the reputation has lingered, keeping a lot of would-be investors away.

On the heels of the S&L mess came the banking industry crisis, resulting in the failure of hundreds of banks and piling even more assets into the laps of federal regulators, this time the FDIC. It too is now peddling these assets right alongside the RTC.

As if that were not enough, in 1988 the sins of those who mismanaged

HUD came home to roost as well, burdening that organization with tens of thousands of repossessed housing units—all of which have to be sold.

Taken all together it's the biggest garage sale in history—homes, condos, office buildings, commercial space, office equipment, cars, boats, planes—if a bank or S&L or their customers could dump money into it, it's for sale today through one of these federal agencies. So, as you can see, there is no shortage of assets for sale from these government agencies. For the ordinary American the meltdown in ethics and common sense during the 1980s has created the best real estate buying opportunity probably since the end of WWII. In the pages ahead we will show you the ropes.

Chapter Two

· ·

Dialing for Dollars

How to Access the System without Even Leaving Home

Dealing with government agencies, whether it's the Postal Service, the IRS, Congress, the RTC, or the FDIC, can be a once-in-a-lifetime experience—you try it once and then promise never to put yourself through such an ordeal again.

Prior to 1991, investors trying to buy repossessed real estate from bank and thrift regulators had a tough time of it. Telephone calls went unreturned, asset lists were not available or slow in coming, properties listed for sale had actually been sold long ago to someone else, and so on. But things began to change in mid-1991 when RTC and FDIC officials finally realized they had to look and act like a private company, not a government bureaucracy. Otherwise, they knew that they would be stuck with their billion-dollar inventories until doomsday.

To accomplish this, the bureaucrats swallowed hard and turned to the private sector, that is, nongovernmental contractors and consultants who sell real estate and other assets for a living. After studying the RTC's sales efforts, these consultants concluded what every businessperson already knew: The most important contact with a prospective customer is the initial contact. If a customer's first impression is a bad one, then the relationship tends to end right there.

For those with no experience whatsoever in buying assets from the government, there are a few different ways to get started:

1) Watch the newspaper for RTC and FDIC auction notices
2) Call the RTC or FDIC consolidated office nearest you and ask for a real estate or loan account executive
3) Call a realtor who specializes in RTC and FDIC properties or
4) Tap the two agencies' easily-accessible computer data bases of available properties

In this chapter we will concentrate on the last option. Only by being the first to get your hands on the inventory list will you be able to beat the competition. The best way to do this is by tapping the RTC's data base of available real estate and loans. By doing so you can quickly and easily discover what properties are available in your area—hopefully before others do. At that point you can buy a property from the government[1] before it goes to auction. Though circumstances differ, chances are you will be able to buy a home, apartment building, or whatever cheaper than if you wait for a public auction.

THE RTC: DIALING FOR INFO

You don't need a computer to tap into the RTC's computer data base, just a touch-tone telephone. (If you do have a computer there is an even better way to get information. We will explain how to conduct an RTC computer search with your home computer later.) The RTC has estab-

---

[1] Throughout this book you will come across the terms *RTC, FDIC*, and *government*. For the most part these terms are interchangeable. Although the RTC only sells S&L assets and the FDIC only sells bank assets, they both use similar policies and methods. Where they do not, it will be noted. Both, of course, are government agencies.

lished a half-dozen different toll-free 800 lines staffed by professional telemarketers who give clear instructions and bend over backwards to provide you with any information you need.

There are a number of 800 numbers you can call to get different kinds of information. (All are listed in the Yellow Pages in the back of this book.) The most important 800 line you will use is the asset specific inquiry (ASI) line. The number is 1-800-RTC-3006 (1-800-782-3006).[2] To access the RTC's data base with just a phone call you will need to have a touch-tone telephone. Old rotary phones *will not* work. The asset specific inquiry data base operates through a computerized voice mail system that does not respond to rotary signals.

Once you get into the system by dialing the telephone number given above, an electronic salesperson will offer you several numbered choices. The choices change occasionally, depending on what kind of special programs the RTC has going at the time. Still, one of the choices will always connect you to a telemarketing service that will mail at your request a computer printout of property for sale in your area. This is called the **Real Estate Asset Specific Program** and it is touch-tone choice number 1.

After pushing 1 you will be given more choices, one of which will again be a list of specific properties for sale. Take your time. This is a toll-free number—it costs you nothing, so feel free to do a little browsing with your ear. Each time you call, pick a different asset category and get to know your way around the system. You should find it an efficient and user-friendly environment in which you can never wear out your welcome.

One of the choices offered allows you to order an RTC catalog of auctions that the agency provides to callers at no cost. The ordering process is completely automated, utilizing the touch-tone features on your telephone. You will be asked to punch in your zip code, then your daytime telephone number. You then will be asked to clearly speak your name and address at the sound of a tone. This will be recorded. About five days later your RTC catalog will arrive in your mailbox. If General Motors operated this well the Japanese would be in serious trouble.

---

[2] This telephone number was current at the time of publication. Though we don't expect it to, the telephone number could change for one reason or another. If it does, call the RTC in Washington to get the new telephone number.

If, when you were given all these choices, you selected the "Asset Specific" choice, you will finally be connected to a live person who will explain what kind of information you can receive from them. These operators sit at a terminal connected directly to the RTC's computers and will conduct up to five computer searches for you on any one phone contact and will mail you a computer printout of properties in your area that conform to your personally requested criteria. This service will cost you only 10 cents per property listed, with a $5 minimum. The only acceptable form of payment is by Visa, MasterCard, or American Express, so as they say, "have your credit card ready." If you find 100 properties that fit your geographical, price, and size needs, you'll be charged $10 on your credit card. (There is no charge if you do not ask that the list be mailed to you.)

The RTC operator will first ask you a few questions to help you narrow down your search. The operator will ask what kind of properties you're interested in and will offer various searchable categories, including single-family residential, duplexes, apartments, commercial, and offices. After you pick a category the operator will ask what part of the country you want searched. They can search by town, city, state, or by the first three numbers of a specific zip code area.

Once the operator has this information the search takes only about 30 seconds. The operator will tell you how many properties there are currently for sale in your category and target area. The operator will then ask if you want a printout of the properties mailed to you. Again, the list takes about five working days to arrive. The operators *will not* give you information over the telephone on these properties. The only information they are allowed to give over the phone is how many properties the computer found that fit your criteria. They are not trying to be unreasonable. These operators are professional telemarketers, not licensed real estate agents. Giving out details of properties over the phone would put these operators in conflict with state laws requiring that only licensed realtors can market real estate to the general public.

The RTC asset specific computer list you receive will provide limited information about the property, including its asking price, size, and type. (Exhibit 1 is an example of an RTC computer printout.) That's all you need to get started. The asset specific computer list will include the name and telephone number of the realtor (or asset manager, as the

RTC calls them) handling the marketing of the property for the agency. If you like, call the realtor and arrange to view the desired property.

If for any reason the realtor gives you the runaround, you should then call the consolidated office in charge of that property (that number will also be listed on the printout) to complain or arrange a viewing. The realtors are contract employees of the RTC. Most of the time you will be dealing with the realtor. The RTC picks these realtors from those who apply for RTC listings. The RTC likes to hear feedback, good or bad, about the kind of service you get from these realtors. With an estimated 80,000 realtors handling RTC and FDIC listings nationwide, they won't know if a realtor is doing a bad job unless you tell the regional office.

Unless you're investing in large commercial properties costing $25 million or more, you won't be dealing directly with the RTC consolidated office at all. The properties are offered through realtors who collect the offers and forward them to an RTC account executive at the local consolidated office in charge of the property who selects the winning offer.

The RTC updates its computer files on a regular basis. Keep in mind that the agency is a big bureaucracy and hasn't worked out all the bugs in its computer and telephone systems just yet. Chances are they never will. So don't be surprised if you find that a property listed on your printout has already been sold or that a sale is pending on it when you call the realtor. Sometimes the computer lists you receive can be up to 30 days old at any one time. If you contact the realtor listed on the asset printout—even if the property has been sold—you will not have wasted your time because you've just met someone important—an approved RTC asset manager, who most likely will be getting more RTC listings in the weeks and months ahead. Because the realtor is paid a commission when the property sells, he or she has every reason in the world to give you a call when new listings arrive.

OTHER TOLL-FREE SERVICES

Asset Inventory Publications, 1-800-431-0600. Through this number you can order and have mailed to you a six-volume set of books that lists every single asset the RTC has for sale. The books are updated every six months and cost $100.

You can also order just the commercial property listing volume

```
                    Residential - Single Family - 1 Family
                          Selected City: San Francisco

Asset Type/Number        : RES SINGLE FAM DET. 1 FAM / 7285
Broker Name/Number       :  (000)
RTC Contact Name/Number: PENA, HENRY (714) 631-8600


Address        : 49     MINERVA      ST   Total Square Feet : 1671
                 SAN FRANCISCO, CA  94112
List Price     : $.00                     Year Built        : 1976
Condition      :                          Construction Type : WOO
Bedrooms       : 3                        No. Fireplaces    : 1
Bathrooms      : 2                        Garage            : 2
Heat           : GAS                      Air Condition     : NON
Amenities      :
--------------------------------------------------------------------

Asset Type/Number        : RES SINGLE FAM DET. 1 FAM / 7285
Broker Name/Number       :  (000)
RTC Contact Name/Number: PETERSON, MARTHA (415) 391-4742


Address        : 763    31ST         AVE  Total Square Feet : 0
                 SAN FRANCISCO, CA  94121
List Price     : $.00                     Year Built        : 0000
Condition      :                          Construction Type :
Bedrooms       : 0                        No. Fireplaces    : 0
Bathrooms      : 0                        Garage            : 0
Heat           :                          Air Condition     :
Amenities      :
--------------------------------------------------------------------

Asset Type/Number        : RES SINGLE FAM DET. 1 FAM / 7828
Broker Name/Number       :  (000)
RTC Contact Name/Number: BILL KIRWIN (714) 852-7700


Address        : 1043   HOLLISTER     AVE  Total Square Feet : 816
                 SAN FRANCISCO, CA  94124
List Price     : $.00                     Year Built        : 1905
Condition      : FAIR                     Construction Type : STU
Bedrooms       : 3                        No. Fireplaces    : 0
Bathrooms      : 1                        Garage            : 0
Heat           : ELE                      Air Condition     : NON
Amenities      :
--------------------------------------------------------------------
```

EXHIBIT 1.   When you call the Asset Specific line and order a computer printout of properties for sale near you, this is what you will receive. Note the $0 prices. This was an early problem with the system and is supposed to be history by the time this book reaches you.

for $25, the four residential volumes for $15 each, or the land volume for $15. If you don't want to spend that kind of money for information that could be months old, you can look at these volumes free of charge at your nearest Federal Depository Library (FDL). The RTC asset inventory publications operator will tell you where the closest FDL is located.

Portfolio Sales, 1-800-348-1484. Operators on this line will tell you about "pools" of property. A pool of similar properties might include a half dozen or so apartment buildings or condo units sold as a single asset—one bid takes all. Sometimes the agency will offer in one package an apartment building, a few office complexes, and a portfolio of nonperforming loans collateralized by small shopping centers. Occasionally the FDIC and RTC might mix and match properties in the same package. Other times it will keep the package to "like-kind" properties only. It all depends on which properties the government can get title to prior to a scheduled offering. These types of packages often are sold through a sealed bid auction in which you will have to compete against other bidders. This number will plug you into the portfolio sales calendar of events.

Contractor Line, 1-800-541-1782. If you're a licensed real estate broker looking for listings, this is the number to call. It will connect you to the Contracting Division of the RTC, where 80,000 real estate brokers have preceded you, and many are now representing the agency.

Seller Financing, 1-800-533-8951. If you need a loan and don't want to go through a bank or S&L or tried and were rejected, this is the number to call. It offers up-to-date information about RTC financing, loans, and terms.

The above numbers will get you started. Feel free to test these telephone numbers until you get a solid sense of how the RTC is structured. Most operators are a wealth of information and the automated lines are easy to use. You should order every brochure and schedule they offer. Not only will the brochures be informative, but the RTC's computer has a wonderful memory and once you enter your name and address the computer keeps it on file. That means that the next time you call in and ask an operator to send you something your information will already be on file.

The RTC also uses this information as a mailing list. If the agency is planning a big event in your area you'll be on their mailing list.

LET YOUR FINGERS DO THE TALKING

If you want to buy more than one piece of property from the RTC, the best favor you can do for yourself is to sign on to RTCNET. This is a private, computerized data base accessible over standard telephone lines with a personal computer. It was created and is maintained for the RTC by Business Information Network (BIN), a private provider of on-line computer data bases. BIN is headquartered in Fort Washington, Maryland.

Once you become a BIN subscriber and are assigned an RTCNET password by BIN you can literally browse the entire current RTC asset portfolio—nationwide—from the comfort of your own home or office through your personal computer. BIN has developed a sophisticated yet simple system for the RTC. RTCNET strikes a balance between the search and retrieval requirements of the sophisticated commercial computer data base user with the needs of the novice. The system is quick, powerful, and simple to use.

BIN updates its RTCNET data base weekly directly off the RTC's own mainframe computer system, called REOM or Real Estate Owned Management system. The RTC's computer system has garnered some criticism from the General Accounting Office because of its lack of timeliness. Our tests of the system turned up a number of properties listed for sale that had already sold. This can be a common problem when dealing with computer data bases for which the data is provided by the federal government.

The time lag is caused by the bureaucratic constraints placed on RTC asset managers. When an RTC asset manager sells a piece of real estate the manager cannot directly update the listing on the computer but must send the sales verification material to an RTC consolidated office, where it must be reviewed and then approved by RTC personnel. Only once all the documentation is found to be in order (and the money is in the bank) does the RTC remove the listing from its REOM system. Only then does the RTC let BIN update the data on RTCNET. This can take up to 45 days in some cases.

Being told a property has already sold when you call can be a disappointment, but we consider this to be a relatively small flaw. It in no way diminishes the value of RTCNET to the serious investor. The good news is that the RTC has been made aware of this problem and has begun a crash program to reduce the lag time involved in updating its system.

But most important to you is the contacts, broker names, and telephone numbers you can extract from RTCNET. Even if a particular listing is sold, the realtor (an approved private-sector RTC asset manager) you telephoned will most likely be handling new RTC listings soon. Tell the realtor what sort of properties you're interested in. Often realtors know about new listings before they hit RTCNET. Developing a personal relationship with several RTC asset managers will give you a leg up. "I have properties all the time that I know I can sell but can't get listed on the REOM computer until all the paperwork is done," says Maryland asset manager Larry Ashbury, whose company manages hundreds of RTC properties. Once RTCNET puts you in touch with people like Larry, you will be alerted to deals even before they hit the computer.

RTCNET EQUIPMENT REQUIREMENTS

To use RTCNET you will need only the simplest computer equipment. Here is the minimum system required:

- An IBM-compatible computer, IBM PS/2, or an Apple Macintosh with minimum 256K of memory
- Either floppy or hard disk drives (hard is much better)
- A modem of any kind 300-9600 baud (Hayes compatible is best)
- A computer printer—any kind

If you don't already own a computer, we suggest you buy an IBM compatible—at least 640K memory with at least a 20-megabyte hard disk and a 1200/2400 baud Hayes or Hayes-compatible internal modem card. A color monitor is nice, easy on the eyes, but not mandatory. A monochrome monitor will work just fine. If you shop around you can purchase a nice 286 IBM compatible with the above minimum requirements for around $1,000. You can buy computers with 386 and even 486 microprocessors now, but a 286 will be plenty fast and a lot cheaper. As for the choice of a printer, you can pay as little as $199 for a cheap dot matrix printer or up to $1000 or more for a laser printer. Your choice depends more on what other plans you have for your printer besides printing out RTC property listings. RTCNET supports any kind of printer.

How to Sign Up

Subscribing to RTCNET is easy. Simply dial 1-800-366-9246. Again, have your Visa, MasterCard, or American Express card ready because that's all they take. The operator will sign you up. Subscription fees are quite reasonable. You will be charged an annual subscription fee of $192, and a one-time software fee. The software fee is $48 if your computer is an IBM or IBM compatible, and $113 if you own an Apple Macintosh.

BIN will mail you their proprietary communications software on either 5¼" or 3½" disk—whichever your machine uses. You will not need to buy a separate communications program. BIN developed its own communications software in order to address two basic problems. First, it did not want computer "hackers" using their own sophisticated communications software to crash into BIN's data base and cause havoc. To access BIN, users must use BIN's own communications program, which identifies the user as a BIN member. BIN's software also allows the "computer-challenged"—techno-peasants—to use its system successfully. About all you have to know is how to turn on your computer. BIN's software takes care of the rest.

When you subscribe to RTCNET on BIN you also become a BIN member. This allows you access to a number of non-RTC data bases that also list properties for sale.

BIN On-Line Charges

Because BIN uses an 800 number to access its on-line service, you will not be charged for a toll call for connecting to the system even though BIN's computer is in Maryland. But once you are on the system you will be charged connect time fees. It will cost 41 cents per minute (32 cents if you are in Maryland) for the on-line charge. BIN recently examined the billings for its three thousand subscribers and said that the average RTCNET user runs up about $13 a month in on-line charges.

SIGNING ON TO THE NET

When your BIN software disk arrives in the mail, just slip it into your disk drive and type INSTALL. The software does virtually all the rest. It first probes the guts of your computer, analyzing your communication and graphic systems. This takes about 30 seconds.

When the grand tour is finished the software will offer a list of modems on your screen to choose from and ask which one comes closest to yours. If your particular modem is not listed, or you don't have a clue, select "Hayes Compatible." The computer will then ask if your telephone system requires a prefix when dialing out. Some company phone systems require that you dial an 8 or 9 prefix to get an outside line. If your modem is hooked to such a line choose "yes" and type the prefix. If you have a call waiting service, the next choice allows you to disable it while using RTCNET. Do so. Incoming calls on call waiting will scramble data coming in from RTCNET.

When all these changes are made the program searches your disk and creates a subdirectory called CALLBIN. All the modified files will be copied to this subdirectory, leaving your original files untouched. Once everything is completed the software will modify itself to fit your machine. This includes setting itself to the maximum baud speed of your modem. You will be able to modify baud speed in later sessions but for now don't worry; all is as it should be.

DIALING FOR DOLLARS

You are now ready to access the on-line RTCNET program. Using your hard disk or C-drive, enter the CALLBIN directory by typing CALL-BIN. Your computer screen will tell you that the software is configuring your modem for the call. Then you will hear it dial and connect to BIN. You will know you are connected because a large "BIN" appears on your screen against a blue background (if you have color). The system will ask for your log-in code, which should have come with your software. Type the four-digit log-in code and hit enter.

You will then be asked to type your secret log-in ID number, usually a five-digit code. Don't worry if you can't see it on the screen as you type.

For security reasons only asterisks appear in case someone's looking over your shoulder. You get three cracks at this before the system disconnects you. If that happens redial and try again. Because they can't see the ID code they're typing, some new users get nervous and make mistakes. Keep trying. Type carefully, and don't give up.

Once you pass through this electronic checkpoint you're all set. The RTC's vast inventory will be an open book. Select "RTCNET" from the BIN main menu and you will get the RTC main menu. Here you get several choices:

1) NEWS: Calendar of auctions, upcoming sales events, and current RTC press releases announcing special sales events
2) USERS MANUAL: Relevant excerpts from the RTC policy manual on bid and sales procedures
3) SILVER LINING: Full text of the RTC's Affordable Housing Program newsletter
4) RTC DATA BASE: Available assets for sale nationwide

THE DATA BASE

This is the heart of RTCNET. When you select this choice a "drop down" menu will appear, giving you three further choices:

- Residential
- Commercial
- Land

Whichever you choose, a new menu will appear at the top of the computer screen. This is the meat and potatoes of RTCNET. Let's assume you picked the residential category. You now will see a residential SEARCH menu that allows you to conduct a broad search (for example, all single-family homes under $20,000) or a narrow search (all single-family homes in Dogpatch, Idaho, listed for under $20,000 that have an acre of land, a pool, four bedrooms, and a two-car garage). The SEARCH menu looks like this:

SEARCH	PropType	City	State	Region	Zip Code
Style	Bedrooms	TotRooms →		Amenities Price	
IntSqFt	Instit#	EDIT	Srch →		CLEARSrch

PropType: If you choose this a drop down menu will give you a number of choices. In this case you will be asked to choose between:

Single-family residential
Single-family duplex
Single-family quadruplex
Single-family attached townhouse
All of the above
Single-family attached condominium
Single-family attached co-op
Single-family attached timeshare
Multifamily—5 + units
Mobile home

City: Type the name of any city. Spelling is important. New York could become Newark.

State: Displays a listing of all states. Pick the one or ones you want.

Region: Lists the RTC's regions: Eastern, Southwestern, Western, and North Central.

Zip Code: The system can search by the entire zip code or by partial zip codes. You might want to try several areas covered by different zip codes: for example 95466, 95472, 95401, 95404, or 95407—all are within one geographical area but each represents different small towns or suburbs. By entering the 954 prefix you will get any available property listed in that area. (This is the smartest way if you are interested in a distinct area and those touching on its main zip county boundary.)

Style: What kind of architecture do you like? Do you want single story or multistory?

Bedrooms: Tell the system how many you want.

TotRooms: How many rooms do you want in your new house?

Amenities: Want a pool? Other choices include laundry room, exercise facility, clubhouse, tennis, playground, storage, and security systems.

Price: Set your upper limits. If you select this option the computer will allow you to specify your price range by selecting: >$xxx,xxx and <$xxx,xxx. For example, you might want to set your upper limit at homes selling for no more than $99,000 but don't want to look at homes selling for less than $65,000. In such a case you would answer the computer's query with: <$99,000 (properties listed for less than $99,000) and >$65,000 (properties listed for more than $65,000). The computer will then cull out all properties above and below your two limits and give you only those which fall between these two parameters.

Lot Size: Want some acreage or just a large back yard?

IntSqFt: How many internal square feet do you need?

Instit#: Institution number. If you want to buy real estate from a specific failed S&L that was once near and dear to your heart, here's your chance. S&L assets listed on RTCNET are in the process of being liquidated or sold by the RTC or might be open to the public under a "conservatorship," which is sort of like an orphanage system for wayward thrifts.

EDIT Srch: Each time you choose search criteria the BIN program keeps tabs on your choices by listing them on screen in a small separate "dialogue box." This way you can always see the choices you've made so far. If you change your mind about a choice, just hit the EDIT function and the program will allow you to change one or more of your choices.

CLEAR Srch: At the end of each search the program will still retain all your search instructions. Select this option to clear those criteria before you start a new search.

MainMenu: Returns you to the RTCNET main menu.

You can choose as many search criteria as you desire. The more you choose the narrower the search and the fewer properties will pop up. Mix and match to your heart's content. The more specific you get the less you will be bothered with listings that don't suit your investment needs.

Once you select all your search criteria move the cursor to the word SEARCH on the menu and hit ENTER. Within seconds you will see the first listings scrolling across your computer screen. A counter on the top of the screen will tick off listings as the computer finds them. When it stops changing you know that the computer has found everything close to your search criteria.

Each listing is comprised of four "pages" or screens of data. (See Exhibit 2). You can use your F keys to move through the data. F2 will take you to page two, F3 to page three, and F4 to page four. Moving the cursor to NEXT will take you to the next listing.

Each residential property listing on RTCNET will contain the following information:

- Property address
- Institution number (failed institution)
- Property type
- Asking price
- Status of legal title
- Acquisition date
- Ownership (full or partnership or joint venture)
- Occupancy status (occupied or unoccupied)
- Year built
- Style
- Total number of lots
- Number of floors
- Number of bedrooms
- Type of heating and air conditioning
- Types of amenities (pool, sauna, etc.)
- Zoning
- Construction type (wood, frame, brick)
- Condition of property (good, fair, poor)
- Total number of rooms
- Total square footage (inside)
- Number of outbuildings

              Copyright (c) 1991 Business Information Network, Inc.
                          1-800-366-9246

                        Residential Database

          Asset Name:
   Property Address: 18475 WEXFORD
   City, State, Zip: DETROIT, MI   48234-
Institution Number: 7194   REO Number: 12517127
      Property Type: SINGLE FAMILY RESIDENCE
              Price: $750   Ownership: FULLY OWNED
        Legal Title: Occupancy: UNOCCUPIED
   Acquisition Date: 09/28/90

                    ZDDDDDDDDDDDD Contact DDDDDDDDDDDD?
                    REO DEPARTMENT
                    (215) 650-8500

   ZDDDDDDD RTC Asset Manager DDDDDDD?   ZDDDDDDDDDDDDDD Broker DDDDDDDDDDDD?
   RTC SALES CENTER   RTC SALES CENTER
   (800) 782-6326   (800) 782-6326

   ZDDDDDDDD Property Manager DDDDDDD?   ZDDDDD Contract Asset Manager DDDDD?
   RTC SALES CENTER   RTC SALES CENTER
   (800) 782-6326   (800) 782-6326

                 Affordable Housing Eligibility: NO
        Year Built: 1928   Construction Type: BRICK FRONT
             Style: COLONIAL   Condition: POOR
      Total # Lots: 1   Total Rooms: 10
 Land (in Acres): 0.10   Total Square Feet: 1862
        # Floors: 2   # OutBuildings: 0
      # Bedrooms: 4   # Bathrooms: 2.0
   Size of Garage: 0.0   Size of Carport: 0.0
     Type of Heat: GAS   Type of A/C: NONE
             Pool: NO   Jacuzzi: UNKNOWN
           Tennis: UNKNOWN   Fireplace: NO
    Zoning Class: RESIDENTIAL
   Description: CONVEYANCE. REQUIRES MAJOR REPAIRS

   Institution Name: EMPIRE FEDERAL SAVINGS BANK OF AMER
            Address: 1000 ADAMS AVEN
                   : NORRISTOWN, PA 19401-
            Contact: REO DEPARTMENT
            Phone #: (215) 650-8500

Search criterion:
Typecode EQUALS All Above: Single, Duplex, Tri, Quad, Townhouse
Price LESS THAN 20000

EXHIBIT 2.   When you pull a residential property file off RTCNET and print them
out on your own home computer printer, this is what they look like.

- Size of garage or carport
- Fireplace
- General description
- RTC asset manager contact (person and phone number)
- Name of failed institution from which asset was acquired
- RTC consolidated office telephone number and contact person responsible for this particular asset

RETRIEVING AND PRINTING RTC DATA

The search criteria you choose might result in a lot of "hits." But don't use expensive on-line time to read them all—you will want a physical record for reference. Here again BIN has made life easy for you. A search we conducted of the RTC's residential data base for "all homes under $20,000" resulted in 1,661 available listings! At four pages each that meant scrolling through 6,644 pages of text. But that's a waste of time and money. Just hit the F5 button and the computer will ask if you want to print the listings out on your printer or save them to disk. Unless it's only a few pages of text, we recommend saving to disk. Before printing you may want to edit the list down to just the useful information. When you choose the disk option the system will ask you for a file name and path, for example, C: RTC HOMES. This saves the file, called HOMES, on your hard disk or C-drive. (You can name the file whatever you like. We chose HOMES as an example.)

When you name the file, a small bar graph will appear on screen, telling you how much data has been transferred and how much is yet to come. When the transfer is complete, sign off RTCNET. You can then view the captured data at your leisure rather than running up on-line computer charges. We found that the best way to view data is to load it into your word processor. If you have a word processor that can handle ASCII text files (like WordPerfect), just load the file like any DOS text file. You will have some line spacing but it's not that big a deal; hit your DELETE button to kill the spaces. (You can save yourself a lot of work in this regard by simply resetting your word processor's margins from the standard default setting of 1" to .5". That's how BIN configures the data when it transmits it to you.)

COMMERCIAL REAL ESTATE ON RTCNET

If under "PropType" you selected COMMERCIAL you will have the following choices to select from:

- Mobile home park
- Office complex
- Retail
- Time share—resort
- Storage facilities/mini warehouse
- Industrial parks/warehouses
- Restaurant
- Hotel/motel
- Marina/boat yard
- Parking garage/lot
- Medical facility/private hospitals
- Nursing/retirement homes
- Resort/golf courses
- Recreation/athletic club
- Churches
- Schools
- Other commercial
- 5+ unit apartment and condo projects
- Office condos

Each commercial property listing on RTCNET will contain the following information, again in four screens (see Exhibit 3):

- Property address
- Property type
- Total number of rental units
- Asking price
- Acquisition date
- Ownership status
- Occupancy status

Copyright (c) 1991 Business Information Network, Inc.
1-800-366-9246

Commercial Database

Asset Name: 1923 N. PAN AM
Property Address: 1923 N PAN AM
City, State, Zip: SAN ANTONIO, TX 78208-
Institution Number: 7334   REO Number: 32373953
Property Type: 5+ APARTMENTS & CONDOMINIUM PROJECTS
Number of Units: 8
Price: $42,000   Ownership: FULLY OWNED
Legal Title: Occupancy: UNOCCUPIED
Acquisition Date: 06/29/90

ZDDDDDDDDDDDD Contact DDDDDDDDDDDD?
NANCY DENNIS
(303) 573-5959

ZDDDDDDDD RTC Asset Manager DDDDDDDD?   ZDDDDDDDDDDDDDD Broker DDDDDDDDDDDDD?
LEE SANDERS   LEE SANDERS
                                         15505 SPUR CLIP
      -                                  HELOTES, TX 78023-
(512) 695-2424   (512) 695-2424

ZDDDDDDDD Property Manager DDDDDDDD?   ZDDDDD Contract Asset Manager DDDDD?
LEE SANDERS   NANCY DENNIS
                                         1515 ARAPAHOE STRE
      -                                  DENVER, CO 80202-
(512) 695-2424   (303) 573-5959

Affordable Housing Eligibility: NO
Year Built: 1930 # of Buildings: 1   # of Units: 8
# of Lots: 1   # of Floors: 2   Land (in acres): 0.00
Style: CONTEMPORARY   Construction: WOOD FRAME
Total SqFt: 8405   Net Rentable SqFt: 5356
Avg. Rent: $0   Avg. Net Income: $0
Avg. Total Expenses: $0
1 Bedroom Units: 6   Average SqFt: 0
2 Bedroom Units: 2   Average SqFt: 0
3 Bedroom Units: 0   Average SqFt: 0
4 Bedroom Units: 0   Average SqFt: 0
Studio/Effic. Units: 0   Average SqFt: 0
Uncovered Parking: 0   # Covered Parking: 0
Elevators: NO   Pools: UNKNOWN   Storage: UNKNOWN
Playgrounds: UNKNOWN   Tennis: UNKNOWN   Exercise: UNKNOWN
Laundry Facilities: UNKNOWN   Security: NO   Clubhouse: UNKNOWN
Condition: FAIR
Zoning: D
Description:

Institution Name: TRAVIS SAVINGS & LOAN ASSOC
Address: 10100 REUNIO PLACE
       : SAN ANTONIO, TX 78216-
Contact: PAT KITTELL
Phone #: (512) 841-8281

EXHIBIT 3.   When you pull a commercial property listing off RTCNet, this is the imformation you receive.

- Year built
- Style
- Total square footage
- Average rents
- Average expenses
- Number of 1-bedroom units
- Number of 2-bedroom units
- Number of 3-bedroom units
- Number of 4-bedroom units
- Studio/efficiency units
- Number of parking spaces (uncovered and covered)
- Elevators
- Playgrounds
- Laundry facilities
- Physical condition
- Zoning
- Lot size
- Construction type
- Net rentable square footage
- Average net rents
- Average unit square footage
- Amenities (pool, exercise rooms, etc.)
- RTC contract asset manager and phone number
- RTC consolidated office and contact name and phone number

LAND ON RTCNET

If you select LAND your search choices will be:

- Unimproved residential
- Residential developments
- Commercial developments
- Agricultural
- Ranch/pastures
- Oil and gas developments
- Mining

"Development," as used by the RTC when it sells land, often means these properties are unfinished, which is why they are listed in the raw land section. This means that someone started something they couldn't finish. Streets and utilities may be incomplete, which means you will have to do the rest. In many cases streets and sidewalks will be as far as they got before going belly up.

Features in the raw land data base are similar to those listed above for commercial properties. "Number of units," for example, will mean the number of units the land is zoned or approved for, not necessarily how many units exist. So don't get too excited if you see a parcel listed for $40,000 that shows "53 units."

If you are buying an uncompleted subdivision you more than likely will be required to meet all the preconditions imposed on the original developer by the local zoning authorities. The purchase price may seem cheap, and maybe it is, but you could be subject to zoning requirements that will cost you more later.

For example, the property may have been approved as a low-income rental project, meaning you *must* set aside a certain number of units for low- to moderate-income renters. Or you might be assuming the responsibility for repaying municipal bonds that were used to finance infrastructure such as sewers, sidewalks, and street lighting. The only place these conditions will appear is in the RTC due diligence package, which is available from RTC asset manager. We will discuss bid packages and due diligence later. If you're still in doubt, call the RTC account executive at the consolidated office who is in charge of the property.

Anyway, be careful when searching through the RTCNET commercial data base. Things are not as they may appear. We did a search with a criteria of "Residential developed in Arizona costing less than $100,000." The computer spit out a number of tantalizing leads. It told about an uncompleted 57-unit townhouse development outside Tempe, Arizona, that was available for just $8,500. It sounded too good to be true—it was.

With a little more research we discovered that when the RTC lists a townhouse development it first lists each lot separately. In this case the project had 57 "lots." We mistakenly assumed the price for just one lot was the price for the entire development. The $8,500 price was listed on the computer without explanation after the address. The $8,500 was the value of just that one lot, which the RTC calls a "sub-asset classification." The entire development later sold for $1.1 million. If you have any questions ask the asset manager (realtor) if the listing you are interested in is a major or sub-asset. Under some conditions the RTC will sell a sub-asset separately, but most of the time they will not want to, shall we say, break up a set.

SHOPPING FOR A LOAN?

If you want to invest in loans that are being offered by the RTC, RTCNET has a LOANS menu selection. This gives you a complete list of loan packages and pools that are available to bid on. However, you cannot search this data base. It lists all the loan pools currently available in one large file. Each listing contains the following information:

- Collateral for the loan, listed by residential, commercial, consumer, and multifamily
- Total dollar amount of the loans
- Yield
- Geographical distribution
- Number of loans in the pool
- Issuing S&L
- Contact person for bid information
- Bid deadline

OTHER RTC INFORMATION ON RTCNET

Besides searching the RTC's data base for specific assets, RTCNET provides other useful investor information. For those interested in keeping abreast of the Affordable Housing Program, selecting SILVER LINING from the RTCNET menu will allow you to read the RTC's own Affordable Housing newsletter. SILVER LINING contains stories about people who successfully purchased homes, condos, or apartment buildings from the RTC. It also posts recent changes in AFH policy and pending legislation. Back issues also are available. Again, the best and cheapest route is to download the whole thing onto your hard disk, print it out, and read it.

RTCNET also offers subscribers the complete Affordable Housing Disposition Directory. This directory lists the names and direct-dial phone numbers of RTC staff in each RTC consolidated office responsible for making this program work for you. The numbers are all toll-free 800 lines. In case you don't get satisfaction from the regional representatives, the directory also gives the names and direct-dial phone numbers of their bosses in Washington.

RTCNET has also added the RTC's *National Investor Newsletter* to its on-line service. The newsletter is put out by the RTC to reach large investors interested in multimillion-dollar assets. The newsletter includes a calendar of major asset sales, including loan pools, commercial projects such as office buildings, and large multifamily residential projects. The newsletter is of little interest to small investors, unless they simply want to see how the other half lives.

NON-RTC DATA BASES ON BIN

BIN contracts data base services with other vendors besides the RTC. All these services are available to BIN subscribers. Access fees vary, and you are warned about them before being granted access. Among the more useful services to real estate investors are:

- **National Foreclosure Data Base.** Lists over 16,000 properties for sale directly from banks and thrifts. These are properties banks and thrifts acquired through foreclosure when borrowers failed to make their mortgage payments. This service will cost you a 55 cents per minute on-line charge.
- **Real Estate Reporter.** Tracks over 80,000 foreclosures nationwide. Also offers investment information for investors who specialize in buying property at foreclosure sales. This service incurs a 55 cents per minute on-line charge.
- **Thrift Liquidation Alert.** A newsletter that specializes in reporting on recently closed thrifts. On-line fee is 49 cents per minute. (*The Resolution Trust Reporter*, another private newsletter that tracks the RTC, is available on the Lexis/Nexis computer network.)
- **Electronic Mail.** BIN offers subscribers, individuals, and com-

panies custom electronic mail services. To get your own BIN electronic mailbox you simply have to ask.

- **Private Networks.** BIN custom designs and operates private networks for corporations, associations, and other organizations. Access to private networks requires special authorization. RTCNET is a private network designed for BIN's client, the RTC.

SUMMARY

The RTC is part of a giant bureaucracy and has built-in inefficiencies. It's not surprising to find that some of its on-line computer information is outdated and occasionally inaccurate. What amazes us is that RTCNET works well despite the formidable odds against it working at all.

For the serious investor, RTCNET is a required tool. Your chances of making serious money off this huge inventory will be greatly enhanced by mastering this data base. It's expected that over time the RTC will increase the accuracy of data on RTCNET. But even as it is now, it's well worth the $250 to $300 a year it costs to use. If the data base does nothing more than introduce you to asset managers around the country who sell for the RTC, it will have paid for itself.

For the noninvestor who is simply looking for a single piece of investment property or a home or an affordable housing opportunity, the system may still be worth the cost. This is particularly true if you are not married to a specific town and are casting your net statewide or regionally. RTCNET can save you a lot of long-distance toll calls trying to find just the right property.

As of this writing Business Information Network is the only public computer access to the RTC portfolio. They are doing a good job and it is unlikely the RTC will contract with another provider. But before subscribing to BIN you might ask your closest RTC consolidated office if they are still the only show in town.

THE FDIC'S DATA BASE

As we went to press the FDIC's computer data base was still a primitive affair. The agency only had a funky computer bulletin board available through its Dallas regional office that performed like it had been designed by someone's brother-in-law. To say it's marginally useful would be an overstatement.

The FDIC says it intends to get its digital act together in 1994, but for now we can't recommend the FDIC's system, which is called the ORE Bulletin Board. ORE stands for *owned real estate*. The system is being developed in-house by the federal agency, which explains why it doesn't work. It's expected, hopefully, that the FDIC will wake up and smell the coffee and hire someone in the private sector such as Business Information Network, CompuServe, or Nexis/Lexis to help them bring their asset data base into the twentieth century. There was talk at press time that the FDIC would contract with a private-sector firm like BIN to manage its data base as well. Another option being explored took the process one step further—using Prodigy Information Network to supply information to would-be investors right in their homes, reducing the cost to the Prodigy fee of $12 per month.

IN SUMMARY

Though the FDIC lags a bit behind the RTC in the "reach out and touch someone" department, both agencies have become increasingly user-friendly. The toll-free phone numbers listed here and in our Yellow Pages will plug you directly into agencies. This may well be the first time in history that such giant bureaucracies have tried to make themselves so accessible to the ordinary citizen.

So you can ease into this process. Start by calling the RTC toll-free lines and order manuals and computer printouts. They have created a nonthreatening environment in which "no salespeople will call" if you change your mind. Go as far as you like, and stop when you like.

The ability to search RTC's data base with your home computer represents a real opportunity for the serious investor.

In short, anyone who tells you that you can't deal with the FDIC or RTC hasn't tried recently.

Chapter Three

....

Finding Home Sweet Home

AFFORDABLE HOUSING OPPORTUNITIES FROM THE RCT, FDIC, AND HUD

Eva Garcia was fed up with New York City. In 1991, after her divorce was final, she needed a more spacious and liveable place to raise her two children. After hearing that the Resolution Trust Corporation was holding an affordable housing auction in Toledo, Ohio, she packed her two children into the family car and drove all night, arriving at the auction an hour before it started. With her kids in tow, Eva bid on every large condominium offered that day until finally she realized that the auctioneer who was shouting "SOLD" was pointing at her. She had just bought a spacious condominium in Stoney Creek, a condo project in suburban Toledo, for $33,500—less than some people pay for an automobile.

Prices for single-family homes and condominium units that day ranged from a low of $2,000 up to a high of $96,000. Eva, a nurse in training and first-time home buyer, couldn't have been happier. She had long ago given up any hope of ever owning her own home.

Eva is not alone. Every week the RTC and FDIC quietly sell homes to thousands of citizens who once thought they were locked out of the housing market. Both agencies have portfolios bulging with residential properties, ranging from "fixer uppers" to luxury mansions.

For low- to moderate-income Americans the S&L and banking disasters have been good news. (The low- to moderate-income label applies to any citizen who makes 115 percent or less of an area's median income. Median is the middle point where half the people earn more and half earn less.) Congress has ordered both the FDIC and RTC to make a portion of their repossessed residential properties available to low- and moderate-income families and individuals. This doesn't make up for the eight years of Reagan administration insiders looting the Department of Housing and Urban Development (HUD), but it offers a great opportunity to those who act now. Together the two agencies will dispose of tens of thousands of single-family homes over the next few years. Some will be earmarked for the Affordable Housing Program; others will be sold on the open market to anyone who makes the highest offer. Each program serves a different pool of potential buyers.

BUILDING PERSONAL WEALTH

Frankly, a penny saved is an underachieving penny. The only reason to save money is in order to collect enough of it to invest in "equities"— real estate or stocks. Only by acquiring property with growth potential (equity) can you break the cycle of wage-slavedom and gain independent wealth.

A family earning $40,000 a year will earn about a million dollars in wages over a twenty-five-year working lifetime. That's a lot of money. Unfortunately, by the time it's over, you'll have precious little left. State and federal taxes will relieve you of at least 25 percent of that, leaving $750,000, and living expenses such as rent or mortgage payments, car payments, food, and utilities will consume most of the rest. If you are lucky enough to save 5 percent of your after-tax earnings (a high percentage by American standards), that means you will have put aside a measly $37,500 (not counting interest)—hardly enough to fund a golden retirement in the Caribbean.

The only way to acquire real wealth and to secure your retirement is by investing in equities *now*. But what equities? Though over the long term the stock market historically far outstrips the inflation rate, individual stocks can plunge without warning—maybe the week before you retire. The trick is to pick stocks that always increase in value. Good luck if you choose that route, and if you figure out how to do it, give us a call.

Since the beginning of time the safest and best investment has been real estate. The reason is obvious: They just don't make the stuff anymore. It's a simple case of supply and demand. There will always be stock splits and new stock issues. But there will *never* be any new real estate. What there is, is already there. And if you own a piece of it you are a fortunate soul indeed. If you don't, the government's Affordable Housing Program is a rare chance to make that giant leap.

THE AFFORDABLE HOUSING PROGRAM

The Affordable Housing Program (AFH) is a program mandated by Congress whereby the RTC and FDIC must first offer to low- and moderate-income residents of a given area homes that are "moderately" priced. For the RTC this means homes appraised at under $67,500.[1] This includes everything from condos and townhouses to mobile homes, single-family houses, and one- to four-family apartment buildings. As of September 30, 1991, 13,000 families had already purchased homes through this program.

Don't be put off by the mistaken belief that this is a program for just the "poor." This is one of the greatest fallacies of the RTC and FDIC's affordable housing effort and has caused countless qualified buyers to turn their noses up at the program. A family of four in Dallas that earns $50,000 annually can easily qualify to buy a home under this program.

Besides the single-family cap of $67,500, the RTC places a price cap on two-family, three-family, and four-family homes that can be purchased through the AFH program. The two-family (or duplex) cap is $76,000; the three-family (triplex) cap is $92,000; and the four-family

[1] The $67,500 is likely to be lifted or increased, probably in early 1993 as the RTC comes under increasing pressure to sell off its large inventory of real estate.

(fourplex) cap is $107,000. When it comes to condos or co-ops, a studio, one-, two-, or three-bedroom unit is considered a single-family unit.

WINDOW OF OPPORTUNITY

Prior to the S&L and banking debacles not many working-class Americans could find properties as cheaply as the one Eva Garcia bought in Toledo. Real estate values—especially homes that moderate-income Americans could afford—were soaring through the roof during the mid- to late 1980s. The S&L and banking disasters that followed changed all that. Today, by law the RTC must make available first to low- and moderate-income residents all residential properties that are appraised for $67,500 or less. The property spends its first thirty days on the market priced at 70 percent of its appraised value. If it doesn't sell, the property is marked down to 40 percent of appraised value and offered for another sixty days. After that, if it still hasn't sold it is removed from the Affordable Housing Program and sold in a multiproperty auction to the highest bidder on a "no-minimum bid" basis. The FDIC goes one step further than the RTC. Realizing that some areas like New York and Los Angeles have very few "affordable" housing units priced at $67,500, Congress mandated that the FDIC establish an affordable housing price cap tied to the median price of a given geographical area.[2]

Median home price is the "middle" point where half the homes cost more and half cost less. In the Washington, D.C., area, for example, the median home price is about $152,000. The affordable housing cap of $67,500 does little for the first-time home buyer. But under its AFH program the FDIC can raise that cap, allowing more properties to be made available to low- and moderate-income taxpayers. Using its discretion, the FDIC can include $120,000 homes (or higher) in its affordable housing auctions. This is a major advantage for moderate-income families in high-priced housing markets such as Boston, Los Angeles, San Francisco, New York, and Washington, D.C.

---

[2] In December 1991 the FDIC was forced into creating an affordable housing program after Congress voted to provide the FDIC with $70 billion in borrowing authority from the U.S. Treasury Department.

HANDYMAN SPECIALS

AFH properties, like all government-owned real estate, are sold by the RTC and FDIC "as-is," which translates into: What you see is what you get. For a low- and moderate-income home buyer who is also handy with tools or has construction skills, buying a two-, three-, or four-family unit could be a gold mine. The worse the physical shape of the house, the cheaper you can get it. If you can fix it up yourself and rent out the other units you can do quite nicely.

> KEY INFORMATION. *Although the RTC cap of $67,500 sounds too low for buyers in some metropolitan areas, the auctions are worth checking out anyway. There have been many instances in which homes that were once valued at $100,000 to $150,000 were dropped into the AFH program and slashed down to the AFH limit. Also, if a home doesn't sell after thirty days its price can be reduced even further by the RTC and FDIC.*

Just how low will the government go to make some housing affordable to qualified buyers? How does *free* sound? It may sound unbelievable, but the RTC and FDIC have given AFH properties away. In 1991 alone, 380 properties were simply given away by the RTC—an average of more than one a day. Most giveaways by the two agencies are to charitable, nonprofit organizations that have an Internal Revenue Service tax exempt identification number. Giveaways must be approved by the local government where the house is located. Church groups with social outreach programs can pick up properties for their local homeless programs or battered women's shelters or to fix up and sell in order to raise hard cash.

AFH: WHO QUALIFIES?

The RTC and FDIC place an income cap on families who are allowed to purchase properties (one- to four-family homes) from the government through the AFH program. The cap is pegged to the median income of the area in which the house is located. The way the law is written, any family that earns 115 percent or less of the area median income is allowed to buy a home that has been placed in the AFH program. If you make between 80 percent to 115 percent of the area median income you are considered a moderate income resident. If you make less than 80 percent of the median income you are considered a low-income resident. In Denver, for example, a family of four that earns $41,400 or less can qualify for the AFH program. A single home buyer in Denver who earns $38,755 or less can qualify as well.

The RTC, FDIC, and local realtors selling AFH properties all provide charts that rank an area's median income. Any local Chamber of Commerce office also carries median income data. However, COCs tend to paint a rosier picture of reality, and their figures can lead you astray. When in doubt telephone the RTC or FDIC consolidated office nearest you and ask what the median figure is for the area you're interested in.

KEY INFORMATION. *If you live in a high cost-of-living area such as New York, San Francisco, or Los Angeles and you barely qualify under the 115 percent of median income rule, your best bet might be to wait for an FDIC auction where the available AFH homes will be tied to the area's median home price and not the RTC cap of $67,500. There is a risk in waiting, though. Some states weren't as hard hit by the S&L and banking messes as other states, and the number of AFH opportunities will be limited.*

Before purchasing a home from the government you will have to fill out a bidder qualification form to show the RTC and FDIC that you make 115 percent or less of the area's median income. This form must be completed before you bid on a property at auction. The government will use this form to determine if you qualify to purchase a home.

Your median income will be calculated by the number of people and dependents in your family. The RTC and FDIC will deduct amounts from your gross income depending on the number of children in your family. Remember, gross income is what you earn, not what you take home each week. The agencies will subtract $480 from your gross income for each family member who is under the age of 18. They will also subtract $400 from the total if you're an "elderly" family whose members are 62 or older. If you have a child who is under 18 and working you *do not* have to count, his or her income on your bidder qualification form. Both agencies will count your liquid assets toward the overall income calculation. Assets that you are required to list include checking accounts, savings accounts, certificates of deposit, rental property, and stocks and bonds. If you have a certificate of deposit (CD) of $10,000 sitting in a bank account somewhere, the RTC will take 5 percent of the $10,000 and add it to your gross income. However, if you have less than $5,000 in liquid assets the RTC *does not* require that you take 5 percent of their value and add it to your gross income. If you have handicapped children and receive public assistance you *do not* have to include it as part of your gross income.

Question: What if I make less than 115 percent of the area median income and I suddenly inherit a lot of money or my spouse dies and I receive a large insurance settlement—do I have to include it as annual income?

Answer: Yes. RTC and FDIC rules are explicit on this. However, government rules allow you to exclude "temporary, non-recurring or sporadic income including gifts." This area could be tricky. If a relative or friend gives you $1,000, technically you don't have to declare it on your gross income qualification statement.

Other forms of income that you *do not* have to declare include:

- relocation pay
- payments you may have received for volunteer work (this is an odd exclusion since most volunteers don't receive pay)
- foster care payments
- reimbursements from medical costs and any combat pay to a family member serving in the Armed Forces (this of course would apply to Desert Storm and Vietnam veterans)

If you happen to be a retiree, the government will count your pension income and social security payments. Again, they will include 5 percent of your liquid assets toward calculating gross income.

FIGURING OUT YOUR INCOME

Each city and town has its own median income. New York, Los Angeles, and Chicago have the highest median incomes of any city. Each year the median could rise or fall, depending on the local economy, so ask the RTC or FDIC what figure they are using before you get too far. Because median incomes change based on shifts in the local economy, we offer, as an example, what the caps were on the qualifying median incomes in Texas at the beginning of 1992:

| | *Family of* | | |
City	*One*	*Two*	*Four*
Austin	$33,000	$37,700	$47,150
Dallas	$35,300	$40,350	$50,450
Ft. Worth	$31,300	$35,750	$44,700
Houston	$33,150	$37,900	$47,350

Before you are allowed to bid at auction the RTC and FDIC will pre-screen you to make sure you qualify. If after calculating your AFH income you still have doubts, just pick up the telephone and call the RTC or FDIC consolidated office that is holding the auction. Most AFH experts can tell you on the spot whether you qualify—but keep in mind they're going by what you tell them. If you "cheat" a little and shave a few thousand off your income, remember the agency will later require a signed financial statement. Filing a false financial statement is a crime. If caught, you'll have to explain your math to a judge. Despite impressions that the RTC is a bureaucratic nightmare where a little fudging will go unnoticed, we've found the AFH program to be well managed, thorough, and staffed by competent professionals.

ARE YOU "TOO RICH"?

If you're a real estate investor looking for bargains, don't let all this low income talk turn you away from the Affordable Housing Program. There's room for you in this program too. The government offers no income limits on AFH buildings that have five or more rental units. In fact, buying an apartment building under the RTC or FDIC's affordable housing programs could be one of the best investments you've ever made. Depending on where the property is, its condition, and how good a manager you are, you could do quite well. The RTC will even lend up to 85 percent of the purchase price to help you buy an apartment building. Detailed information on how real estate investors can make money through the AFH program appears later in this chapter.

GETTING STARTED AND FINDING WHAT'S AVAILABLE

For one- to four-family homes, the first step is to telephone the RTC or FDIC consolidated office nearest you. (Consult the Yellow Pages to find the RTC or FDIC office closest to you or the region in which you wish to buy.) You also can start by calling the RTC's Affordable Housing hot line (1-800-624-HOME).[3]

In general the RTC has a better-organized affordable housing program than the FDIC. The FDIC is moving in the same direction and should be offering affordable housing opportunities in a "user-friendly" environment shortly. Keep in mind that once the RTC winds down its sales effort around late 1996 the FDIC will still be humming along, because the banking crisis followed the S&L meltdown by almost four years. Therefore, the FDIC will be selling billions of dollars worth of land, homes, and commercial properties until the end of the decade.

Because the S&L and banking crisis hit hardest in the Southwest, most of the properties first offered have been in Arizona, Louisiana, Texas, and New Mexico. But the real estate recession in America is a "rolling" recession, meaning it's been rolling around on the nation's deck like a loose cannon. Though Texas was deep in recession by 1988, the New England states didn't feel the full bite until 1990, and California didn't go into serious recession until 1991. Except for Hawaii, very few areas have been unaffected by the real estate recession.

---

[3] Or you can do your own search using the RTC's "RTCNET" computer data base, which you can access with a personal computer. See Chapter 2. Properties in the AFH program are clearly designated as such on the computer printout.

Hot affordable housing markets. As the banking crisis in America worsens, banks of all sizes will fail in cities and states previously untouched by this financial plague. Because New England has been hit like a sledgehammer by the recession, some of the best bargains under the AFH program might be found in Connecticut, Maine, Massachusetts, and Rhode Island.[4]

The Midwest, Illinois, Minnesota, Michigan, and other "rust belt" states are areas to keep an eye on. Parts of southern California and the Pacific Northwest have their share of bargains as well. Be patient and be flexible. So far most of the heavy AFH action has been concentrated in Arizona, Florida, Louisiana, Oklahoma, and Texas. In 1993 the RTC will offer at least eighteen thousand single-family AFH homes, condos, and townhouses and two hundred or more apartment buildings with thirty thousand apartment units under its Affordable Housing Program. The pickings should be good and the geographical spread should include most regions.

WHAT ARE PRICES LIKE?

In Texas the average sales price of an AFH home is around $28,000. Houses haven't sold this low since the 1960s. These are not "fixer uppers." Many are nice suburban homes, townhouse units, or condos built during the mid-1980s. Developers overbuilt with S&L and bank money, and now there's a glut. It's as simple as that. The best news for first-time buyers is that most properties in the AFH program are selling at sizeable discounts compared to nongovernment-owned homes.

In Dallas, for example, the median home price is $90,000, compared to the RTC AFH average in Texas of $28,000. We're not inferring that

---

[4] Interestingly, Vermont has escaped much of the financial damage suffered by other New England states, perhaps because of a perception by some builders during the go-go 1980s that the state wasn't "user-friendly." For much of the decade Vermont's largest city, Burlington, had a socialist mayor, Bernard Sanders, who later was elected to Congress. Sanders was viewed by some in the real estate industry as being anti-development and pro-rent control, which reduced development and therefore overbuilding. Also, tough environmental laws in the state prevented rampant development of ski resorts.

the $90,000 home is in the same condition or part of town as the AFH home. Some AFH properties have been vacant for months and need a bit of TLC. Still, AFH properties represent a terrific opportunity for low- and moderate-income families. A first home is the first rung on the equity ladder—a rung that until now has been too high for many to reach.

HOW TO ACT

There are two ways to buy AFH houses from the government. You can take the passive approach and just check the real estate section of your local newspaper for an announcement of an upcoming affordable housing auction, or you can get serious and call the nearest RTC or FDIC consolidated office and ask it for a list of available properties and upcoming auctions.

KEY INFORMATION. *By contacting the RTC or FDIC first before an auction takes place, you can beat the competition and avoid the auction process, which tends to drive prices up.*

Typically the RTC offers AFH properties with selected local real estate brokers for sixty days. The homes are advertised and listed just like any other home but are designated as "Affordable Housing" properties, the sale of which is limited to those who qualify. If after sixty days the property hasn't sold the RTC will then take the property listing back and try to sell it through a public auction. Ask the realtor how long he or she has had the listing, or ask to see a copy of the listing agreement with the RTC to see the date. If the realtor won't give you this information, call the RTC regional office and ask them when they gave out the listing. Also in the back of multiple listing books is a list of properties that includes a "days on the market" column. Ask to see the most recent Multiple Listing Service (MLS) book.

INVESTOR TIP. *If you want to gamble, wait until the property has been returned to the RTC unsold. Then contact the RTC consolidated office and make a bid. Because the RTC takes its costs into consideration when analyzing a bid, you can point out to an agency account executive that the RTC is now saving the 5 percent real estate commis-*

sion. Under its pricing guidelines, because the home has not sold the RTC can now sell it for 40 percent of its appraised value. This is the perfect time for you to make a lowball offer. The consolidated office will have to balance your offer against the costs involved in holding the property longer. The account executive might turn you down. If so, you'll get another crack at the public auction.

As with other RTC real estate, buyers can use their own real estate broker to buy an AFH property. And the listing broker must present all offers made, no matter how low, to the RTC. If the buyer has his or her own realtor, the commission will be split between the RTC broker and the buyer's broker. The RTC pays a 5 percent commission.

If you, as a buyer, use your own realtor, the listing agent will be less than pleased to split the commission. But this shouldn't hurt your chances. The listing broker must submit all bids to the RTC and the RTC (and FDIC) must accept the highest bid, regardless of who made it. Still, the listing broker has subtle advantages that give him or her a leg up. The listing broker's regular customers will certainly get a phone call the day listings arrive and will get first crack at these properties. This is a good reason to find and cultivate a relationship with a realtor who is an approved RTC contractor and gets listings on a regular basis.

AFFORDABLE HOUSING AUCTIONS

The RTC is increasingly using public auctions to sell its affordable housing properties. Some of these properties had been listed with realtors but did not sell. Others are put in the auction program immediately, without first being exposed to the market. These judgment calls are made by account executives at the RTC consolidated office handling the asset.

Buying through an auction has its good and bad points. The worst part about an auction is that you're competing against an unknown number of other bidders—which means the price of a house or condo, if there's more than one bidder, can be driven out of your reach. On the other hand, auctions can accomplish just the opposite—if few show up to bid, prices will drift lower than you expected. It's a crapshoot.

Many of the professional auction firms hired to dispose of these properties are top-notch marketing experts and publish full-color brochures of the available properties. Since the RTC pays for marketing costs, these auction companies will be more than happy to mail you a complete auction package. The nice thing about the auction process is that you can view hundreds of properties without spending a nickel.

Occasionally the RTC and FDIC will auction AFH homes together with homes that exceed the AFH price limit. AFH homes will clearly be marked in the brochures with an "A" while the other homes will be marked "G," meaning "general" or non-AFH auction. If you qualify as an AFH bidder you can still bid on the non-AFH homes at bid levels that meet your budget. Who knows, you might get lucky. But if you do not qualify as an AFH bidder you *cannot* bid on "A" designated properties. Before bidding you will have to prequalify as an AFH bidder. The prequalification sessions are held at the auction or beforehand at the RTC or FDIC consolidated office sponsoring the auction.

KEY INFORMATION. *A pre-bid qualification session will be held before the auction. If you are going to bid on an AFH property you are required to bring the following information:*

- The name and address of your employer
- A copy of your most recent pay stub and last year's W2 statement
- If you are self-employed, personal and business tax returns for the last two years
- Your bank and savings account statements showing current balances and account numbers
- A statement showing your current monthly expenses, including rent, car payments, student loans, and any other outstanding debts

The information that you bring to the prequalification session will remain confidential. The information will only be used to determine your ability to bid on affordable housing and qualify for a loan. If you qualify as a bidder but for one reason or another can't get a bank loan, the RTC will use the information to see if you qualify for an RTC loan.

THE BIDDER'S CONFERENCE

Several weeks before a public AFH auction the RTC often arranges a "Buyer Awareness Seminar" (also known as a "Bidder's Conference"). Here financial counselors will explain the auction process, how to bid (though not "what" to bid), how to get an RTC loan, financing terms, "good faith" deposit requirements (generally, the agencies require a $500 to $1,000 good faith deposit in the form of a cashier's check to bid), and the general guidelines of the AFH program. Sometimes these conferences are advertised in local papers. But to be certain you don't miss such an announcement your best bet is to simply phone the RTC hot line and select the choice for auctions. After you get the list of upcoming auctions, phone either the RTC regional office in charge of the auction or the auction house listed, and ask if they plan to hold a bidder's conference, and if so, when and where.

The RTC and FDIC also work closely with State Housing Finance Agencies (SHFAs) and local nonprofit organizations to counsel first-time buyers on the rudiments of homeownership.[5] The counselors, some of whom work for nonprofit housing advocacy groups, can provide information on which lenders in town have the best interest rates. The RTC and FDIC consolidated offices can provide the names and telephone numbers of SHFAs.

BIDDING

The RTC uses two types of auctions: "oral outcry" (or "open-cry"), in which bids are shouted out to an auctioneer, and "sealed bid" in which offers are submitted in sealed envelopes.

When it comes to oral outcry auctions, keep a few things in mind. First, people tend to get carried away at open-cry auctions. RTC statistics show that the average price of a home sold at oral outcry auctions averaged $5,000 higher than the price of homes sold through sealed bid

---

[5] SHFAs are state-operated organizations that provide housing and homeownership assistance to citizens through public grants and mortgages that usually carry below-market interest rates.

auctions where everyone stays quiet and calm. Sealed bid auctions are less emotional than oral outcry auctions. Either way, be careful. Set your limits before you bid and then don't go beyond them. Calculate the total price you're willing to pay. Factor in your cash down payment, monthly mortgage payment, and monthly expenses. If your monthly mortgage and related expenses (such as utilities) exceed 35 percent of your monthly take-home pay, keep your hands in your pockets and let the bidding roll on by.

INVESTOR TIP. *You can "ballpark" a monthly mortgage payment (interest, principal, and insurance) by multiplying the number of thousands in the loan by $10 (e.g., a $50,000 loan = 50 thousands × $10 = $500 a month payment). This gives you a rough estimate of what your monthly payments will be.*

If this is your first taste of high finance you should consult a social service counselor before the auction. If you win the bidding on a house you cannot afford, the first thing the government will ask is, where are you going to get the extra money to make these payments? If you don't have a good answer, the property will be offered to the runner-up bidder.

Before the auction begins each home or condo is assigned a lot number, which is used by the auctioneer to refer to that particular property. If you attend an oral outcry auction it will sound something like this: "On lot number 22 we're starting at $30,000. Do I hear $30,000? (Someone makes a bid.) Okay, do I hear $32,000?" And so on and so on.

KEY INFORMATION. *Remember to add 10 percent to the price of your bid. Auction houses are not charities. They earn their money by charging both the seller and the buyer a 10 percent commission. If you bid $30,000 that means you will actually pay $33,000.*

If you want to bid, raise your hand and loudly yell out your bid. It's as simple as that. Because it's a government auction, you won't have to worry about shills or decoys in the audience bidding the prices up. The government wants to get rid of this stuff.

HOW LOW WILL THE GOVERNMENT GO?

KEY INFORMATION. *Whether you bid at auction or contact the RTC directly, keep in mind the government has certain value schedules to follow that limit how cheaply it can sell a piece of property at any one time.*

When it first markets a property the RTC sets a minimum bid price that, rest assured, it will not share with you. If you "lowball" a bid you run the risk of falling below the RTC set minimum and your bid will simply be rejected. If the property has not sold after being on the market for a while, the RTC will begin an orderly process of lowering the price until it attracts a buyer.

As we said earlier, before a property ends up at auction the RTC and FDIC generally list all AFH homes with local real estate brokers. During the first 30 days the house (or any one- to four-family residence) is listed with a broker, you can walk into the realtor's office and make any sort of bid you like. The broker won't tell you yes or no because he or she doesn't have the authority to accept or reject an offer. Instead the broker will call the RTC account executive at the consolidated office in charge of that particular home and relay your bid.

KEY INFORMATION. *What the broker will not tell you is that during the first thirty days the house is on the market the RTC is allowed to accept a bid as low as 70 percent of "appraised" price! This represents an immediate savings to you of 30 percent. Consider it a future, built-in profit!*

LOW AND GOING LOWER

Another thing the RTC won't tell you is that if an AFH house has been on the market from thirty-one to sixty days the RTC is allowed to accept direct bids from buyers of just *40 percent of the current appraised value!* In other words, if a home is listing for $67,000 you might be able to get it for half that if it hasn't sold during the first 60 days on the market. If an AFH house has been on the market for more than sixty days and hasn't sold, then that piggy is sent to market and is auctioned to the highest bidder.

DEALING DIRECTLY WITH AN S&L

Question: Can I go directly to a failed S&L that is still being operated by the government and buy a low-priced house directly from them?

Answer: Yes. When the government moves against an insolvent S&L it first places that institution into a "conservatorship." The S&L remains open to the public while the RTC tries to sell its assets and find a buyer for its deposits. (Usually another bank or S&L buys the deposits.) While an S&L is in conservatorship you can approach it directly and make a bid on any of its real estate holdings. All of the institution's REO, or real estate owned, will be listed with the local consolidated office. If you need a list, start there. As with "receiverships," which are S&Ls that are no longer open to the public, all homes priced at $67,500 or less are placed in the RTC's Affordable Housing Clearinghouse. The clearinghouse is simply a computer listing of all AFH homes available from RTC receiverships and conservatorships.[6]

Conservatorships, which are staffed by RTC-approved employees, are a good place to pick up deals. The RTC wants to get rid of as much REO as it can, as quickly as possible. REO is real estate that has been foreclosed on by the S&L. Where did the REO come from? From the previous management, who made bad loans and has since been booted by the RTC.

KEY INFORMATION. *Although one- to four-family units owned by an S&L in federal conservatorship are subject to the AFH guidelines, low-priced apartment buildings owned by conservatorships are not subject to the AFH guidelines. Only when low-priced apartment buildings, of five units or more, move from conservatorship to receivership do they come under the AFH guidelines. (Again, a receivership occurs when the RTC closes an S&L and begins to sell all of its*

[6] For a short while in 1991 there was a loophole in the law under which homes valued at $67,500 that were owned by conservatorship S&Ls were not subject to the AFH guidelines—meaning anyone, no matter how much they earned—could buy low-priced homes. That loophole was closed in the spring of 1991.

remaining assets. At this point the apartment building will move into the RTC's Affordable Housing Program and become subject to that program's rules and limitations.)

FINANCING

Not only is the government selling these AFH homes at bargain basement prices, but it will even loan you the money to buy that house or condo. In some cases it'll even pay your closing costs. Ideally, the government would rather have you go out and get a loan on your own, but since it wants to sell houses as quickly as possible, the RTC, for all intents and purposes, is in the loan business. So is the FDIC, but to a lesser extent.

When you fill out the bidder qualification form, the RTC is doing two things: First it's making sure you don't exceed the income cap, and second—at the same time—it's trying to get enough information to qualify you for a mortgage. When the government sells homes at auctions it has professional loan underwriters (loan officers) on hand who will take your mortgage application the same day.

Sometimes when auctions are held, the government will distribute information lists on where you might be able to get below-market interest rate mortgages, or state or federal grants to fix up your home. The money comes from a variety of sources, including state and local housing finance agencies, nonprofit pro-housing organizations, and private foundations. The best place to get a mortgage is from a bank, S&L, mortgage banking company, or credit union.

Banks and thrifts. Even though you are a low- to moderate-income buyer you can still qualify for a bank loan. Community Reinvestment Act (CRA) laws passed by Congress require banks and S&Ls to make a certain percentage of loans in lower-priced neighborhoods. CRA laws are enforced by the FDIC, Federal Reserve, and Office of Thrift Supervision (OTS), a federal agency that regulates only S&Ls. Banks and thrifts don't like the law, but most of them work hard to meet their quotas.

Mortgage bankers and credit unions. Mortgage banking companies are independently owned businesses that only make mortgages. They do not take deposits. For many years credit unions were not in the mortgage business but now are making home loans. Not all credit unions make home mortgages. If you have any questions check with your credit union.

OTHER MORTGAGE-RELATED ITEMS TO KEEP IN MIND

Mortgage insurance. Most conventional lenders require a cash down payment of at least 10 percent, but will accept 5 percent if you purchase private mortgage insurance (PMI). Private mortgage insurance is an insurance policy that a borrower takes out to "insure" that you won't default. The premium is figured into your monthly payment and can cost as much as $50 per month, depending on your loan size.

FHA and VA loans. If you qualify you can also get a mortgage from the Federal Housing Administration (FHA) or Veterans Administration (VA). Both will lend on RTC and FDIC properties. FHA and VA loans typically require 3 percent down if you're borrowing $25,000 or less, and 5 percent down if you're borrowing more. Although the borrowing guidelines changed in the summer of 1991, you can still finance up to 57 percent of your closing costs with an FHA or VA loan.[7] Previously, borrowers could finance up to 100 percent of the closing costs. By "finance" we mean that the closing costs—the points, fees, title, and escrow charges—are added onto your overall mortgage amount, costing you nothing up front. However, the FHA and VA *will not* lend you money on a condo or a co-op unless 51 percent of the building's units are owner-occupied—meaning the owner must live there. No renters. FHA and VA loans are available from banks, S&Ls, and mortgage banking firms. Mortgage banking firms tend to specialize in this type of business.

THE RTC WILL EVEN LOAN YOU THE MONEY

The RTC has its own lending guidelines, which we cover in detail in Chapter Five. Briefly, the RTC will make thirty-year loans to qualified buyers of single-family homes who cannot get financing elsewhere.

---

[7] Previously a borrower could finance up to 100 percent of his or her closing costs. It is anticipated that the 57 percent cap will be overturned sometime in the next year or so.

FINANCING FOR RENTERS OF GOVERNMENT-OWNED PROPERTIES

If you currently rent a condo or co-op owned by a failed S&L, you can buy that apartment with an RTC-financed loan. For renters the mortgage down payment is just two months' rent. There is a catch. The program is available only to those who earn 80 percent or less than the area median income. If you make 80 to 115 percent of the area median income, the government will still lend you the money, but only up to 95 percent of the loan amount.

In some areas of the country the government might be your only source of funding on a condo or co-op, because as we noted earlier, the FHA and VA will not extend you a mortgage unless 51 percent of a building's units are owner-occupied. RTC seller financing tends to go smoothly because all parties want the same thing—a completed sale.

RTC FINANCING ON ONE- TO FOUR-FAMILY AFH PROPERTIES

Lending terms offered to low- and moderate-income buyers of RTC AFH properties are better than those offered to higher-income buyers. RTC mortgages on AFH properties are for fixed-rate terms of either fifteen or thirty years. Rates tend to be slightly lower than the prevailing market rate and the RTC does not require private mortgage insurance (PMI).

If the home you're buying costs less than $50,000 the RTC will lend you up to 97 percent of the purchase price, bringing your cash down payment to just $1,500—less than the first and last month's rent for a good apartment! Remember, though, these terms apply only to people who make less than 80 percent of the area median income. If you make 80 to 115 percent of the area median income you have to put at least 5 percent down. If the home costs more than $50,000, the RTC requires a down payment of at least $750 plus 5 percent of the sales amount that exceeds $25,000. On a home price of $51,000 that translates into $750 plus $1,300 (5 percent of $26,000), which comes to a grand total of $2,050.

The RTC places only a few restrictions on these generous AFH loans:

- The buyer/borrower must live in the home for at least one year
- The loan cannot be assumed by a third party
- The RTC loan is due and payable upon the sale of the property

KEY INFORMATION. *Depending on what your personal finances are—and how desperate the government is to unload a house—the RTC will pay a portion, or even all, of your closing costs. Circumstances vary from state to state. As one RTC official told us: "We're more likely to pay closing costs on a house in Texas than in California." That's because the RTC is up to its neck in cheap houses in Texas but doesn't have as many in California. But even in states where properties are more scarce, the RTC will bend over backwards to place a house with a low-income family. The lower your income, the more likely the government will pay your closing costs.*

After you make a bid on a home, ask an RTC account executive or asset manager or realtor in charge of the sale about the closing cost option. The fewer bidders there are, the better your chances of getting government assistance at closing time. Also, your financial statement will have to reflect a level of "poverty" that would support such an act of "charity."

ONE WARNING

Be straight on your AFH financial statement. The entire S&L and banking mess was created by liars and cheats who received million-dollar loans from lenders with phony financial statements. Understandably, Congress is in a nasty mood. Lawmakers have instructed the Justice Department (read: FBI) to have zero tolerance for anyone, even AFH buyers, who doctor their financial statements. The Justice Department will prosecute. The RTC and FDIC have plenty of AFH and non-AFH properties available for purchase. Cheating is not worth it. You just might turn out to be the poor sucker they decide to make an example of.

CAVEATS AND RESTRICTIONS ON AFH HOUSES, CONDOS, AND CO-OPS

Question: If I buy an AFH home from the RTC or FDIC can I fix it up and sell it a few months later at a profit?

Answer: No. If you qualify to buy a home under the affordable housing program the government requires that you live in it for at least one year. This is called the owner occupancy rule. But the day after a year is up, you can do whatever you like with the property—rent it, lease it, or sell it.

Question: Can I fool the government into thinking I live there when I really don't?

Answer: Only at your own risk. From time to time the RTC does follow-up occupancy checks. If you rent it out and you're caught the agency can fine you or have the Justice Department (in extreme cases) prosecute you. Again, it's just not worth the risk.

Question: What if I buy an AFH home and then find I have to move or sell it before a year is up?

Answer: If you sell before a year is up the RTC will step in and claim 75 percent of any profit you make. If you spent money remodeling you will not be able to recoup it.

The government makes exceptions to the one-year rule—in the case of a job transfer or genuine family crisis. The emphasis here is on the word "crisis." The RTC does not consider your need to raise money to pay last year's taxes a "crisis." The agency leans more toward "an act of God" definition of crisis.

Question: As an investor can I use friends or relatives who qualify under the AFH income guidelines to buy a house where I really own it?

Answer: Only if you want to share a jail cell with Charlie Keating. The person whose name appears on the bidder qualification form will be given legal title to the house. You can give him or her "gift" funds toward buying an AFH home but that person must own the property and pay for it. Using a "front" or "straw" buyer to hide true ownership is a federal felony. The Justice Department will indict. Bet on it.

RICH GET RICHER DEPARTMENT— INVESTOR OPPORTUNITIES

Just because the RTC's AFH program focuses its energies on low- to moderate-income buyers, that doesn't mean well-heeled investors are shut out. The opposite is true. For apartment building investors the AFH program can be a golden opportunity.

In December 1991 the RTC sold 26 apartment buildings through the AFH program—20 of which were in Texas—to General Electric Capital Corporation, a conglomerate based in Stamford, Connecticut. The sale price was $75 million. The number of rental units in those 26 properties totaled 5,590. The unit cost on those 5,590 properties came to just $13,416 per apartment (divide $75 million by 5,590.) You can't even buy a decent mid-sized new car for $13,000.

General Electric—not exactly a poverty case—made a killing. And it's not the only one profiting from the AFH program. Since the RTC was created in 1989 the agency has been selling apartment buildings at per unit costs far below market value. G.E. represents an example of a large corporate investor. For the small to mid-sized investor—developers, contractors, doctors, lawyers, and other professionals—opportunities abound in the AFH program.

Here's a sample of AFH apartment buildings (five or more units) that were available from the RTC in Texas in early 1992:

City	Units	Asking Price	Per unit cost
Austin	578	$4,100,000	$7,093
Corpus Christi	40	$500,000	$12,500
Dallas	72	$510,000	$7,083
Dallas	46	$210,000	$4,565
Houston	164	$2,700,000	$16,463

Keep in mind these are asking prices. The final sales price could be as low as 45 percent of the initial asking price. In 1992 the average cost of constructing just one rental unit of public housing from scratch was $78,000. But apartment buildings in the RTC's AFH program were selling at an average per unit cost of between $10,000 and $11,000!

The quality of the apartment buildings offered through the AFH multi-family program ranges from poor to excellent. Why would the RTC put perfectly good apartment buildings into its AFH program? Answer: overbuilding. During the 1980s S&Ls were practically giving money away to developers. It was a "lend now, worry later" atmosphere. Too many apartment buildings were built too quickly, forcing prices down. Because the per-unit asking prices are so low, the buildings must—by law—be offered through the AFH program. As a result, excellent bargains in apartment buildings will be plentiful through at least 1995 in the AFH program. After that, economists predict, prices will begin to stabilize and rise. By mid-decade, as populations continue to swell—especially in Texas, Florida, and California—experts predict that well-built apartment buildings will become cash cows and will remain so for many years to come.

By late 1991 the RTC had almost 15,000 single-family properties and 1,000 apartment buildings available through the AFH program. That inventory will rise and fall depending on sales and future S&L failures. For investors looking to get in at rock-bottom prices, Colorado, Florida, Oklahoma, and Texas remain your best bets. The good buys of the future, however, are likely to be found in New England, New York, New Jersey, and the Midwest. As the FDIC's caseload of insolvent banks reaches critical mass over the next two years, more and more apartment buildings will be coming to market. The greater the pressure from Congress to sell these buildings, the more the prices will be slashed. Watch for the investor focus to switch from the Southwest to these largely untapped regions of the country.

EVERY SILVER LINING HAS A CLOUD

Buying an apartment building through the AFH program, though a great opportunity for investors, does have its drawbacks. First there's the question of eligibility. As we noted earlier, it doesn't matter how much money you make—as long as you're buying an apartment building of five or more units. But not all government-owned apartment buildings are placed in the AFH program. Some are sold at RTC commercial property auctions open to all bidders. An apartment building placed in the AFH program will carry certain burdens. If an apartment building has five or more units it cannot be offered through the AFH program if its studio apartments are valued at $29,500 or more; one-bedroom units at $33,816 or more; two-bedroom units at $41,120 or more; three-bedroom units at $53,195 or more; and larger units at $58,392 or more.

(All values based on current market analysis appraisals by RTC approved appraisers.) The per unit values are reached by prorating the building's appraised value among its individual units. The formula stated above applies only to RTC properties. The FDIC has more discretion to set its own AFH caps, which tend to be more generous to investors.

One negative in buying an apartment building through the AFH program is the federal "set-aside" requirement. Because you're buying the building so cheaply, the RTC requires that you rent at least 35 percent of its units to low-income residents. The low-income set-aside requirement will be written right into the deed. You cannot escape it. Worse yet, the condition encumbers the property for forty years from the date of the sale.

The RTC, not the buyer, decides what the term "low-income" means. The rent formula for low-income units is pegged to the "adjusted" income of a family as determined by its gross income, not take-home pay. Low-income families are allowed to deduct amounts from the gross similar to the deductions allowed buyers of AFH one- to four-family homes. The rent investors can charge low-income residents can be no more than 30 percent of their gross income. For example, if their monthly adjusted gross income is $1,000 you cannot charge a low-income resident more than $300 a month for rent. Is this condition a problem for real estate investors? Yes and no. On the rental end it may be less a problem than it appears. The property manager—not the government—chooses the tenants. Depending on where the apartment building is located, the rent charged on these "set-aside" units may not be too much lower than what you were hoping to charge for rent anyway.

KEY INFORMATION. *Remember—if you buy a low-priced apartment building from a conservatorship S&L and not a receivership you can escape the 35 percent low-income rental set-aside. This loophole could change, but for now, investors are safe.*

DAVID VERSUS GOLIATH

Right now some healthy competition exists for these cheap rental units. Corporate investors like General Electric, as well as pension funds and insurance companies, are showing increasing interest in these RTC and

FDIC apartment buildings. They realize that below replacement cost per-unit prices of $10,000 don't come along everyday. In other words, they know a good deal when they see one—deed restrictions and all. The good news is that these big investors only want the larger, prime apartment buildings with 300 or more units. For the small- to mid-sized investor this is a welcome bit of knowledge. Some of the best deals available from the government are on apartment buildings of six to sixty units. These complexes are not moving as quickly as the others—and since the demand is less, discounts abound.

Question: Can a buyer "flip" an AFH apartment building within a few months after buying it?

Answer: Yes. AFH apartment properties (five units or more) *are not subject to the same one-year rule that burdens the one- to four-unit AFH program.* If you can sell it two weeks later for twice what you paid, more power to you. Uncle Sam will not be around for his share. The RTC can do nothing to you. Remember, though, the 35 percent rent set-aside for low-income residents applies to the next owner— and lasts for forty years from the date of the original RTC sale.

Question: Can a sharp lawyer get the deed restriction quietly removed?

Answer: A lawyer can try but we don't recommend such a strategy. As one RTC contractor who deals extensively with the AFH multifamily program told us, "You'd be looking for trouble if you tried to remove that deed restriction. The RTC would have you in court overnight and I think most judges would be very unsympathetic to your cause."

INVESTOR TIP. *If you buy more than one AFH apartment building at a time you can play around with the 35 percent set-aside rule. For example: You purchase three AFH apartment buildings, each with 100 rental units. Two of the buildings can have set-asides of just 10 percent each while the third has an 85 percent set-aside. It's all legal. By law, if you buy apartment buildings "in-bulk," meaning more than one at a time, you are allowed to make the low-income rent set-aside as low as 10 percent in any one building, but you will have to make up for it with more units in the other buildings.*

For a while there was a loophole in the law whereby you could shift all of the low-income set-asides to one building and have none in the others. GE did this with its bulk purchase of twenty-six apartment buildings. Unfortunately for other investors, the publicity following what GE did killed the loophole. Also, you can only play with the set-asides if you buy more than one building at a time. If you buy one AFH apartment building one month and another the next, you cannot after-the-fact alter the set-aside. You have to buy the two at the same time and tell the RTC up front what the set-asides are going to be in each apartment building.

INVESTOR TIP. *If you're afraid of the forty-year deed restriction that mandates you set aside 35 percent of the rental units for low-income residents, then the best way to buy an apartment building is not through the AFH program but to buy a delinquent or defaulted loan that the RTC has in its inventory of available assets. The RTC is dying to get rid of these loans and would be more than happy to sell them to you. After acquiring the loan you can foreclose on the building and become its owner. (See Chapter 8 on buying loans.)*

BUYING AN AFH APARTMENT BUILDING: THE SEALED BID PROCESS

When it comes to purchasing an apartment building through the AFH program, you will not be doing so at an open-cry auction. AFH apartment buildings are sold through the sealed bid process. This means that any apartment building that falls under the AFH guidelines will first be offered to the public for ninety days. During this three-month period you can view the property by filling out a "notice of inspection" form with the consolidated office. The form is a technicality and allows you access to get a closer look.

If you decide to bid you will have to wait until the ninety-day period ends. The RTC marketing material provided lists the official bid date. After you submit a formal bid the RTC allows another thirty days to conduct an in-depth inspection of the property. If you are not a seasoned real estate investor you may want to hire a structural engineer or contractor to determine the condition of the building. During this thirty-day period the RTC will examine all the bids it received to determine which gives the government the highest present dollar return. Whether you win or lose, your bid will be kept confidential. One caveat here. Not only will the government ask how much you are willing to pay, but they want to know how many of the units you will rent to low-income tenants. Even though 35 percent is the law, they will give preference to higher set-asides. If you bid $400,000 for a building and offer to rent out 35 percent (the minimum) to low-income residents and the Dallas Housing Finance Authority bids $375,000 but offers to rent out 75 percent of the units to low-income residents, the DHFA will probably get the property.

If you manage a nonprofit organization, this is good news. "For-profit" investors should view the consideration like a golf handicap. In late 1991, when Congress voted to allocate $70 billion for the ailing FDIC to prop up the nation's ailing banks, it passed several amendments to the AFH program. One amendment grants the RTC the right to negotiate *exclusively* with nonprofit organizations, cutting for-profit investors out of the loop.

Still, many investors do not see this as that big a deal. Nonprofits have limited resources. Also, the policy is not cast entirely in stone and clashes with the RTC's mandate to sell real estate at the "highest return to the taxpayer." As of this writing the exclusivity clause had not been used, or even tested for that matter. We mention it as a precaution. Of the 115 apartment buildings sold through the AFH program as of year-end 1991, only twenty had been acquired by nonprofit groups or state or local housing finance agencies.

BUDDY, CAN YOU SPARE A LOAN?

FINANCING FOR INVESTORS

Even in the AFH program "cash is king." In other words, the RTC and FDIC will take an all cash bid before they take an offer that requires financing. Having your financing locked in before you go to bid allows you to offer the RTC, in essence, "all cash." If you don't have all cash and need a loan to make a sale happen, you have two ways to go. Try a local bank or S&L for a loan. Don't be surprised if they beg off. Banks and thrifts are under a lot of pressure to reduce their loan exposure on investment real estate.

Still, if you're a regular bank customer, and haven't already borrowed to the hilt, you might get the financing—it all depends—as long as the loan doesn't look too risky. "Too risky" in regulatory-speak translates into owner equity in the venture. In other words, are you, the borrower, able and willing to make a substantial cash down payment of at least 25 percent? Also, does the appraisal show the project is worth what you're willing to pay? Will the rent proceeds allow you a good profit? If the answer to all these questions is "yes," you have a shot at getting a loan from your bank or S&L. Also, try the aforementioned mortgage companies. Mortgage bankers make large apartment building loans as well. If a bank or S&L is in no-loan mode, a mortgage company might have a stable of private investors willing to take you on.

Because you're buying your AFH apartment building at substantial discount, obtaining financing should not be a major roadblock as long as you're willing to make a down payment of at least 25 percent.

RTC SELLER-FINANCING

If you can't get (or you don't want to get) outside financing, don't worry. The RTC will lend you up to 85 percent of the purchase price on an apartment building. The terms are often better than what you can get on the open market. The catch is that the loans offered are only seven-year balloons, which means you'll have to get new financing in, yes, seven years.

KEY INFORMATION. *Although the government would prefer at least 20 percent down, RTC rules (which also apply to the FDIC) state that a down payment of 15 percent is the "absolute minimum" the government will accept. The RTC ties its mortgage interest rate to the weekly Treasury Bill Index published in the* Wall Street Journal. *Again, the loan term is for seven years, but is amortized using a thirty-year schedule—that means you're paying all interest and little or no principal.*

If you're a nonprofit group, the RTC will lend you 95 percent of the purchase price to buy an AFH apartment building. The agency also will make you a longer-term loan—fifteen years rather than seven years. Again, the loan will be amortized using a thirty-year schedule.

THE FDIC'S AFFORDABLE HOUSING PROGRAM

As we've already noted, the FDIC's AFH program is nearly identical to the RTC program. The FDIC's AFH program was late in getting under way and has learned from the RTC's early mistakes. The major difference between the two programs is that the FDIC asked for and received the authority to establish a price cap on one- to four-family units based on a particular area's cost of housing. This is good news for home buyers in high-priced housing markets such as Boston, Los Angeles, New York, and San Francisco, where even a vacant lot often sells for more than the normal $67,500 AFH cap.

Another difference between the RTC and FDIC involves seller financing. Although the RTC offers liberal seller financing on AFH properties, the FDIC offers limited financing. This is likely to change over time. When in doubt ask an account executive at the closest FDIC consolidated office. As the FDIC liquidation process gathers steam, this agency will learn the same thing the RTC learned a couple of years ago: Seller financing moves property.

Otherwise the programs are much the same and you can deal with the FDIC as you do the RTC. Instead of starting out by telephoning the RTC's consolidated offices for AFH properties, you will be calling the FDIC's consolidated offices, which are listed in our Yellow Pages. As with the RTC, you can check out the FDIC's AFH opportunities on your home computer by accessing its computer network, which is called the ORE (Owned Real Estate) Bulletin Board.

AFFORDABLE HOUSING SUMMARY

- The Affordable Housing Program is not just for the poor and disadvantaged. It's also for the most often forgotten Americans—the working middle-class who've been priced out of the housing market. For them, Ronald Reagan's "trickle down" theory of economics is based on the belief that the best way to feed the birds is to first give grain to the horses.

- The RTC has set a cap of $67,500 on homes that can be sold under the AFH program. The cap is adequate for cheaper markets but does nothing for higher-priced areas such as Chicago, Los Angeles, and New York. The FDIC—whose AFH program is similar to the RTC's—can raise the $67,500 cap at its discretion. If you live in a high-priced region, your best affordable housing bet will be with the FDIC.
- Both agencies have become "user friendly." You can access their AFH inventory through a computer or telephone.
- Real estate investors can make money with the AFH program as well. Now's the time to buy. Per unit costs of $4,000 to $16,000 abound. You will not see these prices again.
- When it comes to buying AFH apartment buildings, "cash is king." If you don't have cash or you're having difficulties obtaining financing from a bank or S&L, the RTC will lend you up to 85 percent of the purchase price.

NON-AFFORDABLE HOUSING OPPORTUNITIES

Besides AFH opportunities for investors and low- to moderate-income home buyers, the RTC and FDIC have billions of dollars' worth of residential real estate for sale that does not fall under any AFH restrictions or conditions. Investors can buy anything from suburban homes to mansions, from condos to townhouses. Whatever you desire, chances are good the RTC or FDIC has it—and you won't have to worry about a bunch of guidelines and rules. As with real estate purchases, though, it helps if you have financing lined up.

As explained in Chapter Two, if you're buying from the RTC, start by telephoning its Asset Specific 800 number (1-800-RTC-3006) or by accessing its RTCNET data base with your home computer. When your search is complete you will have a list of properties that fit your price, location, and habitat needs.

Real estate listings mailed to you by the agency will include a telephone number of the RTC asset manager and the listing real estate broker assigned to that property. Call the real estate agent listed. Only call the RTC asset manager if you have a problem reaching the real estate agent. The realtor will arrange to show you the property. After you've seen the property, make an offer through the realtor. The realtor *must* present all offers to the RTC consolidated office—no matter how low those offers might be.

As with any real estate transaction, the RTC will either accept your offer, reject it, or make you a counteroffer. The RTC's response will be communicated to you through the listing realtor. If you require RTC financing, be sure to tell the agency when your offer is made. (See Chapter 5 for RTC financing terms.) The RTC so far has been authorized to make $7 billion in loans. More than $250 million has been earmarked for loans on one- to four-family homes. The RTC has been authorized to make an additional $4.25 billion in loans if the demand is there. If you've already been approved for a bank loan, obtain a letter of credit from the lender. Include it with your offer.

If a non-AFH house has not sold after being on the market for thirty days, the RTC will instruct the realtor to reduce the price. If after ninety days the house still hasn't sold the RTC will take the listing away from the realtor and offer it through a general auction at which it will be sold with other non-AFH homes to the highest bidder.

Purchasing a non-AFH property from the RTC is a straightforward process. You just have to know what's for sale and who to call. Then make an offer. When buying from the FDIC, start by calling the closest consolidated office in the area in which you want to invest. You can also tap into its computer data base, the ORE Bulletin Board, and start that way. Either way, after that the process is the same.

OTHER GOVERNMENT HOMES FOR SALE

BUYING A HUD HOME OR APARTMENT BUILDING

The RTC and FDIC are not the only federal agencies struggling with the residue of the 1980s. When it comes to buying cheap real estate, one of the best bargains around—besides the RTC and FDIC—is the Department of Housing and Urban Development, commonly known as HUD. Created in 1934, HUD's mission in life is to promote home ownership and affordable housing. HUD also is in charge of the nation's public housing stock and is responsible for building new public housing, as well as promoting single-family ownership among low- to moderate-income Americans.

To say HUD lost sight of its mission during the eight years Ronald Reagan occupied the White House would be an understatement. While occupying itself with arranging lucrative development contracts for Republican Party insiders like former Interior Secretary James Watt, the agency paid little attention to its low- to moderate-income federal loan guarantee program operated by the Federal Housing Administration (FHA).

The FHA makes loans to individuals who for one reason or another cannot get a loan from traditional sources such as a bank or S&L. Guaranteed by the federal government, the FHA requires as little as 5 percent down. If a borrower defaults, HUD repossesses the house and then tries to sell it.

Unfortunately for taxpayers, the FHA didn't do a very good job of underwriting the millions of mortgages it insured. This included mortgages on one- to four-family homes as well as entire apartment buildings. When lenders incurred a loss on a bad home mortgage it was a little like the S&L crisis: "Heads we win, tails the government loses." The FHA picked up the tab, not the lender.

FHA loans are available from most lenders—including banks and S&Ls. Interestingly, lenders will make FHA-insured loans to the financially disadvantaged, but not other types of loans. The key, of course, is the word "insured." In making FHA loans lenders earn money by charging the borrower points and loan application fees.

Tens of thousands of FHA-insured mortgages went bad during the 1980s, leaving HUD no other choice but to foreclose. Because the FHA insured billions of dollars' worth of mortgages, it was just a matter of time before the agency started accumulating thousands of single-family properties. And once it repossessed these properties HUD had to sell them—fast. The result has been a bargain market. Over the past two years the average sales price of a home sold by HUD has been around $40,000, leaving HUD with an average loss of $20,000 to $23,000. For buyers that means getting a home for about one-third of what it normally might have sold for had it not been owned by Uncle Sam, who is now forced to sell at fire sale prices.

Property Types Available

HUD sells single-family homes, duplexes, triplexes, fourplexes, single condominium units and cooperatives, and townhouses. It also has apartment buildings available. The homes come in all shapes and sizes and are in almost all fifty states. They have garages, patios, driveways, and some are relatively new.

In 1990 and 1991 HUD foreclosed on 72,092 and 66,648 homes, respectively. During those two years it sold a total of 153,357 homes. In 1992 and 1993 HUD expects to foreclose on at least another 140,788 homes, while anticipating sales of 159,171. These are Bush administration numbers buried in the 1993 budget, which means they are certainly on the "optimistic" side. The number of foreclosures may well be much higher.

Despite HUD's huge inventory of single-family homes each year, it only has a hundred or so multifamily units (apartment buildings) available for sale. In 1991, for example, HUD sold about one hundred apartment buildings with one thousand four hundred rental units. So when it comes to apartment buildings the RTC has a lot more to offer in the way of inventory, while HUD will generally have more single-family units available at any one time. But HUD isn't under pressure from Congress to unload these properties at fire sale prices, so you can still get your best single-family property deals from the RTC. Also RTC and FDIC single-family properties are more varied and include luxury amenities and residences, unlike HUD homes, which tend to be more spartan.

KEY INFORMATION. *HUD homes are most plentiful in the Southern and Southwestern sections of the country. In 1991, for example, HUD sold twenty thousand homes in metropolitan areas such as Albuquerque, Fort Worth, Little Rock, New Orleans; and San Antonio. Southern cities such as Atlanta, Birmingham, Coral Gables, Florida; Greensboro, North Carolina; Louisville, Nashville, and Tampa, also are chock-full of available HUD homes.*

As of the beginning of 1992 the New England area had the least amount of homes available to purchase, but that situation could change as the economy continues to scrape along the bottom in Connecticut, Rhode Island, and other states.

We expect that by mid-decade HUD's inventory of good deals will begin to decline. As far as Western markets are concerned, Fresno, Phoenix, and Tucson have more to offer in the way of available HUD homes than other metropolitan areas.

WHO CAN BUY A HUD HOME?

Unlike homes sold through the RTC or FDIC Affordable Housing Programs, which cater to low- and moderate-income buyers, there are no income limitations whatsoever on who can buy a HUD home. In any city in any state anyone can walk off the street and make a bid on a home owned by the agency. The only individuals barred from buying HUD properties are employees of the agency and members of their immediate families and anyone who has defaulted on an FHA mortgage.

GETTING STARTED

Querying HUD is not as easy as dealing with the RTC. As we noted in earlier chapters, the RTC's multibillion dollar inventory of loans and real estate can be easily accessed via computer or by dialing a toll-free asset specific inquiry telephone number that gives you tailor-made lists of available properties. HUD, unfortunately, is not quite so user friendly. HUD has no computerized real estate data base that is available to the public.

HUD has ten regional offices and eighty field offices. It also has a special Indian Programs office in Phoenix that provides housing assistance to American Indians. The ten field offices are in charge of selling foreclosed homes to the general public.

The 10 regional offices are located in the following cities:
- Boston (Region I)
- New York (Region II)
- Philadelphia (Region III)
- Atlanta (Region IV)

- Chicago (Region V)
- Ft. Worth (Region VI)
- Kansas City, Mo. (Region VII)
- Denver (Region VIII)
- San Francisco (Region IX)
- Seattle (Region X)

Each regional office has a number of field offices. The field offices break down as follows:

Boston: Bangor, Me.; Burlington, Vt.; Hartford, Conn.; Manchester, N.H.; Providence, R.I.

New York: Albany and Buffalo, N.Y.; Camden and Newark, N.J.; San Juan, P.R.

Philadelphia: Baltimore, Md.; Charleston, W. Va.; Pittsburgh, Pa.; Richmond, Va.; Washington, D.C.; Wilmington, Del.

Atlanta: Birmingham, Ala.; Columbia, S.C.; Greensboro, N.C.; Jackson, Miss.; Coral Gables, Orlando, Tampa, and Jacksonville, Fla.; Knoxville, Memphis, and Nashville, Tenn.; Louisville, Ky.

Chicago: Cincinnati, Cleveland, and Columbus, Ohio; Detroit, Flint, and Grand Rapids, Mich.; Indianapolis, Ind.; Milwaukee, Wisc.; Minneapolis, Minn.; Springfield, Ill.

Fort Worth: Albuquerque, N.M.; Dallas, Houston, San Antonio, and Lubbock, Tex.; Little Rock, Ark.; Oklahoma City and Tulsa, Okla.; New Orleans and Shreveport, La.

Kansas City: Des Moines, Iowa; Omaha, Neb.; St. Louis, Mo.; Topeka, Kan.

Denver: Casper, Wy.; Fargo, N.D.; Helena, Mont.; Salt Lake City, Utah; Sioux Falls, S.D.

San Francisco: Honolulu, Hawaii; Phoenix and Tucson, Az.; Reno and Las Vegas, Nev.; Sacramento, San Diego, Santa Ana, Fresno, and Los Angeles, Calif.

Seattle: Anchorage, Alaska; Boise, Idaho; Portland, Ore.; Spokane, Wash.

For a complete listing of addresses and telephone numbers for the regional offices see our Yellow Pages.

Like the RTC and FDIC, HUD to a certain degree is decentralized, meaning that authority to buy the homes is granted by the field and regional offices, not HUD headquarters in Washington. Realtors list the properties for sale and are paid a standard sales commission for selling the homes—up to 6 percent. In general HUD pays brokers the going rate in the local market. If it's 5 percent then the realtor gets 5 percent. (If you're a realtor this is good news because no matter who buys the home you get paid a commission—that is, as long as you're the listing agent.)

HOW HUD HOMES ARE SOLD

All HUD homes are sold through an auction process. That means if you're an investor you cannot negotiate with the agency or the realtor to try to get it to whittle down the price. Besides appearing in the MLS (multiple listing service) book, homes available for sale by HUD are listed in local newspapers (both weeklies and dailies) in the city in which the house is located. Typically, new listings are advertised in the real estate section of the local newspaper on a Friday. All HUD listings are posted on Sundays.

Auctions of HUD homes are listed when the agency amasses enough properties to make an auction cost-effective. All auctions are advertised and are held on weekends in order to maximize attendance. If there are not enough homes to hold an auction, HUD will list the individual properties with real estate agents.

If you want to bid on a home you have two weeks to do so from the time the house first goes on the market. Yes, this is a very short period of time. If you see a good property and blink you could miss it entirely.

The newspaper advertisements taken out by HUD and local realtors typically state the address, a few characteristics about the property, and the asking price.

HUD sets a "bid date" for its sealed bid auction. Anyone can bid. After contacting the listing broker and viewing the home, you submit your sealed bid to the listing broker. Along with your bid you must post an earnest-money deposit of $500. (For particularly expensive properties the earnest money could be as high as $2,000, but not more.) The listing agent will place that deposit in an escrow account for you until all the bids are unsealed. A bid date will be established by HUD and the bids will be collected. HUD then has two business working days to review the bids and choose a winner. HUD rules are cut and dry: Whoever bids the most wins. The winning bid is picked by the regional or field office that has been assigned that foreclosed home. If you do not win the bid your money will be returned to you by the listing realtor.

Unlike the RTC, HUD has not been very willing to share with the public how it determines a minimum "strike" price on a home it wants to sell. If a home is listed for $30,000 HUD may take as little as $25,000. Unlike the RTC it has not disclosed publicly what percentage of the asking price it will accept. (The RTC has already let the world know that it will accept a bid that is 95 percent of the fair market value.) But making a wild lowball offer is not likely to work with HUD. Its strike price is not likely to be less than 90 percent or so of the asking price. If the house checks out, make a reasonable but conservative bid. If a home fails to attract bids, HUD will then remarket the property, likely reducing its price.

BUYING GUIDELINES:
INVESTORS VERSUS OWNER-OCCUPIERS

Although HUD was chartered to promote home ownership among low- and moderate-income families, the agency will sell its repossessed homes to anyone—even investors. But HUD is willing to accept less of a down payment from owner-occupiers than investors. If you're a buyer planning on living in the home, HUD will accept a down payment of less than 2 percent. If you're an investor who is going to rent that home out,

HUD requires that you put down at least 25 percent. Investors who buy single-family homes from HUD can rent them out to whomever they like at whatever price they want. The government imposes no limits on this.

Unlike the RTC, HUD won't loan anyone a dime to buy one of their properties. However, buyers can always obtain an FHA-insured mortgage on a HUD home even though the previous owner defaulted on an FHA loan. FHA loans are arranged through banks and thrifts. Contact one in the general area and tell them you plan to bid on a particular FHA property and want to get prequalified for a loan. Since the house already passed FHA muster once, it is likely to easily do so again. The FHA requires a house to meet some basic structural requirements such as adequate insulation, foundation, and electrical.

In the summer of 1991 Congress passed legislation tightening the FHA's loan underwriting guidelines. Those changes are still in effect today. The changes prohibit borrowers from financing more than 57 percent of their closing costs. Prior to the change a borrower could finance up to 100 percent of closing costs and then add that amount to the overall loan. This was great news for first-time home buyers, but for the FHA it posed a great risk: If a home buyer lost his or her job, or the home went down in value, the buyer could just walk away from the loan and not lose any equity because the entire purchase price as well as the points and other closing costs were financed and "insured" by the FHA (a.k.a. Uncle Sam).

If the property costs $50,000 or more, HUD now requires that the buyer put down at least 2.25 percent of the purchase price. Homes that cost less require a minimum 1.25 percent down payment—compared to the 10 percent to 20 percent required by your friendly neighborhood bank or S&L. Besides the low down payment, the FHA requires that you pay a small up-front mortgage insurance premium of 3.8 percent and an annual mortgage insurance premium of .5 percent. On a $50,000 loan this would mean $1,900 at closing, plus an extra $250 per year, or about $20 a month in mortgage insurance premiums. Considered high by some, the mortgage insurance premiums are scheduled to be reduced to 2.25 percent at closing and .55 percent per year in 1995. (It is always possible that Congress could once again change these FHA underwriting guidelines.)

BUYING APARTMENT BUILDINGS FROM HUD

Buying HUD apartment buildings can be a lot trickier than buying buildings from the RTC or FDIC. For starters, about half of all apartment buildings offered by the agency were built with federal "Section 8" grants. That means that if you're the new owner you *must* rent the units out to low- and moderate-income tenants. (As defined in our Affordable Housing section, low- and moderate-income residents make 115 percent or less of the area median income. Median is the middle point where half the people make more and half make less.)

This iron-clad requirement is going to hold down the value of these multifamily properties. If you get the property cheaply enough, you may want to go ahead. But HUD multifamily properties are better left to nonprofit groups, community organizations, and tenant groups who band together to buy and manage a project themselves. However, because Section 8 housing is so heavily subsidized by the federal government, landlords of Section 8 housing do not need to worry about tenant rents.

BIDDER INFORMATION

Auctions of HUD properties are advertised in local, and sometimes national, newspapers a minimum of sixty days before the sale date. All HUD apartment buildings are sold by federally appointed auction commissioners chosen by HUD. The auction commissioner has the discretion on what type of auction to hold—either an oral outcry, in which buyers shout out their bids, or sealed-bid, in which offers are quietly collected in envelopes. Most HUD apartment building auctions are done through oral outcry.

When bidding on an HUD multifamily property the buyer must post an earnest-money deposit. The amount of this deposit varies from region to region and is determined by the sales manager at each office. In general, anticipate that you will have to post at least 10 percent of the purchase price as a good faith deposit. As with other government auctions, the money is returned if you're not the winning bidder. HUD apartment buildings are auctioned on the courthouse steps of the county seat where the building is located. Sometimes HUD auctions buildings that are still in foreclosure. This means you may not have much of a chance to perform any significant due diligence work on the property. It's not likely that the owner who is being foreclosed on by the government will give you a walking tour of the facility. In some cases the landlord might be an absentee landlord who is less than reputable.

Keep in mind that many HUD multifamily properties are dilapidated and need extensive work. If you buy one you will be subject to HUD maintenance guidelines. After years of abuses HUD frowns upon slumlords and will levy sizeable fines if you buy a Section 8 property and decide to simply collect the subsidized rents and let the property go to seed.

LOANS

If you plan to ask for seller financing, don't bid on HUD multifamily properties. HUD is not RTC or even the FDIC. It doesn't offer any seller financing. HUD wants cash at closing. You will have to get your own loan. If you're buying a Section 8 property that needs repairs, HUD requires that you post a letter of credit to facilitate repairs. No letter of credit means no sale.

MAKING A BID

HUD regional offices will not negotiate directly with investors on the sale of apartment buildings. Buyers have to bid through the auction commissioner. If your bid is accepted you will have thirty days to close the sale. The only time HUD deals directly with buyers is when the purchaser is a nonprofit organization that has pledged to keep the building a rental project for low- to moderate-income residents.

If you have any questions about how HUD works, we advise you to call the regional and field offices. Despite Jack Kemp's housecleaning of HUD, little has been done to improve the quality and responsiveness of HUD's public affairs staff in Washington. From what we found, it often takes days for telephone calls to be returned, and responses to buyer inquiries are less than satisfactory. However, we found sales executives at the regional offices to be well versed in the rudiments of buying and selling properties. Start there.

IN SUMMARY

There are a lot of reasons people give for not buying their own home:

- I don't have enough for a down payment
- I can't qualify for a loan
- I don't make enough money
- I can't afford the price of a home in my area

But with the creation of the FDIC and RTC's Affordable Housing Programs and the sale of HUD properties, such excuses no longer hold water. Now down payments are flexible, low-income people qualify *because* they have low incomes, and the prices can't be beat. Due to congressional pressure to do something about the nation's housing crisis, these agencies are under the gun and eager to deal with the very people banks have traditionally shunned and locked out of the home market. For those who thought they would never own their own home, these programs offer a once-in-a-lifetime opportunity. This is one government program that is working.

Chapter Four

....

Look Before You Leap

How to Assess Properties Before You Bid

Like most things in life, investing in real estate is not as complicated as it may appear once you understand the basics. The fundamentals of investing are just that—fundamental. Nevertheless, industry jargon and terminology can be intimidating, leading the novice investor to believe he or she doesn't have a chance of working through what appears to be a dense bureaucracy (which, as we've already explained, really isn't). The better you can function on your own, without getting outside help from a lawyer, for instance, the greater the return on your investment. If you're a seasoned real estate investor you'll probably want to skip this chapter and go on ahead to the next one.

By following the advice given in previous chapters, you should have found more than enough properties to pique your interest. The question then will be, which one and at what price? To get the answers to those questions you first have to do some research.

LOCATION, LOCATION, LOCATION

After you've researched what the RTC and FDIC have to sell in your area and you've chosen a few target properties, your first job is to inspect the property's physical location. It's a cliché, but true, that the three most important factors affecting the value of a piece of real estate are location, location, location.

In some cases you will be familiar enough with the target area to know what parts of town are on the "right" side of the tracks and what parts are on the "wrong" side of the tracks. But just because a property is in a good part of town, that does not mean its location is automatically going to work for you. Neighborhoods undergo demographic and zoning changes constantly. Before investing you will have to inspect what kinds of social and governmental forces are at work in the area that you've targeted.

A FEW TIPS

- Drive around the property's neighborhood ten blocks in each direction. Do you like what you see? Look at the properties 5 blocks away. Are they being renovated? Can you tell if the renovation trend is moving towards your property? Or do the properties look increasingly neglected as you drive? Is this trend moving your way? Is the property you're considering a rental property rather than your personal residence? If yes, then don't apply your standards to the surroundings or neighbors. You are not going to live there. What you want to consider is, can the property be rented to the kind of people you want as tenants?

- Go to your county or city building department and check out the zoning for the area. Ask if any zoning variances have been applied for in your target area. If you discover that the county or city has just granted a variance for someone in the residential neighborhood to run a kennel, you may want to reconsider. Ask if the area has been the subject of any zoning hearings or if any zoning changes are anticipated.

- As you drive around the area, determine your target property's proximity to conveniences such as shopping, mass transit, and schools. If the property is a commercial project, does its location facilitate such critical factors as customer traffic, parking, and convenient shipping and receiving access?

- If the property is an apartment building or a small commercial complex, check with a commercial realtor in the area to see what the local vacancy rate is.

These site appraisals should be your first considerations. Once the property's location passes muster, and only then, move on to the next consideration.

KICKING THE TIRES

Although the property inspection process differs for residential and income properties, both have common elements.

- How old is the structure or structures? An old building with a lot of "deferred maintenance" will cost you money for new appliances, updating electrical services, paint, and so on. If this is going to be your personal residence, this extra money will come right out of your pocket. If it's a duplex or fourplex rental unit that will be used to help meet the mortgage payment, then the repairs can be written off against that rental income, thereby reducing your tax liability. If this is the case, your tenants and the government, in essence, help pay for the repairs.

- What's the condition of the structure and what will it cost to fix it up? If you do not have the background or experience to make cost estimates, hire a home inspection service in the area. Fees for inspections can cost from $150 to $250. Make it clear to the inspecting contractor that you will not be hiring the contractor to do any of the repair work. This way you can be reasonably sure the estimate you are given is close to reality (see Exhibit 4). If you intend to do the work yourself, tell the inspector so the estimate doesn't include labor, just materials.

   If the inspection report is bad you may be able to use it to lower the seller's asking price. This may not always work when buying from the government because many of its properties are sold "as is" through a sealed bid process. But for RTC and FDIC properties listed with a realtor you at least have an opportunity for direct, one-on-one negotiations. A bad inspection report can result in the government accepting a lower price. An inspection report signed by a licensed contractor estimating that the property needs $25,000 in repairs, material, and labor can become a powerful negotiating tool.

Repairs and maintenance are key considerations in determining what kind of bid you should make to the RTC, FDIC, HUD, or other agencies.

THE DO-IT-YOURSELF INSPECTION

If you don't want to spend the money for an inspection service and you can trust your own powers of observation—which is what most small-time investors do—here are the key things to watch for.

Foundation

Start at the bottom. Does the house have a perimeter concrete foundation that raises the house at least a foot off the ground? Or does it have an old "post and pier" foundation? The answer is important if you want a bank loan. Banks love perimeter concrete foundations and they hate post and pier. A house on post and pier is one that does not have a cement skirt around it on which the perimeter of the house rests. Instead it has concrete blocks on the ground onto which wooden 4 × 4 posts are nailed. Floor joists are then laid across these posts. In essence, the house sits on short "stilts." If your target property is post and pier, figure in the cost of installing a perimeter concrete foundation. In many cases a bank will add the cost of the foundation into its loan and will require proof that the foundation has been installed. Also, if the house is in an earthquake zone be sure it not only has a perimeter concrete foundation but that it is bolted to the foundation.

Beams

Inspect the basement. While you are under the house bring a screwdriver and poke it into supporting beams. Don't stab, just firmly poke. The screwdriver should dent, but not penetrate, the beam. If the screwdriver cuts into the beam like a hot knife through butter, it means the house has dry rot, termites, or both.

```
BUG BUSTERS, INC.
4910 SONOMA HWY., STE. F
SANTA ROSA, CA  95409     (707)538-1080
```

<u>PRICE ESTIMATES FOR RECOMMENDED WORK</u>

THE FOLLOWING PRICE ESTIMATES ARE GIVEN FOR WORK RECOMMENDED ON THE STANDARD

STRUCTURAL PEST CONTROL INSPECTION REPORT ISSUED FOR <u>4980 VINE HILL RD.</u>

<u> SEBASTOPOL </u>. DATE OF INSPECTION <u>4-7-89</u>. COMPANY REPORT NO. <u>A-2699</u>

STATE STAMP NO. <u>1966423P</u>.

```
 1.   $50.00
*1A.   $985.00
 2.   Referred to other crafts
*4.   Time and material approximately $1250.00
 6.   $45.00
 9.   Referred to owner
 9A.   Referred to owner
```

* COMPLETION OF THESE RECOMMENDATIONS WILL BE NECESSARY FOR A STANDARD STRUCTURAL
  PEST CONTROL CERTIFICATION.

FOR FURTHER INFORMATION, PLEASE CONTACT BUG BUSTERS, INC. AT (707)538-1080.

THANK YOU,

EXHIBIT 4.   Termite inspection report and repair estimate.

99

Floors

Once past the foundation, jump on the floors. Do the floors "trampoline"? In other words, are they springy? Though your kids might like this effect, the message is a bad one. It means the floor stringers are too far apart, and you will have to reinforce them.

Walls and Ceilings

Now to the vertical structures. Are the walls plaster or Sheetrock? Are they cracked? Can you see the taped seams of the 4′ × 8′ sheetrock sections? Cracks and seams mean a lot of messy scrapping, taping, and repairs. Separated Sheetrock seams also can indicate that a house is shifting on its foundation. The condition of plaster and Sheetrock walls can also tell you a lot about potential moisture damage inside the walls. Constant moisture will show in the form of black mildew blotches, usually in the corners or where the wall meets the floor or ceiling. In really bad cases you'll have no doubts because paint and wallpaper will no longer stick to the wall.

Even though you can't see through walls, you can get a peek into them by removing plug switch and wall socket covers. This will tell you if the walls have insulation. If the house is in a flood zone, taking off a plug switch will show if the house has ever flooded. Mud or silt in the plug housings is a dead giveaway.

Doors and Windows

A lot can be told about a house by how well its doors and windows operate. Open and close all doors, including closets and kitchen cabinets. Do they swing easily, or do they jam? If they jam it could mean the foundation has shifted or is sinking, thereby throwing the door and window jambs out of square. It also can indicate the house has a moisture problem that has swollen the windows and doors.

Attic

Is it insulated? Most codes used to require R19, which is a six-inch thick piece of Fiberglas. Today R30 is recommended, which is twelve inches thick.

The attic is one of the few places in a house where you can get a good look at the electrical wiring. Is it modern Romex-type wiring,[1] or is it the old-fashioned wiring hanging from ceramic insulators? You don't need to be an electrical engineer here. If you wouldn't let your cat walk around in the attic for fear it would get electrocuted, the wiring needs to be replaced. (Cremated mice remains are another ominous sign of electrical problems.)

While inspecting the attic, take a look up. Are there leaks in the roof? Look for water stains on the beams and roof boards. Inspect areas around the chimney closely. It could be prone to leakage.

Roof

Same as the floor. Is it springy? It shouldn't be. What do the shingles look like? A roof that is flat will have a shorter life span than a steep roof. It's a simple concept: Water runs off a steep roof faster than a flat one. A composition (tar or Fiberglas shingle) roof has an average life span of twenty to twenty-five years. If the house has a wood shingle (shake) roof, you may want to replace it regardless of condition. Insurance companies hate wood roofs for obvious reasons, and if you insist on keeping it you will pay more for fire insurance. The best roofs (if supported properly) are tile or concrete tile roofs. They last forever.

Neighbors

While checking out the roof, you should use this lofty perch to spy on the neighbors. Are the adjoining yards a mess? Do they have packs of snarling pit bulls running up and down the fence line? Are old cars piled

[1] Romex-type modern wiring encloses the positive, negative, and ground wires all within a single, usually white, plastic sheathing.

up like cordwood in the yard? From the roof you can tell a lot about the neighborhood. If you don't like what you see, then pass.

Parking

How is the parking situation? Land in cities and even most suburbs now sells at such a premium that little room may have been allocated for parking. In some metropolitan areas curbside parking has been outlawed where streets are too narrow or curbside services, such as street cleaning and mechanized trash collection services, need easy access.

Sewage

If a property is in a rural area not served by a public sewer, you will have to become acquainted with the mysteries of septic tanks. Does the property have a septic tank or a cesspool? Of the two, a septic tank is preferred. A cesspool is a big covered hole in the ground where household sewage flows. The solids are supposed to decompose into fluids and seep into the ground. Depending on soil type, cesspools often don't work as well as septic tanks.

A septic tank is usually a buried tank built of either redwood, cement, or Fiberglas. Connected to the tank is a system of buried perforated pipes. The sewage flows into the tank. The fluids go off down the pipes (called "leach lines") and are absorbed by the earth. The solids are broken down by bacteria and turn into fluids. Septic tanks are engineered taking into account the absorption factor of the property's particular soil. The less the soil can absorb, the longer the leach lines. County building records contain information about a property's septic system. If you have a question, ask the realtor.

Sometimes it's easy to tell when a septic tank or cesspool isn't working properly. *The Grass Is Always Greener Over the Septic Tank* is the title of an Erma Bombeck book about moving to the country. Well, it shouldn't be. A big square or roundish patch of lush tropical rain forest in an otherwise barren backyard is a solid clue that the septic tank needs attention. Even the best-engineered septic tanks need to be pumped out after time. Occasionally the solids get ahead of even the hungriest bacteria. Some tanks go three years between pumpings. Others go twenty years. It all depends on the soil and how well the system is designed. Pumping can cost anywhere from $300 to $500. Not a big deal.

If you think a tank needs more than just a pumping, it might pay to have a septic tank service inspect the system. To do this a service digs down to the lid of the tank and opens the disgusting thing up. I've seen it done many times, and it has fundamentally changed my vision of Hell. Still, the exercise could be worth the cost and trauma. I once sold a house to a man who had never lived in a rural area before. Because the house had not been occupied for several months, I had no clue about the condition of its septic system. The owner vouched for the system, so we passed on an inspection. A week after he moved in I got a call from the buyer. On Sunday he had dressed for church and decided to take a stroll in his new backyard before leaving. Inspecting a patch of stunningly healthy roses, the man was swallowed by the gates of Hell. The wooden lid of the old cesspool collapsed and the man found himself shoulder deep in a well-aged brew. It turned out the whole tank had rotted through and needed to be replaced. Ditto for his Sunday suit. In this case the buyer was lucky. The seller paid the cost of both. But when the seller is a desperate and broke federal agency, the story may end very differently.

Water

If the house isn't on city water it will have a well. Wells come in two categories: trouble and trouble free. There seems little in between. You have to be concerned about three things with a well. First, how is the water? Is it hard or soft? And how does it taste? Some water is so saturated with iron that it tastes like it was run through a bucket of rusty nails before it reached your glass. If the water is hard you will need a water softener.

Second, how much water is there? Wells are tested by well and pump services for a small fee (see Exhibit 5). They will come out and "bail" your well. The process involves running the pump for a specified period of time at a specified number of gallons per minute. They do this until they figure out how many gallons per minute your well can run before it runs dry. Generally, counties like to see evidence of at least two gallons per minute flow before they will issue a building permit.

Finally, how is the pump? There are two kinds of pumps, surface

DUPLICATE
Retain this copy

Do Not Fill In

№ 141566

State Well No._____
Other Well No._____

(1) OWNER:

Name Jim Dykstra

Address 4990 Vine Hill Road
Sebastopol, California 95472

(2) LOCATION OF WELL:

County Sonoma   Owner's number, if any 76-06-6

Township, Range, and Section

Distance from cities, roads, railroads, etc. Same

(3) TYPE OF WORK *(check):*

New Well ☒   Deepening ☐   Reconditioning ☐   Destroying ☐

If destruction, describe material and procedure in Item 11.

(4) PROPOSED USE *(check):*

Domestic ☒   Industrial ☐   Municipal ☐
Irrigation ☐   Test Well ☐   Other ☐

(5) EQUIPMENT:

Rotary ☒
Cable ☐
Other ☐

(6) CASING INSTALLED:

STEEL: ☒   OTHER:
SINGLE ☒   DOUBLE ☐

If gravel packed

From ft.	To ft.	Diam.	Gage or Wall	Diameter of Bore	From ft.	To ft.
0	186	6 5/8"	.156	12.	0	186

Size of shoe or well ring: Size of gravel: Fine Pea
Describe joint Welded

(7) PERFORATIONS OR SCREEN:

Type of perforation or name of screen Torch

From ft.	To ft.	Perf. per row	Rows per ft.	Size in. x in.
153	186	1	4	3/16 x 6

(8) CONSTRUCTION:

Was a surface sanitary seal provided? Yes ☒ No ☐   To what depth 24 ft.

Were any strata sealed against pollution? Yes ☐ No ☐   If yes, note depth of strata

From _____ ft. to _____ ft.
From _____ ft. to Sand seal at 139'
Method of sealing concrete and float cement on pack

(9) WATER LEVELS:

Depth at which water was first found, if known _____ ft.
Standing level before perforating, if known 50 ft.
Standing level after perforating and developing _____ ft.

(10) WELL TESTS:

Was pump test made? Yes ☐ No ☒   If yes, by whom? Bail

Yield: 45 gal./min. with 60 ft. drawdown after _____ hrs.
Temperature of water cool   Was a chemical analysis made? Yes ☐ No ☒
Was electric log made of well? Yes ☐ No ☒   If yes, attach copy

(11) WELL LOG:

Total depth 186 ft.   Depth of completed well 186 ft.

Formation: Describe by color, character, size of material, and structure

ft. to		
0	–	1	Topsoil
1	–	42	Tan sand
42	–	61	Yellow sand
61	–	68	Orange sand w/ stks black sand
68	–	100	Clayee yellow and orange sands
100	–	131	Cemented tan sand
131	–	133	Sandy blue clay
133	–	140	Sandy brown clay
140	–	142	Sandy blue clay & shells
142	–	186	Cemented clayee blue sand w/ hard ledges and stks shells

Work started 3-6-76 19___ , Completed 3-9-76 19___

WELL DRILLER'S STATEMENT:

This well was drilled under my jurisdiction and this report is true to the best of my knowledge and belief.

NAME Meeks Drilling and Pump Company
(Person, firm, or corporation) (Typed or printed)

Address 6100 Sebastopol Road
Sebastopol, California 95472

By Gerald G. Thompson (Well Driller)
(SIGNED) Gerald G. Thompson

License No. 177681 Dated March 9, 1976 , 19___

SKETCH LOCATION OF WELL ON REVERSE SIDE

Example of Well Test Report

1-8-72 30M TRIP ☉T OSP

EXHIBIT 5.   Example of well test report.

104

pumps and submerged pumps. The surface pump is the easiest to access because it's right there to see. Submerged pumps require an act of faith, since they are deep in a hole. These pumps cost anywhere between $350 and $500 to replace.

You should ask if a well inspection report is available on the property you are inspecting. Most counties require such reports to be put on file after the well is drilled and approved.

Inspection Tools

When inspecting a property yourself, bring the following items:

- A good flashlight with fresh batteries for attic and basement inspections
- A screwdriver to unscrew light switch and plug covers and to check beams for rot
- A twenty-five-foot tape measure to draw out a rough floor plan for your records
- A small carpenter's level to check floors and windowsills to see if the house is level
- If you're inspecting many different properties, you will want to keep them straight in your mind. Bring a Polaroid camera to take pictures of each. Keep a separate file for each property you intend to bid on. A picture of a property's problems can soften the government's bargaining position.

A building's physical condition can be both a curse and blessing. A property in A-1 condition will be priced accordingly and the investor will have little opportunity to inject sweat equity into the project. On the other hand, a building that needs too much "deferred maintenance" can be a real money pit that will bleed you white. The best thing to do is find a building that needs mostly cosmetic repairs rather than structural.

If you feel you can do your own inspection, it can save some money. But if you don't feel comfortable doing this kind of hands-on work, then hire a professional contractor. Consider it "cheap" insurance against an investment disaster.

Some of the best investments are so-called fixer-uppers. A coat of paint inside and out, floor coverings, and landscaping can result in returns of $5 to $10 for every dollar spent. This can be a very profitable way for beginning investors to spend their weekends. Bring a friend and pack a lunch.

NEXT STOP: THE PUBLIC RECORD

If you plan to bid on RTC or FDIC properties, one of the best ways to spend your research time is getting acquainted with the local county recorder's office. At the recorder's office you can find the accumulated knowledge of every single parcel of land in a given county. Real estate professionals call it the legal chain of title. Think of it as a property's family tree. If you want to avoid investing in a lemon, get well acquainted with the county recorder's office.

A recorder's office is to real estate what a library is to books. County documents allow you to trace any property's ownership back through the decades, even centuries. I've done searches that included references to original treaties between Indian tribes and white settlers, Spanish land grants, and presidential gifts to Civil War heroes. Each time a large parcel of land is divided or "split," a new piece of property is "created." It then gets its own deed and that deed is recorded in the appropriate county recorder's office. Each transfer of that parcel is recorded along with any new restrictions or encumbrances that are tied to the use of the land.

GETTING STARTED

Clerks at county recorder's offices are like librarians. They can help you record or find any document you need. Go to the counter and introduce yourself. Don't pretend to be anything but what you are—ignorant. They will guide you through the process.

Computerization has been slow to come to some offices. The ones that are computerized can be a pleasure. Investors can sit at a terminal and type in a property's address or "assessor's parcel number," and all the data will be on a computer screen. Still, most recorder's offices remain in the dark ages of paper. In many, land documents are filed by book and page number. The recorder will show you how to find what you want. After a while you should get the drift of it. It's not complicated, just slow. Most offices keep information on microfilm, which is helpful. With microfilm you can sit at a microfiche machine, and instead of viewing the file on paper you view it on film. It's like a mini-slide projector. Documents are numbered in sequence. You can fast forward or go in reverse. If you want a copy of the document you can put a dime in the machine or ask the clerk to make a copy. It shouldn't cost you more than two bits per document.

LOOKING UP A PROPERTY

Most recorder's offices use the same kind of cross-reference system. If you know the property's address you can find it in the recorder's "address directory," which will list the property's assessor parcel number or AP number. For recording purposes this is the only number that really counts. The AP number is your property's "real" name. Write it down. Take the AP number over to the microfiche machine and begin examining the property's chain of title. *Always* begin with the most recent document filed in the chain of title and then work your way back through time.

Most offices use a seven-digit filing system: 90-04560, for example. The first two digits mark the year the document was recorded. The rest of the numbers are sequential from the first document recorded in that year to the last one. The digits are printed in large letters in the upper corner of each document. Every now and then you may want to stop fast forwarding to see how close you're getting to your target document.

WHAT TO LOOK FOR

By searching through the county recorder's office you can discover a number of things.

Who currently owns the property? Just because the government is selling the property doesn't mean it actually owns it—yet. The RTC may be in the process of foreclosing, which means the property is still in the name of the borrower. Or the property may have been foreclosed on by a now-defunct savings and loan. The last person listed in county records as the title holder is, for all intents and purposes, the current owner. The person's name and mailing address will be listed there as well. If you like, give them a telephone call. Ask about the property's pros and cons. You can go back even further and ask other previous owners.

How much did the last owner pay for the property? This is key information, especially if it's a recent purchase. Recorders charge a "documentary transfer fee" when a property changes hands. The fee is based on a factor per thousand dollars of the sale price. In California the document transfer fee is $1.10 per thousand dollars. The fee, when paid, is embossed on the top of the recorded deed. If you see a stamp fee of $341 in California that means the house sold for $310,000. Ask the clerk what the documentary transfer fee is in your area. Also, look at selling prices of other properties in the same neighborhood. This is another clue to value.

Are there any property tax liens filed against the property? If the property taxes have not been paid, the county will have filed a lien against the property. Before the property can be sold this tax lien must be paid.

Are there any other tax liens? If the prior property owner ran afoul of the IRS, federal tax liens may have been filed against the property to secure payment.

Are there mechanics' liens filed? When professional contractors do extensive work on a property they often file a mechanic's lien to insure payment. When the work is finished a notice of completion is filed and the lien is removed. If a contractor has not been paid the mechanic's lien will stay on the property. The lien will have to be removed (paid) before the property can be sold again.

Are there any easements burdening the property? The property you're inspecting may have once been part of a larger property. When it was divided the prior owner may have granted certain access rights to neighboring properties—such as a common driveway or stairs. These access rights can sometimes constitute a real pain in the neck for future owners. All easements will be described and listed on the deed. Look for the word *excepting*. This is how easements and other rights are described.

Utility easements for telephone and electrical lines are commonplace and should not be a great concern. Watch for any easements having to do with roads. Also, there can be some real zingers from left field. Inspect the language carefully. One property I purchased had an easement dealing with the property's only well. It turned out that a prior owner had deeded 25 percent of the well's water to a neighbor fifty years ago. Only by questioning why the easement existed did I learn of the water deal.

Take a look at the deeds to the adjoining parcels. Read the written description that is called "metes and bounds." Look at the "plat map," the parcel's survey map filed at the county recorder's office (see Exhibit 6). Plat maps show easements as broken lines and mark the width and length. Plat maps also contain information on mineral rights that may not belong to the same person who owns the land.

How is the property being taxed? County assessment rolls show how a property's value, for tax purposes, is split in two. One value is assigned to the land and the other to the building and improvements. (This is done because buildings depreciate while land does not.) The combined total is the taxable value of the property.

Are loans encumbering the property in default? If a property owner defaults on a loan or loans secured by the property, the lender will file a notice of default. The borrower then has a set amount of time to cure that default (make the loan or loans current) or face foreclosure. If the RTC or FDIC is foreclosing on a property you will want to know if there are any junior lien holders. This typically involves a second mortgage. If there is more than one junior lien, junior lien holders could wind up bidding against each other for the property to protect their interests.

Were all prior loans properly reconveyed? When a loan is paid off the lender files a deed of reconveyance, which reflects the fact that the loan no longer encumbers the property (see Exhibit 7). It's a good idea to check back through a couple of past sales to make sure all the reconveyances are there. It's not difficult, but if one is missing you will have "a cloud on title" that could be discovered later on, causing problems when you try to resell.

Are there any "CC&Rs" filed on the property? CC&Rs are Covenants, Conditions, and Restrictions. CC&Rs are draconian little documents created when a subdivision is built. Some very old CC&Rs, for example, prohibit land from being sold to blacks or Jews. Recorded fifty to one hundred years ago, these restrictions have since been ruled unconstitutional. When former Lincoln Savings and Loan owner Charles Keating, Jr. developed the Estrella housing subdivision in Phoenix, his

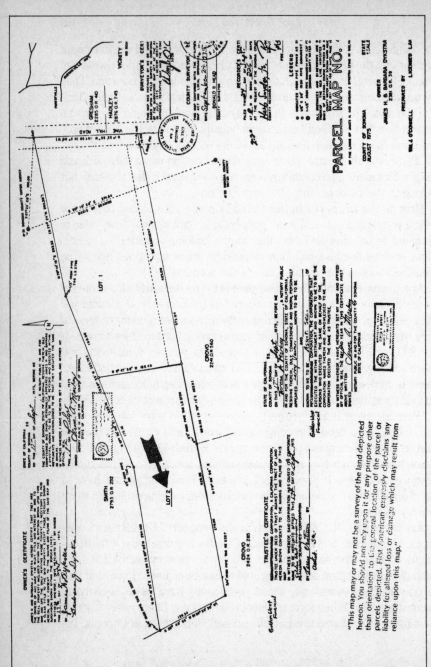

EXHIBIT 6. A property parcel map. Notice the easement through Lot 1 to serve Lot 2. The large black arrow indicates that the

CC&R prohibited home buyers from viewing pornographic material on their properties or having abortions! When the press reported these patently unconstitutional conditions, Keating was forced to remove them. Still, many CC&Rs are perfectly constitutional and bind every owner of the property forever. Some CC&Rs micro-manage every aspect of life in a subdivision, from the height you can build a fence to the kinds of trees you can plant. All CC&Rs have to be recorded and noted on the deed. CC&Rs are very common in condominium projects and planned unit developments for which the care and costs of common areas need to be memorialized.

A FINAL WORD

Get comfortable with your recorder's office. It's a nice place to spend an afternoon browsing through microfilm files for nuggets of information. Before you plan to spend a day there, collect a few property prospects. Bring the addresses. As long as you're at it, poke into the history of the neighboring properties. You can learn volumes from public records—just ask any private eye.

If you really want to be nosy, take the names of your prospective neighbors and look them up in the superior court file down the hall. Are they the subject of a pending civil or criminal case? Did one just get busted for running a crack house?

Don't make an offer or bid without taking a long look at the property's plat map. Check for liens of all types. Check those easements. Look at your recorder's office visit as an "ounce of prevention."

BE YOUR OWN APPRAISER

Before bidding on RTC or FDIC properties you will need to get a grip on what your target property is really worth. This can be done in a number of ways. Some are more accurate than others. The purpose here is not to turn you into a professional appraiser but to arm you with some handy "rules of thumb" for measuring local property values. Don't skip this section. Appraising is an important skill, and it's not as mysterious as some real estate professionals would like you to believe.

Don't be overly concerned with making a mistake in your appraisal.

1991 0043772

OFFICIAL RECORDS OF
SONOMA COUNTY
BERNICE A. PETERSON

FIRST AMERICAN TITLE

AT REQUEST OF:
05/14/1991   08:00:00
FEE: $ 5.00   PGS: 1
TT : $ .00

Space above this line for Recorder's use

DEED OF RECONVEYANCE

(Escrow No. 85469-GR(PAT))

WHEREAS, the indebtedness secured by the Deed of Trust executed by ..STEPHEN P. PIZZO..and

....SUSAN E. PIZZO, his wife,

to **NORTHWESTERN TITLE SECURITY CO.** as Trustee

for .....PAUL PIZZO..and..ANITA PIZZO,..husband..and..wife,..as..Community..Property,

as Beneficiaries,

dated .....August.18th...., 19..86..., and recorded on ..September..15th.., 19..86... in Book ...n/a......,

Page ..n/a......, Recorder's Serial No. ...86072350..................., Official Records of the Office of the County
Recorder of Sonoma County, State of California, has been fully paid.

NOW THEREFORE, the present Trustee under said Deed of Trust does hereby reconvey unto the parties
entitled thereto all right, title and interest which was heretofore acquired by said Trustee under said Deed of Trust.

NORTHWESTERN TITLE SECURITY COMPANY

Dated this ..19th.... day of ....April......., 19..91.   By ...*Patricia Smith*...
                                                          Patricia Smith, Asst.   Vice President

                                                      By ...*Marie Chandler*...
                                                          Marie Chandler, Asst.   Secretary

STATE OF CALIFORNIA   } On ......April 19th......., 1991......, before me, the undersigned, a Notary
COUNTY OF ..SONOMA.. } SS. Public in and for said County and State, personally appeared ....
.......Patricia Smith............ and ....Marie Chandler.........
proved to me on the basis of satisfactory evidence or known to me to be the ...Asst.... Vice President and
..Asst..... Secretary respectively of the Corporation that executed the within instrument on behalf of the
Corporation therein named, and acknowledged to me that such Corporation executed the same.

FOR NOTARY SEAL OR STAMP
OFFICIAL SEAL
NOTARY PUBLIC - CALIFORNIA
Alice M. Barbe
PRINCIPAL OFFICE IN
SONOMA COUNTY
Commission Expires June 30, 1993

Signature ...*Alice M Barbe*...
              Notary Public in and for said County and State

Northwestern Title Security Company
439 College Avenue — Santa Rosa, California

EXHIBIT 7.   A deed of reconveyance.

112

Unless you're paying all cash for a property, the lender, whether it's a bank, the RTC, or FDIC, will serve as a backup. During loan processing the lender's own professional appraiser conducts a formal appraisal, so you'll get a chance to see how close you came. If your bid is too high the lender will sober you up by refusing to fund a loan that is in excess of the property's value. (This assumes of course that your cash down payment is no more than 10 to 20 percent of the sales price and the bank is being asked to provide the remaining 80 to 90 percent.)

WHAT IS VALUE?

When purchasing anything you have to divide the concept of value into two categories: market value and emotional value. If you buy for investment purposes you should eliminate the emotional value and rely totally on profitability. This is business, not pleasure.

When a person finds his or her "dream home," emotions can often distort reality, resulting in "real" value being totally thrown out the window. A couple we knew moved to northern California from Los Angeles, where prices were unconscionably high and living conditions (for them) unbearable. In Santa Rosa they found the quality of life to be idyllic compared to L.A. They found a house on two acres, with a creek, fruit trees, and within walking distance of the local grammar school.

Locals knew the house had been on the market a long time. The seller was in no hurry to sell and had put a high price on the place. A similar home in L.A. would've sold for $350,000. The L.A. couple saw Shangri-La and paid the asking price of $165,000 without quibbling. At the time comparable homes in the neighborhood were selling for $125,000. A few weeks later they moved in. "I went to town and dropped into the local greasy spoon," the husband told me. "During lunch I noticed that the waitress and some of the customers were whispering and looking at me. Pretty soon she came over and said, 'Excuse me, but are you the fellow who bought the Fuller home?' I proudly said I was. The next thing I know they're all slapping each other on the back and laughing. I asked her what was so funny. She stopped laughing just long enough to ask me—'Did you really pay $165,000 for that place?' "

There are no secrets in a small town.

If you're buying for investment you will want to avoid such mistakes.

Rule number one in buying investment real estate is to *never* fall in love with a target property. Eliminate, as much as possible, the emotional component of the valuation process. The only value you want to establish is the property's approximate current market value. Forget how you *feel* about a property until after you've established its market value.

To help with your appraisal, we offer the California Supreme Court's definition of "current market value":

> The highest price, estimated in terms of money, that a property will bring if exposed for sale in the open market allowing a reasonable length of time to find a buyer who buys with full knowledge of all the uses to which the property is adapted and for which it is capable of being used.

TYPES OF APPRAISALS

Professional appraisers use three universally recognized types of appraisal forms. Many busy lenders only require that appraisers submit the *Short Form Appraisal* (SFA). This is a checklist on which an appraiser notes the property's various attributes, amenities, and standard characteristics, like building materials—brick, stucco, or wood. After completing the form, the appraiser makes his or her best estimate of what the property is worth based on the checked categories.

The second is the *Letter Form Appraisal* (LFA). This is generally used when an investor hires an appraiser to do a market analysis of a property. The appraiser writes the customer a letter that gives a brief description of the property, its present condition, and other important observations. The appraiser then gives his or her opinion of its value.

The most extensive type is the *Narrative Appraisal Form* (NAF). Like the letter form, the narrative is written but reads more like a report than a letter. It is extensive, covers local zoning matters, and includes graphs and charts. NAFs generally are required by banks that are lending on income or commercial properties.

For the novice, we introduce a much simpler form: The *Between-the-Ears-Appraisal Form*. We have named it such because that's the only place you should use it. In your head.

If the property you're purchasing is worth more than $15,000, chances are good that it was appraised soon after the government repossessed it. The RTC is required to hire a state-licensed appraiser if a property is considered to be worth more than $15,000. If a property is thought to be worth $15,000 or less, the RTC only needs to obtain a local real estate broker's "opinion of value."

But never mind. You can learn a great deal by doing your own market analysis. First, never accept the seller's appraisal as fact, even if the seller is Uncle Sam. The government's job here is to get back as much money as possible for the taxpayers or, to use its own terminology, "maximize the government's return on seized assets." As fiscally laudable as this may sound, this certainly is not your goal as an investor.

Your goal is to *minimize* the cost of acquisition. Therefore, the only appraisal you should feel comfortable with is your own. It's been said that you don't know a person until you live with them. Any married couple can tell you this. It's also true that you don't really know a property until you've done your own appraisal. The appraisal you do depends on the property type. If you want to purchase single-family or one- to four-family residential homes, the analysis process is straightforward.

Market Data Approach (MDA)

The Market Data Approach uses the appraisal concept of "substitution." Substitution asks, what are other, similar properties selling for in the same neighborhood? Not a tough question to get answered. The easiest way to get this information is through a local realtor. (We have more to say about using realtors later in this chapter.) Most realtors today subscribe to a Multiple Listing Service or MLS, which tracks all current listings, pending sales, and completed sales in a geographical area, usually a county, town, or city. Many realtors also subscribe to a computerized on-line data base that also tracks properties.

Ask the realtor about your target area. Have the realtor pull a list of at least five "comps" off the MLS computer. A comp is a comparable property that has sold during the past six months in the same part of town. Make sure the comps have the same key features: number of bedrooms, baths, lot size, and amenities. The emphasis here should be on "sold," not "listed." You are not interested in what people wish they can get for their homes but what the market actually pays.

If your local MLS is not computerized, then ask the realtor if you can thumb through the latest MLS book. Usually in the back of each book are listed all the recently sold properties. The listings show the asking price, selling price, and how long they were on the market before they sold. If the listing period is long and the property has not sold, it likely means market conditions are soft. A desperate seller is likely to make large concessions. The longer the listing period, the more a seller might give. Such a soft market is bad news for the RTC and FDIC but good news for you.

If you don't have access to a realtor, your job gets a bit more complicated. You can try to use the realtor the RTC hired to market the house, but remember, that realtor is working for the RTC, not you. The more a property sells for, the more he or she makes for a commission. The more a realtor makes for the government the greater likelihood the RTC will want to use that realtor more often. Still, give it a try. The RTC contract realtor can answer questions and might even give you access to raw MLS information without first censoring it.

If you decide to go it alone you'll need to develop a few new skills. To find recent sales you'll have to tap the county recorder's office, which we mentioned earlier. Look up the latest sales price of a property. Inspect the building's county property tax. The most important thing you should remember is this: You can punch your pocket calculator until the cows come home but the ultimate measure of value is what someone is willing to pay for a piece of real estate on the open market. *Therefore, your first step will be to collect at least five comparable properties that closely match your target property in size, condition, and location.* You can stop right here if you feel this process has given you a solid sense of what your target property should fetch on the open market. If you think you need more technical information, here's a few techniques to follow.

Replacement Cost Approach (RCA)

Not as good as the market data approach, estimating the replacement cost of a property can nonetheless be valuable. Telephone a local contractor and tell the contractor you're thinking about having your dream home built. Ask how much the charge per square foot would be. Is it $50, $60, or $100 per square foot? This gives you a sketch of what it costs for labor and materials. Amenities are extra.

Then go visit your RTC or FDIC target property. Get a rough estimate on square footage. Multiply it by the replacement estimates you received from the contractor. From this you should get an estimate on what it would cost to build a new house. Add in the cost of the underlying lot or acreage. This will give you a ballpark value.

The replacement cost approach gives you a sense of what the property, as a physical object, is worth. Depending on market conditions, the actual value of a property might exceed the replacement cost. The opposite also could be true. Here's how an RCA calculation works:

Your target property is a 2,050-square-foot single-story home on a 100′ × 100′ lot. Construction costs run about $55 per square foot. $55 × 2,050 = $112,750 to build that house today. Through a realtor or independently you discover that 10,000-square-foot lots in that part of town are selling for $25,000 or so. Added to the construction cost of $112,750, this gives you a total replacement cost of about $137,750.

The replacement cost approach can at least give you a general idea of what the property is worth. But it doesn't mean you should offer this amount. However, if the RTC is asking, say, $98,000 for the property, then you know right away you could be onto a potential nugget.

The market data and replacement cost approaches are the two main tools you need to evaluate residential property. If your market analysis approach does not satisfy you completely, then try the replacement cost approach and see what you get. Together they should give you a good idea of what the property might be worth. Along the way you will learn more than you ever wanted to know about your local real estate market. If you intend to keep looking in the same market area at the same basic property type, after a while doing quick appraisals will become second nature. By then you should have sufficient knowledge about the local market to do the calculations in your head.

INCOME PROPERTY

If the residential property you've targeted also has income potential (a duplex or fourplex), the process becomes more involved. Besides getting to know your market, you'll need to get better acquainted with your pocket calculator.

Investors like income property because it produces two returns for them rather than just one: appreciation and rental income. With a few geographical exceptions, real estate appreciation in America has outstripped the inflation rate. Ask the vast majority of homeowners and they'll tell you real estate has been the best investment they ever made. Investors in income property want one thing and one thing only—to make money. Investors in income properties want to know what kind of return or income stream can be made from a property. When analyzing income property the first rule is not to count your chickens before they hatch. *Do not* figure future appreciation into your calculations!

If it's apartments you're looking at, figure what the rents will produce. The idea is to make more money in rents than you're paying out in mortgage and maintenance. If it's a commercial property, such as an office building, find out what kind of leases and how much money commercial landlords are getting per square foot. Some of this should be done when doing a market analysis of the property. (See "Analyzing Income Property" for a full explanation of appraising income properties.)

HOW THE RTC APPRAISES

Because it's the seller, the RTC is doing its appraisal for the opposite reason you're doing yours. The RTC began its bureaucratic life sporting an inflated opinion of the properties it had inherited from failed S&Ls. As a result, it spent the first year of its existence turning up its nose at realistic offers made by eager buyers. More than once buyers were referred to as "vultures" because, in the mind of the RTC, they wanted to "steal" properties at the expense of the taxpayer. Buyers told the agency to take a flying leap, and they stayed away from its auctions. When properties didn't sell as well as anticipated, Congress addressed the problem in 1991 with a major reorganization of the agency. One thing Congress changed was how the RTC marked down properties that didn't sell. In short, the RTC became a deep discounter of properties, a sort of Wal-Mart of real estate.

The markdown process works like this: After obtaining a market value appraisal on the property, the RTC immediately trims between 5 and 10 percent off the asking price. If the property does not sell after a few months, it can be marked down by the RTC consolidated office by as much as 20 percent. We'll be dealing more extensively with the markdown process later.

THE RTC VALUATION PROCESS

To give you an edge over other buyers, it helps to know how the RTC's property valuation process works. If you had the time you could read the agency's policy manual, but it's long and arduous reading. Instead, we've read it for you and reduced the RTC-ese to English. The agency uses three very different measures of value when assessing a property. They are:

Appraised Value—the current "as is" value, determined by an independent appraisal.

Adjusted Appraisal Value—the revised estimated value of a property if it has not sold at the appraised value after six months on the market (four months for single-family homes.) The adjusted appraised value must always be at least 80 percent of the appraised value. And the adjusted appraised value can only be reduced by 15 percent of the appraised value at any one time.

Market Value—This represents the appraised value or adjusted appraised value modified to reflect projected holding costs. Because holding costs eat into a property's value, the RTC lowers the price to reflect this dilemma. Overseen by an RTC consolidated office, this new calculation becomes the market value. The actual sales price of a property more than likely will be closer to market value than to the other two.

We offer an expanded overview of RTC pricing strategies in Chapter 7.

OTHER RESOURCES

Investing in real estate is not the cold, cruel world that some think it is. For the novice, many resources are available to help you along the way.

REALTORS

A good local real estate agent can be your most important asset. The secret is to control the relationship and maintain the upper hand. Realtors have access to updated market data through the MLS guide and data base. MLS data is only available to licensed realtors. Regular folks cannot purchase an MLS guide. Only licensed realtors who are members of the MLS can get this information.

Getting free and unlimited access to the MLS is your goal here. Get cozy with your realtor, but don't mislead him or her. Good realtors know when they're being used. Keep in mind that you can use a realtor to represent you, the buyer. This is becoming more commonplace, especially in soft markets. Good realtors will bend over backwards to develop promising clients. If you're looking to invest, interview several local realtors.

If the RTC has already mailed you a list of prospective properties you will notice that many of the listings are with the same realtor. Start with him or her. Because realtors make a commission only when the property is sold, they'll want to work with you. Also, the realtor wants the repeat business when you cash in on your investment.

If you can't find an RTC realtor, then as we mentioned earlier, get a realtor to represent you, the buyer. Don't mislead the realtor. Tell him or her your investment goals and indicate that if all goes as planned you will need a realtor to represent you. The realtor will know that even if he or she doesn't get a commission right away, there may be one down the road when you begin buying and selling properties.

When I was a realtor one of my best clients was a small investor who began investing in real estate for himself and some of his friends. In the beginning our relationship was very one-sided. I provided him with all kinds of information about the area: property values, sales, the "good" parts of town, vacancy rates, rental prices, and the like. Based on this information he acquired a number of properties directly from sellers. But within a couple of years he and his friends were sellers, not buyers. I got the listings, and the sales commissions more than made up for all that "free" advice.

Don't be discouraged if some realtors seem cold to the idea of answering all your questions during the acquisition phase of your program. You don't want a relationship with a realtor who sees you only as a current prospect. Successful realtors cultivate long-term relationships. In time you'll find one of these successful realtors. When you find a realtor willing to work hard for you, show that person some degree of loyalty. Bring properties to him or her. Let that realtor present your offer to the RTC listing broker. In time your realtor will be functioning like a secretary of sorts. If you bring the realtor enough business he or she'll be more than happy to handle loose ends in the paperwork, which frees you up to concentrate on other properties.

TITLE COMPANIES

Title companies are another terrific resource. If you've purchased a home, chances are you've already met your first title officer.

A title company performs three major services for buyers of real estate:

1) It searches the title to determine if the property is encumbered in any way and provides a report to the buyer, seller and lender.
2) It provides title insurance to insure the lender against any undiscovered defects in title.
3) It handles all the paperwork for the buyer and seller and disburses all monies to the proper parties.

Title company employees who manage escrows are called "title officers." Cultivating a personal relationship with a good title officer can save you a lot of work and headaches. A seasoned title officer can manage any title quirks that come along and can research and extract essential information on particular properties for you.

Most big title companies maintain their own computerized property records. They can research almost any property you want using nothing more than an address or assessor's number. Good title companies have what they call a "title plant," which is an in-house collection of regularly updated property records and recorded documents.

Because title companies earn their keep by charging escrow fees and writing title insurance, like realtors they will want to develop a long-term relationship with anyone who conducts a lot of real estate business. Though less likely than a realtor to answer a bunch of questions, they can be useful for certain kinds of problems. For example, say you've completed your own title search on a property and can't find evidence that an old loan was ever repaid. With a good title company you can ask to have their title plant research for a "deed of reconveyance." If they can't find it, the company can tell you how to cure this cloud on the title. Realtors depend heavily on their favorite title officers. Ask your realtor who he or she can recommend.

Other Resources

Besides those listed here, there are other places you can turn for help. As we said in the introduction, this book is not intended to be a complete guide to real estate investing. Many excellent books have been published on the subject and are available at your bookstore.

IN SUMMARY

Real estate is just another commodity, like a car, a washing machine, or a home computer system. But the same consumers who think nothing of reading up on something like a home computer system before buying one avoid doing the same thing with real estate. Somehow real estate has become, in some people's minds, a commodity like stocks and bonds that only experts can understand.

But as we've seen in this chapter, there are no real mysteries about real estate and no codes to break in order to become a knowledgeable buyer. It's just common sense. Follow the instructions in this chapter, and in short order you'll be making your own decisions about real estate investments.

Just remember to keep your pocket calculator at hand and to listen to it rather than your beating heart. "Do the numbers" should be the mantra of every novice real estate investor. Do you have enough income to service the loan? Do you have enough money to make the necessary repairs? What about taxes and insurance? Whatever your heart has to say about a property is only relevant after these questions are answered to your calculator's satisfaction.

That's it—all you need to get started. If you follow these guidelines the process should go smoothly. Only fear of failure now stands between you and some great real estate deals.

Chapter Five

....

Hey Buddy, Can You Spare a Loan?

How to Get Government Financing to Buy Government Property

Okay, so you've found the perfect property. You had it appraised, you inspected it, and finally you've reached a conclusion on bid price. Now it's time to worry about financing. Just how are you going to finance this purchase? In most cases, if you can't get a bank loan the RTC will loan you the money. The RTC can extend credit on any sale over $100,000. In this case, obtaining a government loan can be a pretty good deal.

Congress has authorized the RTC to provide seller financing when appropriate to facilitate the sale of real estate assets. (The RTC and FDIC, however, will not provide financing to buy loans.) Both agencies offer financing on the following: residential, commercial and industrial, raw land, and Affordable Housing Program properties.

RTC LOAN TERMS

DOWN PAYMENT AND INTEREST RATE

The RTC pegs the interest rate charged on its mortgages to the weekly U.S. Treasury Note Constant Maturity Index. This index can be checked by reading the Treasury note and bond tables published in the *Wall Street Journal*. The rate is pegged to whatever the rate was on the previous Wednesday before the auction or contract date.

If you don't read the *Wall Street Journal*, telephone the RTC asset manager handling the auction or sale. He or she will tell you that week's rate. Once you have the rate, the math is easy. The actual interest rate charged depends on the size of your down payment. The RTC prefers 25 percent cash down, but will accept as little as 15 percent. The rate on your mortgage will be a number of percentage points (or basis points) above the Treasury index. One percentage point equals 100 basis points—like a dollar is equal to 100 cents. If someone says a rate is "1.50 percent over the prime rate" the same thing can be expressed as "150 basis points above prime." In this example, if prime is 6.00 percent the rate charged would be 7.50 percent.

In any case, the rate you pay on an RTC loan depends on how much cash you have to put down. The RTC has a sliding scale to determine your rate:

- If you make a cash down payment of 30 percent or more, the RTC loan interest rate charged will be the Treasury Index Rate plus 150 basis points (TIR + 1.5%).
- If you make a cash down payment of 25 to 29 percent, you will be charged the Treasury Index Rate plus 187.5 basis points (TIR + 1.875%).
- If you make a cash down payment of 20 to 24 percent, you will be charged the Treasury Index Rate plus 225 basis points (TIR + 2.25%).
- If you make a cash down payment of 15 to 19 percent, you will be charged the Treasury Index Rate plus 262.5 basis points (TIR + 2.625%).

Example

You want to offer $125,000 for a property. You have $30,000 cash to put down and want the government to carry the balance of $95,000 as a loan. What would your interest rate be on that loan?

Look in the *WSJ*. That week's Treasury Index Rate was 6.25 percent (or 625 basis points). Your $30,000 cash down represents a 24 percent down payment. 625 basis points + 225 basis points = 850 basis points or 8.5 percent. You will pay the government an interest rate of 8.5 percent on your $95,000 loan.

Get an amortization table from your realtor. Look up the 8.5 percent table on a 30-year loan. You will see that your monthly mortgage payment would be $716.

The RTC can be extremely flexible on the subject of down payments. The guidelines given by the RTC to field supervisors reveal just how creative they can be:

While an equity commitment of 15% is the absolute minimum, in certain situations this 15% commitment may be allocated between down payment and a funded escrow to be used solely for capital improvements on the property. While important, down payments should not be viewed mechanically without reference to the overall economics of the transaction. In some cases . . . investment of time and expense by the purchaser may be more relevant than the percentage of down payment. In other cases, especially property sales involving syndication of tax benefits, "equity" may represent only a share of the developer's fee generated by the public subsidy (for low income housing) and not necessarily indicate a serious financial stake in the project.

Talk about wiggle room! As you can see, the RTC is giving its field supervisors a great deal of latitude in deciding how much of a down payment is considered enough.

Unless it's a loan to purchase an AFH unit, single-family residential mortgages made by the RTC that have less than a 20 percent down payment will require private mortgage insurance (PMI). For borrowers that means a few extra bucks a month included in the monthly payment to pay the insurance premium. The amount of premium declines each year along with the outstanding loan balance. (RTC residential loans are made at fifteen-year and thirty-year terms.)

In case you're wondering, these mortgages are not "held" by the government. In other words, you won't be making out your monthly mortgage to Uncle Sam. The RTC will place your loan into a "pool" of similar loans that it will then sell to investors in the form of mortgage-backed securities. As a mortgagor (one who pays a mortgage) you might find that the right to "service" your loan will be sold or transferred to another company. This will not affect your loan payment or terms. From time to time when a loan changes servicers, the paperwork gets messed up, though it's a rare occurrence.

TERMS OF RTC LOANS

Only residential loans made by the RTC have terms of fifteen and thirty years. Almost all other loans carry terms of only seven years. On a seven-year loan the monthly payment is still calculated off a thirty-year amortization schedule. That means that in seven years you'll have to pay the full loan amount or get a new mortgage. When you have a seven-year loan most of your payments are for interest—that means the principal is hardly reduced.

When you make a bid you can ask for a longer-term loan, but you'd better have a good reason. The RTC can grant a loan extension of up to three additional years. The agency is not crazy about doing this. The decision to grant a longer-term loan is made based on market conditions only—not the needs of the borrower. If an extension is granted the RTC requires a 10 percent principal reduction in each of the three extension years. No interest-only loans are allowed on residential and commercial properties.

Raw land is the hardest asset for the RTC to sell, so it bends over backwards to accommodate prospective buyers. Therefore, RTC loans on raw land are a different matter. Here the RTC will break its own rule against interest-only loans and allow interest-only payments on raw land loans. However, before such a loan is made the borrower must agree to make periodic principal payments at set intervals during the life of the loan.

LIEN PRIORITY

The RTC always wants to be the first mortgage (or lien) holder on the property it sells to you when it's providing the financing. However, even here there is some flexibility. If a bank is providing most of the loan amount, the RTC will consider making a small second mortgage on the property. However, the combined loans cannot exceed 85 percent of the sales price.

> KEY INFORMATION. *If the RTC makes you a first mortgage, you cannot go out later and get a second mortgage on the property without the agency's permission. If you get a second mortgage without the RTC's permission and they find out, your RTC loan could be called due at the RTC's discretion.*

ASSUMABILITY

All RTC loans are "due on sale." This means RTC loans cannot be assumed by subsequent buyers. If you sell the property, the loan has to be repaid in full.

PREPAYMENT TERMS

As we noted earlier, the RTC wants to sell your loan into the secondary market. Investors who buy securities backed by home mortgages like certainty and dislike the prospect of having the loans paid off early and therefore having their anticipated return diminished. (A prepayment occurs when you sell the home or pay it off early.) If mortgage borrowers pay off a loan before maturity, the investor in that loan loses all the future interest payments. To protect mortgage securities investors from "prepayment shocks," lenders can impose a prepayment fee on borrowers that can sometimes get costly.

The RTC does not always insist on a prepayment fee. Like everything else, it's negotiable. Still, the agency tells its field supervisors to impose the fee when it can get away with it because it increases the marketability of the loans on the secondary market. RTC prepayment fees are as follows: 5 percent of the principal balance if the loan is prepaid in the first year, 4 percent in the second year, and so on down the line. When you make your offer on the property, designate in your offer that you want an RTC loan without a prepayment fee clause.

PERSONAL LIABILITY

If you borrow from the RTC, you are personally liable for fraud, misrepresentation, waste, enforcement costs, real estate taxes, and environmental indemnifications. If you lied on your loan application and doctored your financial statement to qualify for the loan, the RTC will fine you or take the house away. If you destroy the RTC property you bought (without first paying off your RTC mortgage) or you dump toxic waste in your backyard or build a nuclear reactor (you get the message), the RTC will hold you personally, and legally, responsible forever—and a day.

COMMERCIAL PROPERTY DEBT-SERVICE RATIOS

The RTC is idealistic when it comes to debt-service ratios. In a good debt-service ratio situation the rents on a property meet or exceed the monthly mortgage payment, insurance, taxes, and maintenance costs. When this happens the lender can rest easily.

Unfortunately, the RTC does not often find itself in this sort of good situation. Even in its own policy manuals, the RTC admits to field supervisors that "many RTC properties are leased well below traditional break-even levels at 75% of financing."

Therefore, when it comes to making loans the RTC has to be flexible. When it appears that a debt-service ratio is going to be low—meaning rents may not right away cover the mortgage payment—the RTC looks away from the property and to the financial strength of the borrower for added comfort. If the property *and* the borrower are weak, the likelihood of a meeting of the minds is low.

INSURANCE

The RTC, like all lenders, requires the borrower to have fire, liability, comprehensive, and general liability insurance on the property it acquires. The RTC remains as the property's co-beneficiary until the loan is repaid.

RELEASE PRICE

Let's say you purchase a townhouse development from the RTC and the RTC makes you one blanket loan covering the whole asset. Then six months later you sell half the development to someone else. If you want to release a portion of a real estate development from an RTC blanket loan, the RTC requires 105 percent of the pro rata debt allocated to the released collateral. In other words, if the RTC loan was $200,000 and you sold half the project, the RTC would require that you pay the loan down by $105,000, and then the RTC will continue to carry the balance of $95,000.

COMMERCIAL LOAN FEE

When it makes commercial property loans the RTC charges a $1/10$ of 1 percent application processing fee with a floor of $1,500 and a ceiling of $7,500. The fee is due when the application is submitted and is nonrefundable.

BRIDGE LOANS

The RTC will provide a temporary "bridge" loan to facilitate a sale as long as you can get financing elsewhere shortly after the deal closes. Bridge loans are available on commercial property and carry a maximum term of 18 months. A 25 percent cash down payment is required to get a bridge loan.

If these RTC loan terms don't thrill you, then shop around for a better deal. We doubt there's one out there. Conventional lenders—banks and S&Ls—will nick you for appraisal fees, document preparation fees, extra points, and so on, which the RTC does not charge for.

But the RTC doesn't care who lends you the money. The agency just wants to sell as much real estate as quickly as it can. If they have to lend you the money to make that happen, they'll do that at pretty fair terms. The worst thing about an RTC loan is that it's not assumable. If you sell the property a year after you buy it from the RTC, the new buyer cannot assume (begin paying) your RTC loan. The new buyer will have to get his or her own bank loan. It's a minor point, but one worth mentioning.

Anyway, after your RTC loan actually closes, you can always shop around for a better loan later on. Once the property becomes yours you have seven long years to play the interest rate waiting game. When rates dip to a low point, you can refinance the property.

MULTIPLE PROPERTY PURCHASES

What if you want to buy four separate RTC properties? Will the RTC still provide financing? Will it roll the total amount into one big loan covering all the properties? The answer is yes and no. Yes, the RTC will provide financing on the four properties, but no, it will not issue a blanket loan on all four. Instead the RTC will handle each as a separate sale. Each is eligible to get its very own RTC loan.

Again, remember the RTC motto: Cash is king. In its policy manuals, the RTC tells its field supervisors: "If there is an all-cash offer on the table, it may be considered advantageous for the RTC to accept the offer even if the sales price is less than the terms sale alternative." In other words, if you bid $25,000 for a property and want the RTC to make you a $20,000 loan, and then someone comes along and offers $21,500 in cash, you will probably lose that fight.

If you can arrange your own financing before making a bid you will be better off. This way the RTC can "cash out" and be done with the property, hopefully forever. If you arrange for outside financing, make sure you have something to show the RTC that documents this fact when you make your offer. A loan commitment letter signed by your banker is the preferential way to handle this.

Still, it's nice to know that during times of tight credit you won't be closed out of the game. If no one else will, both the RTC and FDIC can make you the loan you need.

RAW LAND LOANS?

Few lenders will make loans on raw land, and often those that do will not lend more than 50 percent of the purchase price. Not the RTC. Beginning in 1992 the agency adopted a policy where it will loan any purchaser up to 85 percent of the purchase price for fifteen years.

IN SUMMARY

The RTC provides seller financing on all sorts of real estate: residential, commercial, multifamily, and raw land. Terms differ for each, but it's an easy and straightforward way to buy. Later you can shop for permanent financing at your leisure.

Only loans on single-family homes made by the RTC have terms of 30 years. Most other loans carry seven-year terms. That means you have seven years before the loan is due. Because you have no points or other fees to pay on an RTC loan, government financing is a good deal—particularly if you intend to sell the property before the loan is due.

The one downside to requesting RTC financing is that when it takes bids the agency will give first consideration to all-cash offers. If you request RTC financing you may never make it to the final round of bidding. That's the risk you run. If you can't get financing anywhere else, then that risk doesn't seem so bad.

Keep in mind that many private banks and insurance companies that are auctioning off their real estate holdings also now provide seller financing. Getting a loan from the bank selling a foreclosed home is easier than obtaining financing elsewhere. Chances are that the bank will also grant you very favorable terms just to get the property off its books.

Chapter 6

....

Crunching the Numbers

Analyzing and Buying Income Property

The RTC and FDIC have a bellyfull of income properties. To say the least, high-flying bank and thrift owners were the world's biggest optimists. Failed banks and thrifts financed everything from office buildings and shopping centers to apartment complexes and health spas—you name it. And they built these projects whether they were needed or not. Former FDIC Chairman Bill Seidman once said his "favorite" piece of FDIC-owned property was a "spec airport"—an airport built in the middle of nowhere by a developer who was anticipating urban sprawl. When the government seized Charles Keating, Jr.'s palatial Phoenician Hotel resort in Phoenix, an FDIC official remarked that the landscaping was "very nice." A loyal Keating employee shot back, "Nice? Let me tell you, sir, that's the way God would have done it—if He'd had the money."

Well, they had the money—yours and mine—and now the RTC and FDIC own their thousands of pet projects. Not all of the income properties built (hotels, malls, luxury housing developments) were pipe dreams, though. In fact, most are properties with great long-term potential just looking for a new owner. The reasons these projects

132

ever worked are many. Unscrupulous developers skimmed money out of the construction loans and into their own pockets, leaving the projects with insufficient funds to be completed or marketed properly, or money was diverted in the form of kickbacks to crooked loan officers. But often the problem was only that during the 1980s banks and S&Ls got a little carried away and over-lent to developers, creating a glut of properties.

Some income properties should never have been built because no one needed them. But demographics will eventually cure that problem as the marketplace absorbs these excess units. Other projects were poorly designed for the purpose for which they were built. But such buildings can often be adapted to other purposes. All these income properties are creations of value simply waiting for the right time, the right use, and the right owner.

Buying income property from the government is radically different from buying government-owned residential property. Income property, for the most part, is a lot more expensive and the risk of loss is much greater—but so are the potential gains. When purchasing a home, your criteria are personal and emotional as well as financial. Investors in income property buy for one reason only: to make money and benefit from the income a property produces. The trick is to be able to calculate your risks and income opportunities for a given property before you bid. Analyzing income property is not as arcane as you think. There are no mysteries or hidden formulas. Done right, the math is simple and straightforward, and you don't need an MBA to reach an informed investment conclusion.

INCOME PROPERTY GIVES A DOUBLE WHAMMY

If you already own a home, any additional real estate you purchase will likely be income property. What you're doing here is investing—hoping to make money on the rent or down the road through appreciation. That's the "double whammy" of income property: *appreciation and income*. Appreciation is realized when you sell or refinance income property years from now. In the meantime, rental income gives an immediate return and helps pay the mortgage and—hopefully—most other costs.

At its best, rents can provide regular added monthly income and cover carrying costs.

A well-chosen income property should at least cover your total mortgage payments, insurance costs, and taxes. "Great" income properties yield a positive cash flow—covering all your mortgage and operating costs and leaving you a little extra (or a lot extra) each month, called "net spendable income." Good positive cash flow properties became increasingly rare during the 1980s. But thanks to the S&L and banking disasters, positive cash flow properties are again available in the form of apartment buildings, strip shopping centers, warehouses, and even office buildings, though you'll have to be extra careful with the latter due to severe oversupply in many areas.

Why Income Property Is Such a Good Investment

In 1976 my wife (Susan Pizzo) and I had saved about $8,500. The money sat in a bank account earning about 8 percent interest, which meant with compounding it would about double in ten years. At the time inflation was running in the double digits and we wanted this money to work a bit harder than that.

We had already purchased our own home, and so we began looking for a small piece of investment real estate. The property we finally decided on was an unassuming twenty-five-year-old wood-frame duplex in a small rural town sixty-five miles north of San Francisco. The town was changing from an old resort community to a year-round suburb of growing Santa Rosa, California, 12 miles to the east. Since this little town was rapidly becoming a bedroom community to Santa Rosa, we decided it would be a good idea to buy some bedrooms.

The absentee owner of the duplex had tired of maintaining a property eighty miles away and listed the property for $36,000. We offered $29,000 with $7,500 down, and asked that the seller carry the balance at 7 percent. He countered at $31,500 with $7,250 down. He would carry the balance, $24,250 at 8 percent. Our payments would be $175 per month. We accepted. Averaging income and expenses for the period owned, here's how that little investment has worked for us:

Gross Rents:	$1,000/mo.
Annual Gross:	$12,000
Less Annualized Expenses:	
Mortgage:	$ 2,100
Insurance:	$ 250
Maintenance:	$ 850 (avg.)
Property Taxes:	$ 934
Utilities	$ 0 (Tenants Pay)
Total Expenses:	$ 4,134
Net Rents:	$ 7,866

(Or $655.50 per month net spendable income)

For simplicity purposes we will not discuss here depreciation, mortgage interest, and capitalized deductions taken for tax purposes. Such deductions reduce your taxes on this income, and we'll cover them later.

Now, let's see how that investment compares with a simple savings account. If we had left our $7,250 in the bank for the same fifteen years, drawing an average 8 percent interest, compounded it would have increased to $23,975. By comparison our little duplex did much better than that. The net rent collected over fifteen years was $62,010. Annualized, that comes to a return on our cash investment of $7,250 of 57 percent a year! ($62,010/15 = $4134, $4134/$7250 = .57).

In the meantime, the building increased in value significantly, further compounding our gain. We bought the building for $31,500 in 1976. In 1991 it was worth $145,000, a gain in value of $113,500, or an additional annual gain of $7,567 on top of rents. With net rents of $4,134, plus appreciation of $7,567, we were really earning $11,701 per year on our little $7,250 cash investment, or a return of 160 percent—just a bit better than the 8.32 percent compounded rate of return we would have earned at the bank.

By the time our first son is ready for college in 1996, the duplex will have plenty of equity. We can either sell the property or borrow against it to cover his tuition and that of his younger brother four years later. By then the building should be worth at least $200,000—or $25,000 per year per kid for four years. Thanks to this little building my wife and I do not lie awake nights worrying about how we are going to pay for our kids' college education.

That investment, made fifteen years ago, was the best decision we ever made. It opened our eyes to the compounding gains that can be had by investing in real estate, particularly income-producing property. Since then we have purchased other properties, even a "fixer upper" operating dairy farm in Wisconsin. All of our real estate investments have produced wonderful returns and a peace of mind that comes only from financial security. That little duplex was not our last income property investment, but the one that most clearly answers the question, "Why should we buy real estate?"

HOW TO ANALYZE INCOME PROPERTY

Using such arcane phrases as "uneven cash flow analysis," "present value of future dollar calculations," and "sinking funds," professional real estate investors can make income property analysis look like quantum physics. The pros find great comfort in these calculations, but for the novice or small investor they can often be just a frustrating waste of time. The small to mid-sized investor needs to know one thing only: After my down payment, will the rental income on the property exceed my monthly mortgage and holding costs? (In a nutshell, this is what the pros want to know too, but they couch it in more sophisticated terms.)

ANALYZING RTC OR FDIC PROPERTIES

Case Study

(Property description of a sample RTC listing)

Asset Name: **Broadmore Manor Apartments**
Property Address: 1111 Broadmore St.
City, State, Zip: Walnut Hill, CA 92401
RTC Asking Price: $200,000

Occupancy: Fully rented
Condition: Good

Number of Units: 4 (Two 2-bdrs, two 3-bdrs)
Year Built: 1984
Acquisition Date: 08/14/91
Construction: Stucco
Total Square Footage: 5,436

ANALYSIS PROCESS OF PROPERTY

Vacancy Factor

Your first task is to establish the local vacancy ratio. Your goal is to keep the four units fully rented. But if the local vacancy ratio is 50 percent, you're going to have a problem. Before making an investment decision and calculation you first need to know what the vacancy rate actually is.

There are a few different ways to go about this. Contact a professional property management company in the area. Tell them what you have in mind and ask if they can provide any hard data on the local rental market. Property managers make their living by managing other people's income properties. Once they hear you're considering a property—and because they will want to manage your property—they might paint a rosier picture of the rental market than what really exists. Keep this in mind. On the other hand they won't exaggerate too much, because if they wind up managing your property and rentals don't match their predictions they run the risk of losing your business. Property managers can be found in your telephone book in the real estate listings section.

A simpler way to get a feel for the rental market is to drive by similar apartment buildings in the neighborhood early in the morning on a weekday. We mean EARLY! We're talking 3 A.M.—before anyone leaves for work. Check out the parking areas. Are they full of cars or half empty? If you see lots of empty spaces there might be trouble. Weekends are not a good time to check for vacancy because people might simply be away.

If the property has a rental history and current tenants, the RTC will include this information in the property's due diligence package. Due diligence packages are available at RTC and FDIC auctions or are given to serious bidders who show they have at least enough money for a down payment. The income history of a property tells you the current rent, the occupancy ratio (how many of the units are now rented) and which renters are in arrears (behind in their rent.)

If the building is vacant—which is not the case in our above example, but is sometimes the case with RTC properties—then you need to investigate similar buildings in the neighborhood.

If you discover the local vacancy factor is much higher than 10 percent and your target property has a vacancy rate of that or higher, you may want to pass. Even if the building you are considering is fully rented, for purposes of this analysis, assume a 5 percent vacancy factor—meaning your units will be empty 5 percent of the year, and you will not receive any rental income.

Establish Rents

Next, investigate what rents are in the immediate area. How much will your apartments fetch each month when compared to similar units? Drive around and copy telephone numbers off "Apartment for Rent" signs. Call landlords. Tell them you want to rent a place. See how willing they are to dicker. In a strong rental market no one dickers.

Now that we've established the vacancy ratio and the rental price, it's time to do our first calculation. We've discovered that the two 2-bedrooms in Walnut Hill rent out for $500 each. That comes to $1,000. The two 3-bedrooms rent out at $700 each. That's $1,400. Together, all four rent for $2,400. Now subtract the vacancy calculation of 5 percent. This represents the property's Gross Operating Income or GOI. To summarize:

- Total rents: $2,400/month or $28,000 per year
- Vacancy ratio: 5%, or $1400/year
- Gross Operating Income = $26,560

We now have the first element in our income analysis. Write that figure down and let's move on.

The next calculation we need to do is the property's estimated Net Operating Income (NOI). This is an easy calculation, but requires some research. First list the property's annual operating expenses, *excluding* the loan payments. If you're lucky the RTC or FDIC asset manager might have a breakdown handy, but don't count on it. Do your own anyway. And be conservative, not liberal. You can't fool yourself into making a profit.

Annual operating expenses
- Property Taxes: $2,000
- Fire and liability insurance: $1,000
- Utilities: $0 (tenants pay)
- Sewer assessment: $950
- Maintenance (5% of gross income): $684 (unless the building and its systems are old and break down a lot)
- Advertising and misc.: $1,800 (including a sinking fund for appliance and floor covering replacement, etc.)

Total Operating Expenses = $6,434

Next, subtract the annual operating expense of $6,434 from your gross operating income of $26,600. You should arrive at $19,354.00. This is your net operating income. The end is now in sight. There's just one more calculation to make. In a moment you will subtract your estimated financing costs (monthly mortgage payment) from the NOI. But before you do, there are a few important things to consider:

- What is the most you are willing (or able) to pay for this property? The government is asking $200,000, but during inspection you concluded it needs $20,000 in repairs.
- You decide to offer no more than $150,000. For your down payment you have only $10,000 cash. You will have to borrow the rest, including the $20,000 needed to remodel. You already know the RTC will finance an 80 percent mortgage that amortizes on a thirty-year schedule. More than likely you'll be getting an RTC seven-year balloon mortgage. If you can swing it, a bank or S&L might offer you an 80 percent loan that also amortizes on a thirty-year schedule but is not due in seven years. Either way, you'll need a $120,000 mortgage (80% + $150,000 = $120,000).

If you've done this simple math correctly, you will learn that you're about $20,000 short. Don't forget the repairs. Also, factor in closing costs, which will be at least another $5,000. So in total, you're $25,000 short. The solution (for this example) is to take out a "second" mortgage from a source who agrees to be junior (subordinate) to the bank or RTC loan. (If the RTC is making the first loan, you will need its permission to get a second.) Let's assume you find private-sector lenders willing to make both loans on the following terms:

The bank loan: $120,000 at 9 percent interest for twenty-five years = $985 per month.[1]

A second mortgage of $25,000 at 10 percent for ten years (interest only) = $208 per month.

Total monthly loan service = $1,194

Total annual loan service = $14,328

Now subtract the annual loan service from your NOI to get your Net Spendable Income (NSI): $19,354 − $14,328 = $5,026 NSI.

Even with your second mortgage this property has positive cash flow. If the RTC takes your bid, you're all set.

After completing these sorts of calculations a few times it should become second nature. There's no magic to it, no hidden tricks. Just simple math and common sense. You don't have to be a rocket scientist. Still, we recommend that before you spend thousands of dollars on an investment property you first spend $29.95 and purchase a *business* pocket calculator. Prices for these little wonders range from under $20 to more than $150. For most small investors the Texas Instruments BA-35 calculator is more than adequate and priced at under $30. The BA-35 will calculate loan payments, balloon payments, compound interest calculations, present- and future-value calculations, loan balances, and many other commonly used business formulas. You don't need to learn the mathematical formulas that make it all happen. Just tap in the appropriate information and the machine coughs up the answer you need.

---

[1] All figures are rounded.

APPRAISING INCOME PROPERTY

As we noted earlier, compared to residential real estate, the stakes are higher when it comes to investing in income property. To separate the "dogs" from the "cash cows" there are a few different quick calculations you can do that will tell you if an income property is a waste of time. Some short cuts are more useful than others, but we'll briefly touch on them all.

PRICE PER UNIT METHOD (PPUM)

Take the per-unit price attributed to the units by local real estate experts and multiply it by the number of units in the building. A marginally useful tool, this gives you a theoretical value of the property. For example, if local experts are using a $40,000 per unit factor, then your four-unit property could be worth $160,000, not the $200,000 the RTC is asking.

The flaw with the price per unit method is that it does not differentiate between different-sized units. A studio apartment is given the same value as a three-bedroom unit. PPUM is often used by large investors who control one hundred or more rental units in the local market. They often figure lump sum costs on all holdings and then divide by the number of units they control. Included as lump sum costs are such factors as maintenance, expenses, and taxes. Considered a "broad stroke" technique, PPUM reflects a certain degree of reality, but it is not perfect. It's useful for quick "on-the-run" calculations for which you can divide the asking price by the number of units in a building.

Before you can make this calculation, you'll need to know what the average cost of rental units is in your particular area. Commercial real estate managers should have those figures readily handy and be happy to share them with you.

GROSS MULTIPLIER METHOD (GMM)

The GMM method is slightly more precise than the unit price approach. It uses a "rent multiplier" to gauge value. (Again, local realtors can tell you what rent multiplier is being currently used in your area.) For example: The gross rent multiplier in your area is 7. The apartment complex you're considering produces gross annual rents of $28,000. Multiply 7 × $28,000 = $196,000. Theoretically your target property is worth $196,000.

The weakness with GMM is that it does not take into account any property's expenses. Still, it can be used to determine if the seller's asking price is above or below the local norm.

NET OPERATING INCOME METHOD (NOIM)

One of the more accurate gauges of value, NOIM deducts property expenses from gross rents and factors in the vacancy ratio. (However, it does not take into consideration mortgage payments.) If your property produces $28,000 in gross rents and has $8,646 a year in expenses, then your NOI is $19,354. Ask a local realtor or two what the rent multiplier is in your target area. For sake of argument, one tells you it's 10 and another says it's 11. Split the difference at 10.5. Then multiply 10.5 × $19,354 = $203,217. Theoretically, that's now the value of your property.

CAPITALIZATION RATE METHOD (CRM)

This method takes you down to the bottom line right away. When you open a savings account you want to know what your rate of return (the interest rate paid by the bank) will be. The same holds true when investing in income property. Instead of interest income you'll be receiving rental income. Like a passbook account, rental income can be calculated as a rate of return to determine what a particular property might be worth.

Ask a commercial realtor what the current "cap rate" is. The realtor replies that it's 10. A 10 means that before investors buy they'll demand at least a 10 percent return from a building's net operating income. Keep in mind that income properties must compete against other investments such as stocks, bonds, and Treasury notes. Using the cap rate method we're trying to compare the property's investment value in the current investment climate.

Cap rates rise and fall with the condition of the local market and are often based on anticipated price appreciation. Take the cap rate and multiply it by your net operating income (NOI). For example, your property's net operating income is $19,354. The cap rate, according to your realtor is 10. Multiply the 10 by $19,354. Your investment value is $193,540.

The higher the cap rate demanded by investors, the lower it drives the value of an income property. It's common sense: The more investors demand in return on an asset's value, the less they'll pay for it based on a given net income stream.

Seasoned investors routinely use these shortcuts when analyzing income property. For the most part these methods are quick, easy, and, more often than not, come close to the mark. As you may have noticed we used the same NOI figure in all these examples and the values we came up with did not vary greatly. Nevertheless, don't rely exclusively on these shortcuts. Always complete your full-blown market value analysis and get comps.

Again, there are plenty of different ways to calculate the value of income property. Bookstores are full of them. But for making a bid on RTC or FDIC properties, the examples given above are enough to get you in the neighborhood. If you bag an investment property a good tax advisor can tell you all about depreciation schedules and how they're used to lower your investment income for tax purposes. Don't worry. It's just more good news.

With income property the biggest mistake you can make is to let your emotions overrule your calculations. No matter how much your eyes and heart love a property, you must be able to put those considerations aside and follow the simple steps above. Your heart will lie to you. Busy divorce courts are a testament to that truth. It's a cliché, but *numbers* don't lie. Numbers have no feelings, and they don't care. Numbers always tell the truth. We will say it over and over: *do the numbers*. Better that you let the numbers break your heart than to let your heart break your bank account.

SOME THOUGHTS ON BEING A LANDLORD

Many hardball real estate investors will advise you not to fall in love with your rental properties. They also warn you not to get too chummy with tenants. Both are sound pieces of advice but should be taken in moderation.

Your investment is going to be someone else's "home sweet home."

Treat it accordingly. You may have reached a point in your life where you can live in a better property than the one you're renting—that's all well and good. In fact, that's the whole point of this book—to raise your standard of living. But when buying and operating rentals, always ask yourself: Would I put my family, or for that matter my mother, in one of these units? If the answer is no, then calculate the cost of upgrading the rental in your cost estimates before you bid. You don't have to love your income property, but you should still be able to love yourself after you cash your tenant's rent check.

Do not purchase residential rental units unless you are prepared to become that building's superintendent or are prepared to hire a super to perform regular maintenance. Water heaters and plumbing are the two most frequent problems you'll have. Early on Thanksgiving Day I was called by a tenant because the element went out in her oven just when she put the turkey in. Guests were coming and all repair services, of course, were closed. I contacted another tenant who was having Thanksgiving at a relative's home and got permission for the woman to cook the turkey in her oven. That's the lot of the landlord.

If you don't like being bothered by other people's problems, then find a more passive investment. Also, it's better that you not think of your renters as "tenants." You'll do a lot better in this business if you consider them to be what they really are—your *customers*. Treat them accordingly. I have sometimes felt uncomfortable in the role of landlord. Having control over a family's hearth and home is a unique responsibility. Too many landlords abuse it. If you've never been a landlord, remember that you may own the building, but always remember also, you are a guest when in your tenant's home.

COMMERCIAL AND INDUSTRIAL INCOME PROPERTY

Commercial and industrial property investing is a venue in which you can lose serious money fast. A lot of losers have preceded you. A large chunk of the real estate being offered by the RTC and FDIC is the direct by-product of those earlier follies. On the other hand, the opportunities for gain are equally large.

Commercial and industrial properties are generally rented by the square foot. Calculations you make on square foot income are the same as on the rental and lease income we discussed above. Find out what the square foot rate is for the kind of property you're considering. Then apply the cap rate method to the result.

Commercial and industrial property investments are not for the faint-hearted or the amateur investor. A glut of office space exists in most major markets—we're talking double-digit vacancy ratios in such previously hot markets as Los Angeles, New York, and even the formerly recession-proof Washington, D.C. Double-digit vacancy ratios will remain in most major office markets through 1995 as both the RTC and FDIC dump more real estate at fire sale prices.

A small retail shop across the street from a regional shopping center may look like a real buy. But if half the shops across the street are vacant, your square footage estimates will be theoretical at best. Do your homework. National commercial real estate companies such as JBS Associates in Chicago and Cushman and Wakefield in Los Angeles spit out commercial vacancy rate data every month. National real estate companies track vacancy trends in—usually—the fifty largest markets. The National Association of Realtors in Washington also has readily available residential and commercial vacancy data.

Most vacancy studies conducted by these large organizations are free for the asking. Watch the business or real estate section of your local newspaper—firms like Cushman and Wakefield regularly supply vacancy data tables to business and real estate editors hungry for easy copy. The graphs are simple to read. At the bottom of the graph or list of statistics the paper will credit the company or organization that provided the numbers. Give them a call and ask for a copy of the full study.

Cushman and Wakefield data can be extremely useful to an investor thinking of purchasing an RTC office building because it compares a city's vacancy ratio over the past years with its current vacancy ratio. Investors should look to see if the vacancy trend is headed up or down. For example, in 1991 in Washington, D.C. the office vacancy rate was 12 percent, compared to 8.9 percent in 1988. This is a sign that vacancies are increasing, not a bullish indicator. (The only ones renting new office space these days are the RTC and FDIC.) In San Francisco, the vacancy ratio on office space in 1988 was 15.3 percent. In 1991 the vacancy ratio had fallen to 13.2 percent—a good sign. Unless you can get office buildings for a song, stay away from Los Angeles office properties. In

1988 the city had an office vacancy ratio of 16.5 percent—which was horrible. Nevertheless, some fools, flush with easy S&L and bank loans, kept building anyway and by 1991 the vacancy rate had jumped to 25.2 percent, creating what locals have dubbed "see-through office buildings." Clearly, it's going to be a decade before L.A. stabilizes.

Investment returns on commercial property can be handsome when the property is researched and purchased properly—as long as favorable market conditions provide renters. Unless you're buying office space for your own company for the long haul, make sure you understand the market. Otherwise, you will be just the latest in a long line of fools who thought it would be a real ego trip to own an office building or a complex of shops or a small shopping center. Megalomaniacs are poorly suited to be real estate investors.

IN SUMMARY

As you gain experience analyzing income properties, you'll soon be doing the calculations in your head. You'll know you are getting better at it when you can glance down a list of properties for sale and eliminate most of them without even leaving home or picking up the telephone.

But when a property makes its way onto your short list it's time to put the mental calculator away and take out the silicone brain in your desk drawer. Open a file on the prospective property. Start crunching the numbers—expenses, taxes, mortgage payments, the real vacancy factors. Start narrowing things down. Always do the numbers. Always.

Commercial real estate may be too much of a leap for first-time buyers. But it shouldn't be avoided. There are plenty of small—two-to four-unit—properties that are both residential and income properties wrapped in one. Buyers can live in one unit and rent out the others.

For the professional investor, now is a great time to buy apartment buildings. Immigrants are pouring into America throughout the Southwest. In California alone, more than 800,000 new households were formed in 1991, but only 500,000 housing units were built. What does that tell you as an investor? Fewer and fewer Americans can afford their own home and must rent. All this adds up to a very bright future for landlords.

The commercial and industrial real estate glut is concentrated in certain big cities, the Southwest and the Northeast. But throughout Main Street America thousands of government-owned commercial properties are available and remain a solid value. A lot of them are former S&L and bank branches, and if you don't mind having a Ft. Knox vault in the middle of your building, you can get them cheap. Turn the vault into a wine cellar, or rent out space to other businesses that have security needs that can't be filled by a bank safety deposit box. If nothing else, it's a great conversation piece.

Income property that can carry its own debt load and expenses is a terrific investment. It will appreciate in time while costing you virtually nothing to own. If it also throws off net spendable income, so much the better. Income property is where you find serious investors because it's where you can make serious money.

Chapter 7

....

Do I Hear a Bid?

How to Bid at Government Auctions

When the S&L mess first reared its ugly head, the government tried, without much luck, to sell repossessed assets itself. But would-be real estate buyers were unanimous in their conclusion that "You just can't do business with these people."

Ironically, federal bank and thrift regulators—who spent the 1980s in a near coma while their wards were being looted—swung suddenly to the other extreme, becoming overdiligent, hyperactive watchdogs when it came to peddling the real estate they ended up owning. Prospective buyers were treated rudely, calls went unreturned, and good offers were often ignored. Instead of being welcomed with open arms, private-sector investors were treated as "vultures" looking for a free lunch at the government's expense. Rather than welcoming their interest in these assets, bank and thrift regulators showed them the door.

Yes, a few vultures certainly flew among the flock, but most of the prospective customers were just real estate professionals trying to buy something at a good price—hardly an un-American inclination. Instead of working with these buyers, government "liquidation specialists" drove them away through inattention and distinctly unprofessional conduct.

That was the past—but a past that continues to haunt the RTC.

Though the RTC has ironed out most of its operating wrinkles, to this day those early buyers will not go anywhere near another government property sale. That's bad news for taxpayers, but good news for investors just discovering the RTC, FDIC, and HUD. Old rumors die hard, however. During your initial search phase don't be surprised if fellow investors warn that, "You can't deal with the RTC or FDIC." Our message couldn't be clearer: Those rumors are no longer true.

What happened to change things? By the end of 1990 Congress was up to its neck in complaints about the RTC. Constituents kept telling elected officials that RTC account executives wouldn't return telephone calls, that someone else bought the property they wanted but at a lower price, and on and on. Congress,[1] which holds the purse strings to the S&L bailout, told the RTC to fly right, or the ball game was over—no more money.

With a new chief executive, Albert Casey, appointed in mid-1991, the RTC began to get its sales act together and was up and running. It hired outside private-sector sales and computer experts to organize and manage its real estate and loan portfolios. In time the RTC (as well as the FDIC) was actually advertising in the *Wall Street Journal*, trying to get the word out to the investing public.

ROUND THEM UP—HEAD THEM OUT

As we noted earlier, when the RTC takes over a savings and loan it usually leaves the S&L open for a time through a conservatorship. Old management is replaced and the RTC tries to sell the thrift to a new owner. But even if successful in this effort, nine times out of ten the new buyer doesn't want all the real estate, loans, and other assets left behind by the prior owners. To accommodate a new buyer, the RTC will take over those assets and place them into a separate receivership through which it will market them to the public.

Rather than repeat old mistakes, the RTC does not try to sell these assets themselves. The RTC lists these properties with approved asset

---

[1] Congress must approve all taxpayer funding of the savings and loan bailout. After an RTC funding bill is approved by Congress it must be signed by the President.

managers. Approved asset managers manage properties for the government under what is known as a Standard Asset Management and Disposition Agreement, or SAMDA. Managers who have these contracts are known as SAMDA contractors. Today, thousands of different firms manage, auction, and sell properties for the RTC through a SAMDA contract. Some national firms just manage, some just auction, and some just sell. Many, like the Los Angeles-based Cushman and Wakefield and the Alexandria, Virginia-based J.E. Robert & Co., do all three.

Often the RTC or FDIC will hire a SAMDA contractor like C&W or J.E. Robert to sell assets "in bulk" at large public auctions. Most of the assets sold at these large bulk sale auctions are income properties such as apartment buildings, hotels, offices, shopping centers, and warehouses.

HOW THE AUCTION AND BULK-SALE PROCESS WORKS

In general, auctions are advertised at least sixty days ahead of time in large national newspapers such as the *Wall Street Journal* and the *New York Times*, as well as in local newspapers. If you miss an auction notice you can always call the RTC auction hot line (1–800–RTC–3006). A prerecorded message will tell you about all upcoming RTC auctions. The hot line recording gives the name, address, and telephone number of the SAMDA contractor in charge of the auction. Auction information is also listed on RTCNET, the agency's computer data base. The FDIC does not yet have an auction hot line, but information about upcoming auctions can be obtained by calling the consolidated office nearest you. Both the RTC and FDIC encourage their asset managers to advertise auctions aggressively.

When the RTC hires a SAMDA contractor to conduct an auction, the asset manager always sets up a toll-free number that you can call for further information. (In early 1992 when C&W was auctioning off $180 million worth of RTC commercial real estate properties, it assigned 120 of its employees to work exclusively on just that auction.) Operators should be able to answer most of the basics. One of the primary responsibilities of the operator is to mail out auction catalogs to interested investors. The catalog should arrive on your doorstep within five working days at the most.

Most of the catalogs put together by the SAMDA contractors come in an 8″ × 11″ color format. Auction catalogs carry a photo of each property, its address, a description, zoning, listed price, and the name and telephone number of the SAMDA contractor, or asset manager,[2] in charge of the property.

If a property catches your eye, don't rely solely on what's in the catalog. Catalogs give a thumbnail sketch of a property but fall short of what you'll need to make an informed bid. If you like the property call the asset manager and ask for its due diligence package—which is a detailed, blow-by-blow description of the property's key features and credit history.

At this point the free ride is over. The SAMDA contractor will charge you a fee of between $15 to $25 for the detailed due diligence package. But for anyone seriously thinking of making a bid on a property the price is cheap. In return for your $15 to $25 you will receive an information-packed ringbinder that will tell you more than you ever need to know about an RTC property.

Inside the due diligence package you should find the following information:

- A detailed description of the property
- The property's income history (if it's income property)
- A list of all current tenants, their names, rent amounts, and overdue rents
- The property's expense history, including utility expenses, taxes, and special assessments
- Notice of any special environmental concerns, including notifications (if there are any) about possible toxic contaminations or easements
- A current demographic breakdown of the surrounding area
- A property type vacancy ratio analysis for real estate in that particular area
- A trend analysis for the area showing increases or decreases in occupancy, rents, and employment
- A traffic analysis for both auto and foot traffic (if commercial)

[2] For discussion purposes, *SAMDA contractor* and *asset manager* are considered to be one and the same.

- An overview of area amenities, including parks, schools, and public transportation
- A demand analysis showing the current marketability and rentability of similar property types
- An analysis of the area's employment picture (jobs, job type, major employers, employment trends)

As you see, the modest cost of this due diligence package is money well spent—cheap at many times the price. Due diligence packages contain the kinds of income analysis and demographic information on a property that are usually only available to well-heeled professionals. If you paid for these studies yourself, the cost would easily run into thousands of dollars for each property.

The due diligence package contains all the information you'll need to make an intelligent bid. *Keep in mind that SAMDA contractors are employed by the RTC* only *to market the property*. Although you will mail your bid to them, they do not become involved in the bid consideration process. The SAMDA contractor forwards your *sealed* bid envelope to the RTC consolidated office overseeing the auction. Your sealed bid is then opened by RTC personnel on the day after the bid deadline.

Think of SAMDA contractors as a convenience provided to you by the RTC. They are required to bend over backwards to help you. Besides studying their due diligence package, you can contact the SAMDA contractor to arrange a physical inspection of the property. SAMDA contractors hold open houses on all properties that are being offered. Most open houses are held at least a month before the bid date. (Besides viewing the property, it might be a good idea to take a quick trip down to the county recorder's office to get a look at the property's title and zoning histories. Also take a look at the title and zoning history of neighboring properties. The SAMDA contractor will be of no help here. You have to do this on your own.)

PUTTING MONEY WHERE YOUR MOUTH IS

After inspecting the property, its due diligence package, and its title history, you should by now have a rough idea what you're going to bid. The next step will be to telephone the RTC consolidated office in charge of the auction and request what is known as a *Direct Bid Brochure*. This package is free and contains specific instructions on bid procedures. Also ask for a copy of the agency's booklet, *General Terms & Conditions*. This booklet contains a lot of "contract-ese" and boilerplate jargon, but slog through it anyway. Buried in all the grey text may be some "need to knows."

The bidding process itself is cut and dried.

WHO CAN BID?

Anyone over eighteen years of age can bid, regardless of sex, race, citizenship, or marital status. Before bidding, though, you must submit proof to the RTC that you are financially capable of coming up with the purchase price. If you offer to put $25,000 cash down, bank statements showing that you indeed have $25,000 will be required along with your bid. If you state in your offer that you plan to borrow the balance from a certain lender, then a signed loan commitment letter from that lender is required. A general financial statement showing your current assets and liabilities may also be required, particularly if you are asking the RTC to carry the loan.

CASH DEPOSIT

When you submit your completed bid form, attach a personal check for 1 percent of the price you bid. If you offer $55,000 for a property, enclose a check for $550. This deposit check will not be cashed unless yours is the winning bid. If you win the bid, not only will your check be cashed, but you will be required to cough up another 4 percent, bringing your total deposit to 5 percent. You have *three working days* to come up with the 5 percent. If you fail to do so, the RTC will discard your bid and accept the next best bid.

The RTC does not fool around. It will not give you additional time to "come up with the rest of the money." Despite what some members of Congress may think, the agency is not in the business of providing social services. If you make a bid, have the money in hand. The RTC has a good computer system that tracks all registered bidders. If the agency pegs you as a flake, chances are that any future bids you make will get short shrift.

UNACCEPTABLE BID TERMS

The RTC *does not* accept bids that request option agreements, creative financing schemes, or lot splits. The agency does not like to divide parcels of land. It's all or nothing. The lot-splitting process takes too much legal work and time. The government also ignores requests by bidders that the RTC repair property defects prior to closing. All properties sold by the RTC and FDIC are on an "as is" basis. Don't even bother asking. Keep your bids simple and straightforward.

ACCEPTABLE FINANCING TERMS

The RTC likes all-cash bids. Aside from that, the RTC will also entertain bids calling for seller financing. The whole purpose of an auction is to make the *government's* life easier, not yours. Still, as we detailed in earlier chapters, the government will extend seller financing to eligible buyers. Except for loans on single-family residences, most of the mortgages offered by the government are seven-year balloons. After seven years you'll have to find another loan.

BROKER COMMISSIONS

A licensed real estate broker representing a buyer can receive a sales commission from the RTC and FDIC. But before the broker can receive his or her cut, the buyer has to fill out and submit with the sealed bid a signed "Purchaser/Co-broker Certificate." Included in the bid package, the form must be signed by both the buyer and the broker. (See Exhibit 8.)

If a bid is accepted, the broker receives half the sales commission, for which he or she will be most grateful to the buyer. The RTC pays the same commission amount whether or not you have a broker representing you. Having a broker will not prejudice your chances of winning a bid. RTC and FDIC commissions begin at 5 percent for most residential properties, but decrease for large commercial properties as the selling price climbs into the millions. When in doubt, ask the SAMDA contractor what the broker commission will be on a given property.

Resolution Trust Corporation
Comprehensive Advertising and Marketing Program

Direct Bid Offering
California Commercial Properties
Winter 1991 - 1992

<u>BID FORM</u>

PLEASE NOTE: THIS BID FORM AND ATTACHED PURCHASER/CO-BROKER CERTIFICATE (IF APPLICABLE) ARE THE ONLY DOCUMENTS TO BE COMPLETED BY BIDDERS. HOWEVER, ALL BIDDERS SHOULD CAREFULLY REVIEW THE FORM OF PURCHASE AGREEMENT TO BE USED, AND ALL EXHIBITS TO THE PURCHASE AGREEMENT.

Dated: _____

To:
Cushman & Wakefield
300 South Grand Avenue, Suite 3750
Los Angeles, California 90071
Attention: Direct Bid Offering

     Re: Resolution Trust Corporation
               Comprehensive Advertising and Marketing Program
               Direct Bid Offering - Property No. _____
Gentlemen:

    The undersigned Bidder hereby submits the following Bid, in accordance with the Resolution Trust Corporation ("**RTC**") Direct Bid Offering Instructions. If RTC accepts Bidder's bid, Bidder agrees to be bound by the terms and conditions of the Purchase and Sale Agreement and Joint Escrow Instructions in the form previously furnished to the undersigned (the "**Purchase Agreement**"), and to execute five (5) copies thereof, duly completed by RTC with the particulars of this transaction, promptly upon receipt. Bidder acknowledges that it has reviewed a copy of the form of the Purchase Agreement, including all exhibits thereto and the documents to be executed for Seller financing, if applicable, and Bidder approves of their respective terms and conditions.

1. Direct Bid Offering Property Number: _____

2. Property Address: _____

     _____

3. Purchase Price: _____

     _____ ($ _____)

4. Seller Financing Requested: Yes _____ No_____

EXHIBIT 8. Five-page RTC real estate bid form for sealed-bid auctions. These forms are included in the auction bid package. They must be returned to the asset management firm in a *sealed* envelope.

5. Amount of Financing Requested: $_____

6. Percentage of bid amount to be financed (not more than eighty-five percent (85%)):____%

7. Name of Bidder: _____

8. Type of Entity, e.g., Corporation, Partnership, Trust, etc.: _____

9. Bidder's Taxpayer Identification Number:_____

10. Bidder's Address for Notices: _____

11. Bidder's Telephone Number: _____

12. Bidder's Fax Number:_____

13. Name and Title
    of Bidder's Contact Person: _____

    _____

14. Bidder hereby submits with this bid the following items:

    A.   A check in the amount of $_____, representing one percent (1%)
            of the Purchase Price (the "**Bid Deposit**").

    B.   If Bidder is represented by a co-broker, a fully-executed Purchaser/Broker Certificate in the
            form of **Exhibit "1"** to this Bid Form.

    C.   Financial statements or evidence of ability to close the transaction, as follows (check if
            applicable):

      (i)   __   A copy of the Bidder's latest personal and/or corporate tax return;

      (ii) __   A letter addressed to RTC from the Bidder's institutional lender, or bank, on that
                 institution's letterhead, stating the bidder's financial capabilities;

      (iii) __   Identification of any equity partners and such partner's financial capabilities;

      (iv) __   Financial statement that sets forth in detail the Bidder's assets and liabilities;

      (v)   __   Other (Explain)   _____

                                       _____

    The undersigned Bidder agrees to furnish any additional evidence of financial capability that may be
    requested by RTC or the DBO Underwriter, and acknowledges that if this bid is conditionally accepted
    and Bidder has made a request for Seller financing that RTC recommends to the DBO Underwriter,
    the undersigned shall be obligated to pay a NON-REFUNDABLE underwriting fee equal to one-tenth
    (1/10) of one percent (1%) of the loan amount, with a minimum fee of One Thousand Five Hundred
    Dollars ($1,500) and a maximum of Ten Thousand Dollars ($10,000), within seven (7) days after

Broker identified above, if any, for commissions or other reimbursement arising in connection with any sale of the Property to the undersigned by RTC.

2. CO-BROKER CERTIFICATE.

The undersigned Co-Broker hereby certifies, represents and warrants to RTC that it has not associated with any other broker other than Broker in connection with the interest of the above-named Purchaser in purchasing the Property from RTC. Co-Broker acknowledges and agrees that: (a) Co-Broker's commission shall be paid by Broker, rather than RTC, through the escrow process directly and solely to the undersigned Co-Broker; and (b) RTC shall have no liability to pay a commission to Co-Broker. RTC shall have no liability to pay a commission to any Co-Broker. The undersigned Co-Broker hereby agrees to indemnify, defend and hold RTC harmless from and against the claims of any other Co-Broker who claims that it was acting by or through the undersigned Co-Broker in connection with any such sale to the above-named Purchaser.

The undersigned Co-Broker hereby agrees that it shall be entitled to fifty percent (50%) of the gross commission paid by RTC in connection with the sale of the Property to the above-named Purchaser. The commission shall be paid only upon full and complete closing of sale and payment of such purchase price in full to RTC (for the purpose hereof, the purchase price shall include the amount of any financing provided by RTC in connection with such sale).

The undersigned Co-Broker agrees and acknowledges that no commissions will be paid by RTC to a broker, which directly or indirectly acquires any interest in the Property being purchased or otherwise financially participates in the purchase of the Property in any way. The undersigned Co-Broker hereby certifies he/she is serving in this transaction only as a broker and not as a principal or direct or indirect owner, lender, or other financial participant.

IT IS UNDERSTOOD THAT A COMMISSION FROM RTC SHALL NOT BE PAYABLE TO ANY CO-BROKER UNLESS THIS PURCHASER/CO-BROKER CERTIFICATE IS EXECUTED BY THE PURCHASER AND CO-BROKER AND SUBMITTED TO BROKER ON OR BEFORE 5:00 P.M. P.S.T., JANUARY 30, 1992.

PURCHASER:

Date:_____   _____

_____

By:_____

Name:_____

Title:_____

CO-BROKER:

Date:_____   _____

_____

License #:_____

By:_____

Name:_____

Title:_____

1823BID.WXT   xi

RTC has indicated its conditional acceptance of this Bid. This underwriting fee shall not be applied toward the Purchase Price.

(If applicable): Bidder is making multiple bids and the Bidder's financial information is submitted with the Bid Form for DBO Property Number _____.

15. Bidder acknowledges it is not relying on any legal or tax advice from RTC in connection with the transactions contemplated by this Bid.

16. The undersigned Bidder understands that properties may be withdrawn from the Direct Bid Offering at any time prior to closing, and that if the undersigned becomes the successful Bidder, the undersigned will not have the right to assign or transfer its right to purchase the property covered by this Bid.

17. The undersigned Bidder represents that the execution and delivery of this Bid have been authorized by any and all necessary parties.

18. Bidder is not acting as a nominee, agent, or trustee for any person or entity who will be the true or beneficial owner of the property that is the subject of this Bid; and Bidder is purchasing the property for its own account and not with the intent of selling the property to, or exchanging the property with, any other person or entity who has requested or arranged with Bidder to enter into the Purchase Agreement for such purpose. There are no agreements, written or oral, express or implied, between (i) Bidder or any of the persons executing the Purchase Agreement on behalf of Bidder and (ii) the previous owner of the property or any person or entity affiliated or connected with the previous owner of the property (collectively, the "Previous Owner") for the payment of any additional amounts to the Previous Owner in connection with the sale of the property or which contemplate the retention by or conveyance to the Previous Owner of any interest in the property or any interest in any entity which may own or hold title to the property, including, without limitation, Bidder.

IN WITNESS WHEREOF, the undersigned hereby submits this Bid.

_____

By: _____

Name: _____

Its: _____

RESOLUTION TRUST CORPORATION
COMPREHENSIVE ADVERTISING AND MARKETING PROGRAM
DIRECT BID OFFERING

PURCHASER/CO-BROKER CERTIFICATE

NAME OF
PURCHASER: _____

PURCHASER'S
ADDRESS: _____

_____

PURCHASER'S
TELEPHONE
NUMBER: _____

NAME OF
CO-BROKER: _____

NAME OF SALES
PERSON, IF OTHER
THAN CO-BROKER: _____

CO-BROKER'S
ADDRESS: _____

_____

CO-BROKER'S
TELEPHONE NUMBER: _____

PROPERTY
NUMBER: _____

PROPERTY
ADDRESS: _____

_____

1. **PURCHASER CERTIFICATE.**

The undersigned Purchaser hereby certifies, represents and warrants to the Resolution Trust Corporation ("RTC") and Cushman & Wakefield ("Broker"), acting as RTC's exclusive agent, that the above-named Co-Broker is the sole Co-Broker through whom the undersigned has considered and shall consider the Property described above (the "Property") for purchase from RTC. The undersigned Purchaser hereby agrees to indemnify, defend and hold RTC harmless from and against any and all claims of brokers, other than the Co-

1823BID.WXT   X

BROKER-BUYERS

A licensed real estate broker can purchase properties from the government but don't expect the RTC to pay that broker a commission. If you're a licensed real estate broker bidding for yourself don't count on the commission to reduce your down payment.

BROKER-NONBROKER PARTNERSHIPS

If you and a broker friend decide to invest together in RTC properties it might be wise if the broker remains just that—a broker—during the acquisition phase. After you receive full title there's nothing to stop the broker from using his or her commission to buy into the property with you as a partner.

RETRACTING A BID

In some cases the RTC will ask you to bid on a property without fully inspecting it or, for that matter, having a chance to see a title report. Therefore the RTC allows for a thirty-day inspection period that begins *the day after* your bid is accepted. During this thirty-day period you can bail out of the property without penalty by submitting a "termination notice" to the consolidated office. After the thirty-day period expires, your deposit becomes nonrefundable.

ACCESS TO THE PROPERTY

Initially you may have had limited access to the property during an open house. After your bid is accepted the RTC allows expanded access, which gives you the opportunity to bring in a site engineer. Before bringing in an engineer the RTC requests that you give "reasonable" notice so they can make arrangements with the asset manager and tenants. Before being granted access to the property you must accept personal liability for injury or damage done during the inspection. Depending on just how much poking around you intend to do, the RTC may require that you provide proof of liability insurance.

Besides allowing you to inspect the physical property, the RTC also grants unlimited access to the building's books, records, leases, and contracts.

CLOSE BIDS

Until title changes hands, you will have no way of knowing how close your bid was to the winning bid. After closing you can visit the county recorder's office to see how much the winner paid. The RTC will not disclose to anyone what the winning bidder paid. However, if your bid and the winning bid are close the RTC will hold your bid during the thirty-day inspection period. If the winner bails out or cannot perform under the contract, the RTC will award the property to you—if you still want it. You then have to increase your deposit to 5 percent. If you don't want it, the next closest bidder gets the property.

RTC BID ANALYSIS

Once the bid deadline passes, you will have to wait. It takes the RTC about thirty days to choose a winner. This is not just a "red tape" delay. The RTC brings in a staff of private accountants to analyze each individual bid to determine which bid nets the RTC the most money in today's dollars.

This bid opening and analysis process is not open to the public. And the RTC will not disclose what formula it uses to judge bids. The only thing they tell bidders is the oft repeated: Cash is king. In fact, the RTC accountants are simply holding each bid up to a standard net present value analysis that you can do on your own business calculator. Nothing mysterious here. The only thing the government wants is to return as much money to the taxpayers as possible.

Still, the behind-closed-doors process upsets some bidders who wonder if, perhaps, someone's brother-in-law isn't getting a sweet deal at their expense. Actually the process is kept confidential for a number of sound reasons:

- The RTC does not want to encourage expensive lawsuits by litigious bidders. By opening up the process the agency could find itself in the middle of constant arguments between bidders who for one reason or another claim their bid is superior even though on the surface everything looks equal. Such litigation could tie up a sale for months, or worse, years. Multiply that times the thousands of properties the RTC has to sell and you can understand its worst nightmare.

If all bids were cash this would not be a problem, but rarely are all bids cash. In most cases bids are a combination of cash plus financing. Therefore the need for accountants to calculate the net present value of each, based on the unique details of the offers.

- If successful bids were made public, a sore loser with time to spare might try to halt the sale by filing a lawsuit. Such suits often result in a "leis pendens"—legal notice filed at the recorder's office that someone else has a claim against the property. Once the property is so encumbered, no one will buy it, and the winning bidder (as well as the taxpayers) will be left twisting in the wind. Under the present system, the burden of proof is on the plaintiff, not the RTC. It is much harder to reverse a sale than to stop one.

As working journalists the authors have a built-in dislike and suspicion of anything the government does behind closed doors. It's certainly not outside the realm of possibility that on occasion favoritism may have been given to certain bidders. But from what we've seen, the process— for the most part—has been fair. Because the RTC—not the SAMDA contractor—decides who gets the property, there is little chance that an asset manager's favorite client (or brother-in-law) will be given the inside track during the bid consideration process. Moreover, RTC personnel operate under strict conflict of interest rules that can land them in jail if they show any form of favoritism to a buyer. In case you were wondering, RTC employees and their relatives are prohibited from purchasing any assets from the agency. It's a felony.

If you were treated unfairly in an RTC or FDIC asset sale, both agencies have an office of inspector general in Washington, D.C. that investigates such matters. Solid evidence helps, but at the very least you can file a letter of complaint. If you lose a property through favoritism, still, it might be best to simply move along to another property. As long as you get your bid money back, squabbling over a lost property usually turns out to be a major waste of time. There's plenty of fish in the government pond.

KEY INFORMATION. *Your bid must arrive at the real estate manager's office in its original sealed envelope. It is extremely important that you write on the outside of your bid envelope on both the front and back in large readable letters:* Bid Enclosed. *If you don't, the SAMDA contractor has no way of distinguishing your bid from all other mail coming into the office. If your bid letter is opened by accident, the real estate manager must return it, which means you'll have to submit it all over again. If this happens the day before bid deadline you could miss the boat.*

When deciding what to bid, once again review all that's available: the due diligence package provided by the RTC, your own income property and market analysis, and your financial statements, and then figure out what you're willing to pay. One of the most useful pieces of information to keep in mind is how the RTC appraises and values property and adjusts it downward during the marketing phase.

It's rare, if not unheard of, for sellers to disclose so much about how they value assets, but the RTC is just such a seller. When the RTC began seizing S&Ls in late 1989 it quickly learned that establishing a value on properties is not easy. Many S&L properties had been valued by appraisers who were "on the take." During the mid- to late 1980s some appraisers were taking kickbacks to inflate their appraisals. These artificially inflated appraisals allowed crooked developers and bankers to skim loan proceeds and embezzle money out of loan proceeds. Compounding the RTC's problems, the national real estate economy went into a tailspin in 1991, dragging the value of already overvalued assets down even further.

After several fits and starts the RTC finally got serious about helping its field personnel reappraise properties by issuing a set of government-backed appraisal guidelines. The RTC also created bid acceptance rules, giving its employees a set of parameters to follow if bids fall short of appraised values. Here's an inside view of how the RTC appraises its properties:

When the asset is acquired by the RTC:

1) The agency's asset managers order a new appraisal on the property using an RTC-approved appraiser.
2) The appraisal is reviewed by asset managers at the closest RTC consolidated office to see if it follows agency guidelines.
3) The real estate broker chosen by the RTC to market the property is then asked to comment on the appraisal.
4) If all passes muster the new appraisal becomes the RTC's "starting point" on value.
5) From that value, the RTC then subtracts estimated holding costs and sets a new value.
6) The property is listed on the open market through a broker, asset manager, or SAMDA contractor at the new, adjusted value. RTC personnel monitor the property closely and if it doesn't sell, consider a price reduction.

If a property does not sell at its adjusted appraised value within a specific time frame, the consolidated office in charge of that asset has been given the power to reduce the asking price. There are limits to how much a property can be reduced at one time, but some reductions can be substantial. Two events can trigger a price reduction:

- A property has been aggressively marketed for six months (four for residential properties) and no offers are received or
- Offers are received but are significantly below the property's appraised value.

If either occurs the consolidated office can lower the asking price, with certain limitations:

- A property's asking price cannot be lowered more than 15 percent at one time.
- A second price reduction can occur only after the property has been exposed to the market for another three months.
- If a property's asking price has been reduced by more than 20

percent of its original asking price, further reductions cannot occur without first obtaining a new appraisal on the property.

EXAMPLES OF RTC APPRAISALS

The following are based on actual examples given by the RTC to its field personnel.

Example 1. A single-family residential home on the outskirts of Houston, Texas

- Appraised value: $100,000
- Date of appraisal: 1/1/90
- Estimated marketing period: 6 months
- Average holding costs for area: $200 per month (taxes, insurance, maintenance)
- RTC's current cost of money: 9% (based on current one-year Treasury bond yield)

Date: 4/1/90

Scenario: The property is listed with a broker for $100,000. During its first three months on the market the RTC has received only one bid, for $89,000.

Is this an acceptable bid by RTC guidelines?

No. When the bid is received the RTC immediately calculates the property's *present value*. The present value is used to measure all offers and gives the RTC a clear picture of what a property is worth at any time during the sales process.

The RTC sets a present value formula that assumes the property will sell six months from the appraisal date. It then prorates holding costs, which in this case come to $591 for three months' time:

- Future Value: $100,000 in three months
- Current discount rate: 9% annualized
- Holding costs subtracted from asking price: present value of $97,783

The result is a new present value (as of 4/1/90) of $97,192.[3] With only three months on the market, the RTC cannot yet sell this property for less than 95 percent of the property's adjusted value. That means the lowest bid the RTC can accept at this point is $92,332.

Date: 5/1/90

Scenario: The property still has not sold and the highest bid is still $89,000. Even though the RTC asset manager now has the right to lower the price 15 percent, in his opinion an 8 percent reduction should do the trick. He then decides to lower the asking price to $92,000. The RTC then adjusts the current value downward by again subtracting holding costs and calculating present value based on a two-month holding period. (Remember the original estimated holding period was for six months.)

- Future value: $92,000 in two months
- Discount rate: still 9%
- Present value: $90,635
- Minus two months' expenses of $395.54

New adjusted market value (AMV) = $90,239. Because the RTC can only accept bids that are at least 95 percent of its adjusted market value, the new asking price translates into a minimum acceptable bid of $85,727.

The RTC now decides to take the $89,000 offer.

Example 2. An office building in North Dallas, Texas

- Appraised Value: $1 million
- Date of appraisal: 1/1/90
- Estimated marketing period: 12 months
- Income generated: $40,000 per month

---

[3] The property is assumed to sell at the appraised value of $100,000 six months from the appraisal date, or in three months from 4/1/90 at a 9 percent discount rate. Subtracting three months' remaining holding costs of $591 gives a present value of $97,192.

- Expenses: $50,000 per month
- RTC current cost of money: 9% (based on current one-year Treasury note rate)

Date: 5/1/90

Scenario: The office building has been marketed extensively and the best offer received is $850,000. Should it be accepted? RTC officials at the consolidated office get out their calculators and figure:

- The building's present value is determined to be $941,975. This figure is achieved by taking the $1 million appraised value and calculating its future value eight months from now at the 9 percent discount rate.
- Then the RTC subtracts from the present value the anticipated building income for the next eight months. (This income would not be realized by the agency if it accepts the offer.) The value of that "missed" income comes to $309,464, which is achieved by calculating a present value of this cash flow stream, discounted at the 9 percent annual rate.
- The agency also subtracts the building's holding costs, which, if it accepts the offer, it will not have to pay. The anticipated holding costs = $386,609. Again the present value of expenses ($50,000 per month) is discounted at the 9 percent annual rate.

The result is an adjusted market value of $864,609. This means the minimum acceptable bid (95 percent of AMV) is now $821,379.

Example 3: Same as in Example 2, but let's change the circumstances. Let's say the RTC never received the $850,000 bid, and the property stays on the market.

Date: 7/1/90

Scenario: The property has been for sale for a full six months without receiving an acceptable offer. Six more months remain in the original marketing period. Based on a market analysis and an examination of low bids already received, the RTC asset manager decides a full 15 percent reduction in the asking price is justified. The property's new adjusted market value becomes *$850,000*.

Date: 8/1/90

Scenario: The RTC receives a bid of $650,000 from a qualified buyer. Five full months remain on the marketing period. Does the offer have a chance? The RTC first determines the property's present market value:

- $850,000 for five months at the 9 percent discount rate equals a present value of $818,830
- Plus PV of income (five months at $40,000 lost) = $195,000
- Subtract PV of holding expenses ($50,000 × 5 months) = $244,472

The result gives the agency a new present value of $769,936. The minimum acceptable bid (95 percent of value) is now *$731,439*. Therefore a bid of $650,000 is deemed unacceptable.

Date: 10/1/90

Scenario: The property still hasn't attracted acceptable bids, and the RTC asset manager orders an additional 5 percent reduction in the asking price. Since the property was first listed for sale, its price has been reduced by 20 percent to $800,000.

Date: 11/1/90

Scenario: The RTC receives a new bid for $700,000. Two months remain in the original marketing period. What chance does this offer have? Let's look:

- PV of adjusted appraised value = $788,134
- Plus PV of holding period income = $79,109
- Minus PV of holding costs = $98,886

This gives us a new present market value of $768,357. The minimum acceptable bid (95 percent of PMV) is now *$729,939*.

But the RTC asset manager is concerned that a 20 percent price reduction may not be enough and on November 15 orders a new appraisal, which is required when a manager seeks a reduction of greater than 20 percent. (The bidder would not know this.)

During the newest appraisal roof damage of $50,000 is discovered.

Date: 12/1/90

Scenario: The RTC receives a new offer of $675,000 from the same bidder who made the rejected $700,000 offer a month earlier. The bidder knows the property hasn't sold for almost a year and decides to make a lowball offer. The RTC calculates present market value:

- PV of adjusted appraised value of $800,000 = $794,045
- Plus PV of holding income = $39,702
- Minus PV of holding expenses = $49,628
- Roof repair costs (which have been disclosed to the bidder) = $50,000

New present market value = $734,119. Therefore the new minimum acceptable bid is *$697,413*.

If the RTC is selling this property through a real estate broker and is paying a 4 percent commission, this offer would be unacceptable. But because it's saving $27,000 on commissions by marketing the property itself, the $675,000 offer is deemed acceptable based on a minimum PV price of $670,413.

Example 4. A 100-acre tract of raw land outside Tucson, Arizona

- Appraised Value: $650,000
- Date of appraisal: 1/1/90
- Estimated marketing period: 24 months
- Holding costs: $2,000 per month
- RTC's current cost of money: 8% (based on current two-year Treasury yield)

Date: 6/1/90

Scenario: The property has been marketed, and the best offer received to date is $400,000. Can the RTC accept this offer?

- PV of appraised value = $572,908
- Minus PV of holding expenses = $35,572

Present market value = $537,336, and the minimum acceptable bid is $483,602.

Date: 8/1/90
Scenario: After seven months on the market the RTC asset manager adjusts the appraised value down 15 percent. The new adjusted appraised value is $552,500.

Date: 10/1/90
Scenario: A bid of $420,000 is received. Will it fly? Let's see:

- PV of adjusted appraised value = $500,090
- Minus PV of holding expenses = $28,452

Present market value = $471,637, and the minimum acceptable bid is $424,475. Though this bid doesn't quite meet RTC guidelines, it's off by only $4,475. The RTC would more than likely make the buyer a counteroffer and a happy ending for all would be reached.

As you can see, it's worth your time to learn the marketing history of an asset you're bidding on. Investors looking for a great deal can afford to wait six months and gamble that the price will be reduced another 15 percent. However, if there's a particular property you really want and it's in good shape, playing the waiting game can sometimes lead to disappointment. The property might be sold the first month it's out for bid.

The guidelines illustrated above show how hemmed in asset managers can be. Managers at the RTC consolidated offices often lack authority to go outside the guidelines. On the other hand, these guidelines also show that the RTC is ready and able to reduce its asking prices when the marketplace is telling it that the price is too high. Also, on properties that are difficult to sell, good faith offers that fall short of the guideline limits are often taken "upstairs" by the consolidated office to Washington, where regional RTC officials will go to bat for a bidder if they believe the bid is in good faith and that market conditions are such that they may later regret rejecting the bid.

"Our policy of disclosing our pricing strategy caused a lot of controversy in the marketplace to begin with," said RTC Southwest Regional Manager Carmen Sullivan. "But instead of holding all this information to our vests, which inhibits buyers from negotiating, we just lay it all out in front of everyone."

As an investor, your "bottom line" bid should fit *your* bottom line, not the government's. It pays to do the math. The above examples should give you a leg up on the competition. When playing poker, if you can see someone else's cards your chances of winning are greatly improved.

WINNER TAKES ALL

If your sealed bid is accepted, the RTC likes to close the sale quickly— within sixty days. From the moment you achieve a meeting of the minds on a bid, the buyer and seller have clearly designated responsibilities.

CLOSING COSTS

The RTC pays half the escrow costs and the buyer pays the other half. The purchaser pays all prorated property and transfer taxes and title insurance premiums.

RENTS

Rents are prorated to the day of closing. Any portion of rents due to the RTC but collected after closing must be paid by the seller to the RTC.

OPERATING EXPENSES

If the sale closes before maintenance expenses for the month have been determined, the RTC will estimate those expenses for the month. After closing the two parties will compare the estimate to actual expenses and balance the account.

Delivery and Possession

The RTC transfers title to the buyer through the use of a quitclaim deed. A quitclaim deed gives the buyer all the seller's rights to the property, though the RTC makes no warranties as to precisely what those rights might be. In essence, a quitclaim deed conveys property without guaranteeing that it is "free and clear"—that no one else has some right or interest in it. The RTC uses quitclaim deeds because it's the quickest and cleanest way for *them* to transfer a property without incurring any future liabilities should the title be marred, but both the RTC and FDIC are very good at "clearing title" before putting properties up for sale. This makes it even more imperative that the buyer conduct his or her own title search. Don't be lazy. Get down to that courthouse. At closing the RTC turns over the keys to the property and the sale, as they say, "is a done deal." At that moment the buyer becomes responsible for all valid leases and contracts encumbering the property.

FAILING TO PERFORM ON THE BID

If a purchaser makes a bid, it's accepted, and then the bidder fails to come through on the purchase price, he or she is then considered "in default." The RTC and FDIC can then legally keep whatever deposit money was posted (as we noted earlier, usually 5 percent). The greater the bid, the larger your loss if you fail to follow through.

If the RTC fails to perform on any part of its agreement with the buyer, the contract states that the RTC's only responsibility to the purchaser is to return the deposit money. The RTC bid contract shields the agency from any legal damages for failure to perform.

IN SUMMARY

Bidding at an auction can be intimidating the first time. It's sort of like audience participation in a play or nightclub act. But once you get in the swing of it, it's a lot of fun. And the feeling of bagging a great deal at an auction can only be compared to reeling in a big one when fishing.

Bidding at a sealed-bid auction is less exciting than attending an open-cry auction. But statistics show that buyers get better deals at sealed-bid auctions. Open-cry auctions create a frenzied atmosphere in which buyers tend to get carried away. Sealed-bid auctions are quiet, dignified affairs. You submit your bid from the privacy of your own office or home any time prior to the bid deadline. Then you wait. Within thirty days you'll get an answer. If your bid gets chosen, expect a telephone call, followed by a request to increase your deposit to 5 percent. If you lose a bid, the consolidated office will send back your 1 percent deposit in the mail within thirty days.

Remember, you control the process. Before you make a bid imagine that your bid was accepted and you now have to perform (i.e., cough up the money). How would you feel? If the answer is "delighted," submit your bid and hope for the best.

Chapter 8

....

Buying Paper

*Buying Good and Bad Loans from
the RTC and FDIC*

Who in their right mind would want to buy a delinquent loan?

Many investors will argue that if an obligation is "delinquent" it must
be worthless. But savvy investors know that one person's shipwreck is
another's sunken treasure. If purchased intelligently, buying a delinquent or "late" mortgage loan or note from the government can yield
healthy returns for investors. However, keep in mind that buying a loan
or a group of loans (called a "pool") from the RTC and FDIC is not
without risk. You can make some expensive mistakes investing in
"paper."

But investing in delinquent loans is no longer uncharted territory. In
fact, it's catching on as more and more investors come to understand the
opportunities underlying these ugly duckling loans. As one RTC official
told us, "We're seeing a lot of new faces at our loan auctions. It's no
longer the select group it used to be." Buying loans is unfamiliar territory
for most Americans, but it's not as complicated as some of the terminology would lead one to believe. We'll try to demystify the process while
also explaining the rewards and risks involved.

UGLY IS ONLY SKIN DEEP

Together the RTC and FDIC hold about $100 billion in assets. About 60 to 75 percent of what the two have to sell start out as loans. Some stay loans while others are foreclosed on and the underlying real estate sold. Knowing how to buy a delinquent loan from the government gives you another avenue to purchase assets at a discount.

Loans come in all shapes, sizes, and conditions. Some are delinquent, some are not. Some are secured, some are not. Just because an S&L failed doesn't necessarily mean all of its loans are bad. To sort out this diversity the RTC and FDIC divide their loans into four basic categories.

1) Good Quality Loans (GQL). Also known as "current" loans—the borrower is paying the loan on time and the loan has no apparent problems. Because the loan is in good shape, the RTC doesn't offer much of a discount. If it's a large loan (over $50,000), the RTC tells its asset managers to hold any discounts offered to buyers to 5 percent of the loan's outstanding balance. (On smaller-performing loans the RTC will offer discounts of up to 10 percent of the loan balance.) The only time that discount will be increased is if interest rates begin rising or falling rapidly. If rates go up quickly, then the loan (by comparison) will yield a lower return than competing interest-paying investments (i.e., newer mortgage loans being sold on the secondary market). If rates fall by more than two percentage points, then the likelihood that borrowers will pay off their loans early increases greatly, which in turn decreases the loan's value. When such shifts in the market occur, the RTC will increase its discount to match market conditions.

2) Fair Quality Loans (FQL). FQLs generate sufficient cash flow to cover at least 75 percent of the outstanding principal balance should the loan go into default. On FQLs that are $50,000 to $250,000 in size, the RTC will offer discounts of up to 90 percent. On loans smaller than $50,000 the RTC will offer larger discounts.

3) Poor Quality Loans (PQL). PQLs in general are considered "delinquent," meaning the borrower is not paying. Once these loans go into default the RTC expects to recover 25 to 75 percent of the outstanding balance. Some PQLs are, or could become, the subject of litigation. The RTC will dump these loans at 85 percent of their outstanding balance. But keep talking. PQLs are a major headache and the agency is open to all sorts of offers.

4) Distressed Loans (DLs). DLs are in default or just about to go into default. At best the government may recoup 25 percent of the loan's outstanding principal. DLs that have balances of $50,000 or less can be sold by the consolidated office for 75 percent of the Estimated Cash Recovery (ECR). ECR is not the same thing as "the outstanding balance." ECR is a much lower value—often a fraction of the outstanding loan balance.

DLs are only for investors with strong stomachs and stout nerves. You can get them cheap enough, but you're buying a real pig in a poke. If you can work with delinquent borrowers to turn loans around or are emotionally prepared to foreclose on someone's house, you can do well buying DLs. Otherwise, it's best to leave these opportunities to others.

DELINQUENT LOANS

WHY INVEST IN A DELINQUENT LOAN?

Investing in delinquent loans sold by the RTC isn't as crazy as it sounds. In one regard it can be viewed as an "alternate route" to gaining title to the underlying real estate. With delinquent loans you have several possible plays:

- Buy at discount a loan that's "just a little delinquent" and then work with the borrower to bring the note current. If you are successful, you can sit back and collect interest, knowing that the discount has boosted your effective yield well beyond the interest rate being charged the borrower.
- Buy a deeply delinquent loan at a steep discount. Work with the borrower to either bring the loan current, or ask the borrower to

relinquish a portion of the property's ownership to you in return for renegotiating the terms and balance of the loan. In this case you become a partner in the property with the borrower, gaining an equity interest as well as retaining a portion of the original loan.
- Buy a deeply delinquent loan at discount and foreclose on the underlying property.

CAVEATS

Buying troubled loans is a lot more stressful than buying real estate. The potential profits are larger, but so are the headaches. When you purchase a delinquent loan you acquire someone else's problems—the borrower's. Unless you hire an attorney (and attorneys can get expensive), you will have to personally contact the debtor to inform him or her of the wonderful news that you now own the loan. As we noted, purchasing delinquent loans is not for the fainthearted. Every default brings with it a tearjerking explanation. If you're a bleeding heart, turn the page. This part of the book is not for you. On the other hand, if you can maintain an emotional distance from other people's problems and keep a cool business head, buying troubled loans is a terrific way to make money. It can also be a way to get property cheaper than if you wait for the RTC or FDIC to foreclose and sell it: As soon as the borrower goes into default, you can foreclose.

Example. The RTC is selling a troubled loan on a duplex in your neighborhood.

- Original loan amount: $108,000
- Original down payment: $27,000
- Principal paid so far: $1,330
- Outstanding balance: $106,670
- Original appraised value: $135,000
- Monthly mortgage payment: $830
- Terms: 8.50%, 30-year, fixed-rate

The borrower kept the loan current for two years and then stopped making payments. He is three months late. To get rid of the loan quickly, the RTC sells it to you at 90 percent of its outstanding balance. You pay around $96,500. The borrower (also known as mortgagor) lives in one of a duplex's two rental units and leases out the other. After researching the property you find that similar units will produce gross rents of about $925 per month.

You have two scenarios to analyze before deciding whether to bid. First, what if the borrower reinstates the loan by making all of his past overdue payments? How does this affect your investment? This consideration relies on probability. Statistics culled by the National Association of Realtors show that the average life of a California mortgage loan is six to seven years. (The borrower might move or refinance—that's why very few thirty-year mortgages ever really last that long.) The loan you bought is already two years old. Chances are the borrower will not stay for twenty-eight more years. It's a gamble, but not a particularly risky one, according to the statistics. If the loan becomes current—meaning the borrower is now paying on time—you can feel satisfied because you bought the loan at a 10 percent discount and you're gaining monthly income—at least 8.50 percent worth. Prevailing CD rates (in 1993 for example) are under 4 percent. You're making at least 4.50 percent more than what the bank is offering. The now-current debtor probably will repay the loan within five years, returning most of your principal. If that occurs the combination of the discount you got buying the loan from the RTC, together with the loan's higher interest rate, could combine to give you an effective return well into the double digits.

But even better is scenario number two. The borrower continues to miss loan payments. As the loan's new owner you decide to get the property appraised and come up with a minimum value of $135,000, the original purchase price. You foreclose on the property. If you gain title you will have successfully acquired a $135,000 property for $96,000. You just made $39,000.

Or you might consider playing landlord, renting the property out after you gain title. You already know that the units can bring in gross rents of $925, which comes to $11,100 a year. Subtract estimated expenses of 25 percent of gross rents ($2,775), which leaves you with a yearly net operating income of $8,325. On top of this income you will also garner whatever market appreciation occurs during your period of ownership.

As you can see, a rotten loan can be converted into a very sweet investment.

To figure out which of these two scenarios is the most likely to occur, you need to do a little sleuthing at your county recorder's office. Look at the property's title. Are there any other liens filed against the property or its owner? Are there mechanics' liens and tax liens filed against the property? If there are, it means the borrower is in deep over his head and is unlikely to pull out of this tailspin.

Loans come in all sizes, secured by all kinds of real estate, and you don't have to be a high roller to play in this league. I once advised a client who bought a $9,500 note for just $7,125—a hefty 25 percent discount. The loan was collateralized by a subdivision lot in Clearlake, California, a rural area being settled by soon-to-be-retired "grey-collar" aerospace industry workers. Because of the cyclical nature of the aerospace industry, similar loans had become late but were usually "cured" or brought current before foreclosure. After first inspecting the lot (a nice corner lot near the lake), I advised my client to go ahead.

The borrower was late with his payment a few times, but paid a 10 percent late fee without complaint, further increasing my client's return. Everything was fine for a while. Then the borrower defaulted—three months went by without payment. My client and I moved into action, instructing the title company trustee to file a Notice of Intent to Foreclose. To fend off foreclosure, the borrower immediately cured the default, bringing the loan current. In addition, he paid all foreclosure costs and still more late fees. Then, just two years into a ten-year note, he suddenly paid the loan off in full.

It was a profitable experience. The interest rate on the note was 9 percent on a $9,500 balance. But my client had purchased the note at a discount, paying just $7,125. Between interest payments and late fees the total annualized return on the investment approached 30 percent.

As you can see, buying loans can be a terrific way to diversify your investment portfolio and boost the effective yield. The trick is knowing when to buy and when to pass, when to hold them and when to fold them.

ARE THERE MANY LOANS AVAILABLE?

When most Americans read or see news accounts about the RTC, they incorrectly believe that most of what the government is selling is real estate—usually raw land or office buildings in Texas. But actually, as of the beginning of 1992, 55 percent of what the RTC had to sell was in the form of loans—both performing and nonperforming. The loans that are available for purchase are located in virtually every part of the country.

As we've noted, not all the loans the RTC and FDIC sell are bad loans. Some 45 percent of what the RTC has to sell includes "performing" loans backed, or "collateralized," by one- to four-family homes and commercial construction projects such as shopping centers and office buildings. The borrowers are making all their loan payments on a regular basis. Loans in this category will be of little interest to you. In fact, unless you are a Wall Street broker, you're out of this game entirely. Performing loans are packaged together in pools and sold to Wall Street firms, pension funds, and institutional investors in $100 million-plus pools.

That's not to say you can't buy a performing loan from the RTC or FDIC. Both agencies have loans they call "nonconforming loans," which are difficult to sell to institutional buyers because they don't fit the narrow standard secondary-loan market criteria. If you are interested in performing loans tell the regional RTC or FDIC/loan representative and the representative will contact you when he or she gets a small nonconforming loan that fits your needs. But the pickings are more plentiful over in the nonperforming loan arena. That's where the real action is.

FIRST MORTGAGES

Depending on how delinquent the loan is, nonperforming first mortgages can be purchased from the RTC for 10 to 90 cents on the dollar. That means if you purchase a delinquent loan from the RTC that has an original mortgage amount of $100,000, you can acquire the loan from the government for $10,000 to $90,000. The cheaper you can buy the loan, the higher the risk that you'll never recover your money. That's how the game is played.

SECOND MORTGAGES

Delinquent second mortgages on one- to four-family homes, shopping centers, office buildings, and raw land also are available for purchase from the RTC and FDIC. But "seconds" mean just that—you will be in second position if the borrower defaults. Someone else has a first mortgage in front of yours on the same property. As the second lien holder, if the borrower defaults on the first you will have to step in and keep the first mortgage current. If not, the first lien holder can foreclose and wipe you out. Once you reinstate the first loan, you then foreclose on the second (your loan) and take control of the property, subject to the first. You will gain title to the property but you now will be responsible for the first mortgage.

When buying seconds, make sure the property has some equity left in it. At the very least the property should be worth more than the first and second mortgages combined. A minimum of 20 percent more is a good cushion because it allows you to absorb foreclosure costs and legal expenses tied to the default.

Do not get lax with seconds. Perform your due diligence. Go down to the county recorder's office and make sure that you file a "Request for Notice of Default." This document requires the recorder to notify you if the borrower defaults on the first loan and is being foreclosed on by the lender. When a notice of default is filed on the first, be prepared to pounce. If you fail to do so the first lien holder can foreclose, take the property, and wipe you out. Once the property is in the first lien holder's name your second mortgage becomes worthless, since he or she has no obligation to you whatsoever.

Besides firsts and seconds on real estate, the RTC and FDIC offer a wide array of other types of nonperforming loans: consumer loans, credit card loans, student loans, automobile loans, mobile home loans, loans secured by furniture, and construction and land loans. Construction and land loans account for about 7 percent of all RTC assets. Timeshare loans on vacation properties also are available—and plentiful. Each type of loan brings its own opportunities and risks. Be certain you understand both before jumping into these waters.

GETTING STARTED

The quickest way to discover what sort of loans the RTC has to sell is to pick up your telephone and call the RTC consolidated office nearest you. As you may remember from earlier chapters, the RTC and FDIC have consolidated offices in every region of the nation—even in such formerly robust economic markets as Southern California, New England, and the New York/New Jersey metropolitan area. If you're looking to buy a nonperforming loan in Florida, for example, you would call the RTC's consolidated office in Tampa.

Each consolidated office holds regular auctions of nonperforming loans. There are two types of auctions: closed, or "sealed," bids, and oral outcry. (More on that later.) Besides being offered through the RTC's consolidated offices, delinquent loans are auctioned—on the RTC's behalf—to the highest bidder by national loan auction companies such as Hudson & Marshall in Macon, JBS Associates in Chicago, and Ross-Dove & Co. in San Francisco. Each auction company has a toll-free telephone number and will gladly mail you a brochure or list of loans that are available. (Consult our Yellow Pages for these numbers.)

> INVESTOR TIP. *When inquiring about a loan or loan package, you should ask for the loan number (or the loan pool number), what the loan was yielding in terms of interest when it was performing, the outstanding balance on each loan, and how long the loan has been delinquent. (Believe it or not, some borrowers stopped paying their loans after their bank or S&L went out of business because they didn't know who to direct the payments to.)*

FINDING OUT ABOUT LOAN AUCTIONS

Announcements of auctions of nonperforming loans (and real estate) are advertised regularly in the *Wall Street Journal* and business trade publications such as the *National Mortgage News* and *American Banker* as well as in local newspapers. But spotting such ads leaves too much to chance. Instead of relying on the media, call the closet consolidated office or telephone the RTC hot line (1-800-RTC-3006) and listen for the updated calendar of auctions. All upcoming RTC loan auctions are also listed on-line on RTCNET, the agency's computer data base.

FINDING A GOOD BAD LOAN

Typically, loans are sold in pools that are groups of loans. If you want to buy just one loan that is collateralized by a single-family house, you will have a tougher time of it. Still, some single nonperforming home loans are available for purchase—usually on large luxury properties. If you're a capital-rich investor in search of a larger home, buying a delinquent mortgage on an upscale property will be cheaper than buying that same home through your friendly neighborhood realtor. (Your play here is to buy the loan, foreclose, and then take over the house.)

Single delinquent loans are plentiful on commercial properties such as office buildings, "strip" shopping centers, hotels, motels, warehouses, and even raw land.

At auctions sometimes the loan is big and the price small. At an RTC auction in Denver one investor bought a delinquent business loan with a face value of $1.8 million for just $30,000. Now all the investor has to do is figure out how to collect.

BUYING PERFORMING LOANS

Many of the RTC and FDIC's performing single-family loans are packaged into securities and sold through Wall Street to financial companies or wealthy investors. These loans tend to be "vanilla" in nature—that is, they all have the same loan maturity, terms, down payment, and so on.

If you want to buy just one vanilla performing loan, forget it. The government won't bother selling it to you. But both the RTC and FDIC have a number of small performing (or "good quality") loans whose terms are so weird or awkward nobody else wants them. These loans have earned the nickname of PITA loans (Pain-in-the-Ass loans). The reason they're a pain is because they're difficult to service. For example, instead of paying monthly a PITA loan might have a semiannual or an annual payment term. Because they're so odd, PITA loans foul up a bank's loan servicing department, where computers are programmed only to handle standard loans.

Typically, PITA loans were originated by a small-town S&L or bank that tailored mortgages to the specific needs of individuals. They range in size from $5,000 to $30,000. PITA loans may not even be listed for sale by the government because they're too odd and puny. Other times they might be packaged with a group of other "nonconforming" loans and sold in bulk. But one thing is for certain—the government hates these small performing loans and likes to get rid of them as soon as possible. The smartest thing an investor can do is call the closest RTC or FDIC consolidated office and let them know you're in the market for these "oddball" loans. The government would love to hear from you. As one FDIC official put it: "Small, nonvanilla loans are just impossible to handle. It costs money to service them and because of their size few big bidders want them. We'd like to get them out of our hair as soon as possible."

Go in and meet with an RTC account executive in charge of loan sales in your region. Tell him or her what you have in mind and how much you are willing to pay. Keep in mind that because these are performing loans you won't be able to purchase them at particularly deep discounts. Government regulations mandate that the RTC should try and sell performing loans at 90 percent or so of the outstanding balance. For investors that still represents a 10 percent discount, which increases the effective yield. If you bid close to 90 cents on the dollar, the government probably will take the offer.

KICKING THE TIRES

Once you decide to bid on a loan or a loan pool, the first order of business is to analyze the loan file. When bidding on loans you will be dealing with either the RTC or FDIC consolidated office or the auction company charged with selling that particular package of loans. Loan files are available for review at the consolidated offices and can be examined free of charge. At this point investors will not have to post any sort of good faith money, but they must fill out an investor survey. (For a copy of what's on the investor survey, see Exhibit 9.) The investor survey will ask you, the potential purchaser, a number of general questions, including what type of loans you're interested in, who you're investing for, what type of loans you want, what part of the country you're interested in, and so on.

KEY INFORMATION. *Interested bidders in RTC loans also must complete a "fitness" certification survey. Although filling out the form is mandatory, there are only six questions, which are short and to the point. Among the questions asked are whether you've ever been convicted of a felony or defaulted on any loans that caused $50,000 or more in damages to a federally insured bank, S&L, or credit union. (Convicted felons who have caused a loss of $50,000 or more at a federally insured bank or thrift might be more interested in the authors' previous book,* Inside Job: The Looting of America's Savings and Loans. *You might even be in it.)*

For larger RTC loan auctions, loan files can often be reviewed either on microfiche or "in the flesh," which means you'll be reviewing the original loan files. The RTC and FDIC will not mail investors copies of the loan files. It is against the law to do so. Loan files are the key to unlocking the quality of your investment and determining how much to bid.

KEY INFORMATION. *The loan file should give you the following:*

- The borrower's annual income and current address
- The latest appraisal on the property
- The payment history of the loan
- Remaining unpaid balance and the interest rate
- The loan's origination date
- A credit report and financial statement on the borrower
- A current title report showing other liens against the property

All are essential in determining whether you want to buy a loan. Review the information carefully. Ask about missing data.

By the way, before the RTC or FDIC lets investors review a loan file they must sign a confidentiality agreement. Loan files contain some very private information, such as the borrower's income. The confidentiality

OMB No. 3064 - 0089
Expiration Date 6/30/94

FEDERAL DEPOSIT INSURANCE CORPORATION
DIVISION OF LIQUIDATION - ASSET MARKETING DEPARTMENT

INVESTOR SURVEY - LOAN SALES

INSTRUCTIONS: *PLEASE PRINT OR TYPE*

NAME (Last, First MI) ☐ MR. ☐ MRS. ☐ MS.	TITLE
COMPANY NAME	AREA CODE & TELEPHONE NUMBER
STREET/P.O. BOX NUMBER	

CITY	STATE	ZIP CODE	FAX: AREA CODE & NUMBER
COUNTRY *(If other than the United States)*			S.S.#:

(CHECK THE APPROPRIATE BOXES BELOW)

SURVEY COMPLETED FOR:	HOW DID YOU HEAR ABOUT FDIC SALES?
☐ CORPORATION ☐ PARTNERSHIP	☐ FDIC ADVERTISEMENT ☐ CONTACTED BY FDIC
☐ BROKER ☐ INDIVIDUAL	☐ BROKER ☐ OTHER

TYPE OF LOANS DESIRED

☐ ACCOUNTS RECEIVABLE, LOANS SECURED BY
☐ AGRICULTURAL
☐ AUTOMOBILE LOANS
☐ BANKRUPTCY, LOANS IN
☐ CHARGED - OFF LOANS
☐ COMMERCIAL - SECURED
☐ COMMERCIAL - UNSECURED
☐ CREDIT CARDS
☐ ENERGY RELATED
☐ GOVERNMENT GUARANTEED - SBA
☐ GOVERNMENT GUARANTEED - OTHER THAN SBA
☐ INSTALLMENT - SECURED
☐ INSTALLMENT - UNSECURED
☐ INTERNATIONAL

☐ INVENTORY, LOANS SECURED BY
☐ JUDGMENTS
☐ LEASES
☐ LOAN SERVICING RIGHTS
☐ MOBILE HOME LOANS
☐ MORTGAGE (COMMERCIAL) - 1ST LIEN ONLY
☐ MORTGAGE (COMMERCIAL) - ALL OTHER LIENS
☐ MORTGAGE (MULTI-FAMILY) - 1ST LIEN ONLY
☐ MORTGAGE (MULTI-FAMILY) - ALL OTHER LIENS
☐ MORTGAGE (RESIDENTIAL) - 1ST LIEN ONLY
☐ MORTGAGE (RESIDENTIAL) - ALL OTHER LIENS
☐ PARTICIPATED LOANS
☐ STUDENT LOANS
☐ TIMESHARES

LOAN QUALITY DESIRED	PAYMENT RATE DESIRED
☐ CURRENT	☐ FIXED RATE
☐ DELINQUENT OR NONPERFORMING	☐ ADJUSTABLE RATE

PORTFOLIO BOOK VALUE DESIRED		LOAN SIZE DESIRED WITHIN PORTFOLIO	
☐ UNDER $2.5 MILLION	☐ $10 MILLION - $25 MILLION	☐ UNDER $25,000	☐ $250,000 - $500,000
☐ $2.5 MILLION - $5 MILLION	☐ OVER $25 MILLION	☐ $25,000 - $100,000	☐ $500,000 - $1 MILLION
☐ $5 MILLION - $10 MILLION		☐ $100,000 - $250,000	☐ OVER $1 MILLION

GEOGRAPHICAL AREAS DESIRED

☐ ALABAMA	☐ FLORIDA	☐ KENTUCKY	☐ MONTANA	☐ OHIO	☐ TEXAS
☐ ALASKA	☐ GEORGIA	☐ LOUISIANA	☐ NEBRASKA	☐ OKLAHOMA	☐ UTAH
☐ ARIZONA	☐ GUAM	☐ MAINE	☐ NEVADA	☐ OREGON	☐ VERMONT
☐ ARKANSAS	☐ HAWAII	☐ MARYLAND	☐ NEW HAMPSHIRE	☐ PENNSYLVANIA	☐ VIRGINIA
☐ CALIFORNIA	☐ IDAHO	☐ MASSACHUSETTS	☐ NEW JERSEY	☐ PUERTO RICO	☐ VIRGIN ISLANDS
☐ COLORADO	☐ ILLINOIS	☐ MICHIGAN	☐ NEW MEXICO	☐ RHODE ISLAND	☐ WASHINGTON
☐ CONNECTICUT	☐ INDIANA	☐ MINNESOTA	☐ NEW YORK	☐ SOUTH CAROLINA	☐ WEST VIRGINIA
☐ DELAWARE	☐ IOWA	☐ MISSISSIPPI	☐ NORTH CAROLINA	☐ SOUTH DAKOTA	☐ WISCONSIN
☐ DISTRICT OF COLUMBIA	☐ KANSAS	☐ MISSOURI	☐ NORTH DAKOTA	☐ TENNESSEE	☐ WYOMING

FDIC 7240/01 (8-91)   **SEE REVERSE FOR MAILING INSTRUCTIONS, PRIVACY ACT STATEMENT, AND BURDEN STATEMENT**

EXHIBIT 9.   Survey form used by the FDIC and RTC for loan sales. Those filling out these forms will be notified when the agencies have loans fitting their needs available.

PRIVACY ACT STATEMENT

The primary purpose of this information is to match qualified prospective investors with specific loan portfolios for sale. Furnishing the information is voluntary; failure to furnish all or part of the information may result in the prospective investor not receiving notice of the availability of a portfolio. Information may be disclosed to other federal or state agencies that also have loans for sale; to appropriate federal, state, or local agencies for law enforcement purposes; to persons involved in the conduct of judicial or administrative proceedings; and to a congressional office in response to an inquiry made at the individual's request. The information is collected pursuant to 12 U.S.C. 1819, 1821, and 1823.

BURDEN STATEMENT

Public reporting burden for this collection of information is estimated to average 15 minutes per response, including the time for reviewing instructions, searching existing data sources, gathering and maintaining the data needed, and completing and reviewing the collection of information. Send comments regarding this burden estimate or any other aspect of this collection of information, including suggestions for reducing this burden, to the Assistant Executive Secretary (Administration), Office of the Executive Secretary Room F-400, FDIC, Washington, D.C. 20429; and to the Office of Management and Budget, Paperwork Reduction Project (3064-0089), Washington, D.C. 20503.

RETURN TO:

F.D.I.C
PO BOX 802090
DALLAS TX 75380
ASSET MARKETING DEPARTMENT

FDIC 7240/01 (8-91) REVERSE

agreement is your promise not to blab the information all over creation. If you do and you're caught, you will be fined.

> INVESTOR TIP. *The riskier a loan file looks, the lower you should bid. The amount depends on the condition of the underlying collateral (property). When in doubt, drive by the property and take a look. Ask yourself: How would I feel about owning this? If the property and its loan file make you queasy, pass. Then again, you could bid next to nothing—and win.*

First-time investors should only consider a loan, or loans, whose collateral is in your own backyard—so you can keep an eye on it. Knowing that your collateral (a house or apartment unit) is within "checking out" distance lets you sleep easier at night. It also allows you to review (or perform due diligence) on the loan before bidding on it.

Buying delinquent loans is a specialized investment, but it is not as complicated as it sounds. However, it takes hard work, diligence, and a willingness to work with troubled borrowers. If you have the capital to invest, but not the expertise, keep in mind that the expertise can be bought—by hiring a collection agency, collection specialist, or a consulting real estate lawyer who specializes in working with troubled borrowers. However, hiring someone else will increase your overhead without necessarily increasing your return. Be careful who you choose. It will be the difference between making a killing and getting killed.

When an auction is announced and a bid date is established, you will have anywhere from three to four weeks to review a loan file. So will your competitors. Don't rely solely on the offering circular and brochure put out by the marketing company hired by the RTC. It's the company's job to try to sell you. Alone, this will not provide enough detailed data to allow for an intelligent bid.

The condition of the loan files can vary. Depending on how well managed the bank or S&L was, the loan file may be void of appraisals, credit history, and other key data. Expect the worst. After all, if the loans had been well managed, the S&L might not have failed in the first place. Study all information in the loan file carefully, paying special attention to the borrower's income and where the collateral is geographically located. Verify as much of this information as you can.

KEY INFORMATION. *Investors in loans can also order from the RTC that loan's due diligence bid package. The cost is about $50. The bid package provides you with essential information such as loan balance, rates, delinquencies, and so on. When ordering the bid package, you still will need to complete a confidentiality agreement and investor fitness certification form.*

Depending on the size of the loan auction, loans may be ranked by interest rate, age of delinquency, location of collateral, or location of lender. Concentrate on the features you find most attractive. Again, if you're just getting into this ball game, select a loan whose collateral is nearby.

LOAN AUCTIONS

The RTC and FDIC hold two types of loan auctions: sealed-bid or closed auctions and oral outcry or open-cry auctions.

SEALED-BID AUCTION

At a closed or sealed-bid auction investors submit bids on a form provided by the RTC or the marketing company. Along with a 5 percent down payment check (which is refundable), the form is then handed over to the marketing company, which forwards the sealed envelope to the consolidated office sponsoring the auction. *Remember to write* Bid Enclosed *on the outside of your envelope.* Your bid and everyone else's will be opened together on a specified day. The final decision on who gets the loan or loan package is made by the RTC and FDIC, not the auction company.

ORAL OUTCRY AUCTION

Like cattle at a ranch auction, here the loans are trotted out one at a time before an assemblage of bidders. The auctioneer will identify the loan or pool by a specific loan number, which corresponds to the number in the auction catalog. The auctioneer then starts the bidding by saying, "This pool is starting out at $10,000. Do I hear $10,000?"

The bidding has officially begun. The auctioneer then asks for bids from the room. Most government auctions take place in hotel ballrooms. If you want to bid just shout it out. After registering, you will be awarded a little stick with a number on top. Just raise your stick and you'll be in the game.

Bidding on loans at auction will cost you earnest money up front. As with other RTC auctions, if you don't win your money is returned. Before bidding, investors must present the auction company or RTC with a cashier's check to establish a good faith relationship. The requirement keeps out charlatans, dilettantes, and nonserious bidders.

The size of the good faith deposit is determined by the size of the loans the government is trying to auction. At some auctions the government sells as much as $200 million in nonperforming loans. If it's a multimillion-dollar bulk sale your good faith deposit might be as high as $10,000 to $20,000, maybe even more depending on the size of the auction. At smaller auctions the good faith deposit will be less, maybe as little as a couple thousand dollars. Once you know what size loan or pool you want, check with the auction house about the deposit size. Again, you will need a cashier's check. The RTC does not accept personal checks at auctions.

KEY INFORMATION. *If you win the bid your good faith deposit is applied toward the purchase price. You then have twenty-four hours to bring your total deposit up to a minimum of 10 percent of the purchase price. You have seven business days to come up with the balance and close the transaction. At closing you must provide the balance before the government turns over the loan portfolio. You are now the owner of a second-hand loan or loans.*

All sales are "nonrecourse," which means if you don't like what you bought, too bad. Neither the RTC nor the FDIC make refunds.

SELLER FINANCING ON LOANS

Unlike its policy on real estate or its affordable housing program for low- to moderate-income home buyers, the RTC *rarely* provides seller financing on loans or loan pools. Only when large financial companies or Wall Streeters are bidding (and usually if the loans are delinquent) will the RTC provide any form of seller financing. When it does, the loans made to buyers are usually five-year or seven-year balloons.

Most investors, whether they're bidding on a $100,000 loan or a $1 million loan, will have to come up with their own financing. As we've often said: Cash is king. The government does not look kindly upon bidders who come up short on closing day. Depending on the circumstances, if you welsh on a bid you could lose your deposit money.

TAKING THE COLLATERAL

Once you become the proud new owner of a nonperforming loan, the real work begins. Because many nonperforming loans sold by the RTC and FDIC are backed by real estate, you just foreclose and take the real estate. But keep in mind that foreclosure laws differ from state to state. You may have to wait up to 120 days after the first loan payment is missed before you can foreclose. There are also redemption periods in some states, which allow defaulted borrowers up to one year to redeem their property. But to do so they have to pay all that is owed, all costs, and accrued interest. Most states have straightforward foreclosure laws. After gaining title to the loan you can use the loan's trustee (usually a title company) to foreclose on your behalf.

If the loan never had a trustee, or the borrower files bankruptcy, you may need an attorney to sort matters out. A good real estate lawyer can cut through the red tape of bankruptcy and foreclose quickly. The faster you gain control of property, the sooner you can sell it or rent it out to gain rental income.

Once a borrower learns the loan has been sold to an investor and that he or she is no longer dealing with some impersonal bureaucracy, the borrower may bring the loan current. On the other hand, the borrower may say, "I don't have any money" and offer to give or sell you the property. When this happens you can take the property through a "deed in lieu" of foreclosure.

A deed in lieu has advantages: It's fast, cheap, a foreclosure isn't involved, and nine times out of ten you won't need a lawyer. But never be too quick to accept a desperate borrower's offer. A formal foreclosure process wipes out all liens on the property, while a deed in lieu allows liens to "run with the property." A hard-pressed borrower might offer a deed in lieu to escape contractor bills and other obligations. As the new owner through a deed in lieu you will be on the hook for these debts unless they are removed before you take title.

The RTC loan file may not list any junior liens. Be careful. If the property is large enough, it's worth a trip to the county recorder's office. Examine the chain of title and look for mechanics' liens. Again, a foreclosure wipes out any junior liens, a deed in lieu does not.

NON–REAL ESTATE LOANS

AUTO LOANS

Only specialists should consider buying paper secured by anything on wheels. Car loans can be tricky. When analyzing auto loan files, make sure the cars still exist and aren't sitting in a "chop shop" somewhere up in the Bronx or East L.A.

Most auto loans are sold by the government in pools. In late 1991, for example, the RTC's Denver office sold a pool of nonperforming car loans with an outstanding balance of $56,000 for just $35,000, leaving the investor with a potential profit of $21,000—if the investor can find the cars and their owners. Car loans are a nice niche for someone already in the car loan servicing business.

STUDENT LOANS

Uncollateralized, student or college loans can be highly risky. There's nothing "physical" backing these up. Do not acquire from the government *any* student loans taken out to attend a vocational institution (e.g., a beauty academy, truck driving school, or air-conditioning maintenance college). Although many vocational schools are legitimate, these loans have been subject to considerable fraud—especially in Florida. Consumers have been enticed into taking out student loans through various "incentives" programs in which cash gifts or kickbacks are offered. The student is then told by the vocational school that he or she does not have to repay the loan because it's "government guaranteed." Such fly-by-night vocational schools don't care if the student drops out or finishes the course because the school has the money even before the semester starts. Only after borrowing the money does the student discover the school is less than what he or she thought, and the student drops out, thinking—incorrectly—that the loan does not have to be repaid.

Trying to collect on a student vocational loan is like waiting for Godot. If you decide to focus on this area, stick to loans written on four-year accredited colleges and universities. Today a lot of confusion surrounds student loans. As noted, some young borrowers think they don't have to repay their college loans. They're wrong, but do you really want to be the person to tell them that?

The richer the student or parents (who may have co-signed the loan), the better the chance you'll get repaid. Analyzing the risks here requires more resources than the casual investor possesses. But again, any company with easy access to credit reporting services and collection agencies can make a profitable sideline out of chasing down delinquent student loans.

TIMESHARE LOANS

Be careful here, too. One $489,000 package of timeshare loans was sold by the RTC Valley Forge consolidated office for just $97,800—that's about 20 cents on the dollar. Not bad if the new owners can collect 30 cents or more on the dollar. But the timeshare marketplace is notoriously cyclical, with long periods of decline marked by brief flurries of interest.

The key to timeshare loans is rental income and "tradeability." With a timeshare you "own" anywhere from three weeks to three months of a single unit, usually a studio or one- or two-bedroom apartment. You can either live in the timeshare for that period, trade it for time somewhere else (in Hawaii, for example), or rent it out, pocketing the income.

Timeshares in popular vacation spots such as Hawaii, Florida, and California and Colorado ski areas more than likely will hold value as long as the project is well maintained. If the timeshare can be traded for two weeks in Europe or the Caribbean, all the better. But during the 1980s unscrupulous developers borrowed tens of millions of dollars to finance timeshare developments in places such as Georgia and Tennessee.

Developers misled investors into thinking that these units were readily tradeable. When buyers discovered that no one wanted to spend time in their backwoods timeshare unit, they defaulted.

If the unit is located in a popular region, the next thing to look at is the unit's rent potential. If you foreclose on a timeshare without incurring a lot of legal costs and the property is a good rental vehicle (a timeshare in Honolulu or on Maui would of course be ideal), you can do well. Professional timeshare management companies in the area can give you a good overview of the local market.

Investigate timeshare projects thoroughly. Some have been rife with fraud, not just misrepresentation. Projects can be "oversold," meaning that two people show up for the same week only to discover that they own the same share. As you might recall, this sort of "double selling" landed televangelist/developer Jim (as in Jim and Tammy) Bakker in the Big House for forty years (the sentence has since been reduced). It's sort of like that scene from Mel Brooks's *The Producers* where Zero Mostel sells 25 percent interest in his play to one hundred different people. Each person owns one-quarter of the whole only to find out that ninety-nine other people do also.

Home mortgages, apartment loans, loans on raw tracts, and office building loans are all a lot less speculative than timeshare loans. Still, the higher the risk, the cheaper you can buy.

MORTGAGE SERVICING RIGHTS

Here's an interesting idea: How would you like to own a failed bank or S&L's mortgage servicing rights? The buying and selling of mortgage servicing rights is a booming business that the general public knows virtually nothing about. Investors in RTC and FDIC servicing rights have experienced returns on their investments of 20 or 30 percent and even higher.

But what is a servicing right? A servicing right is a legal contract whereby a company or person is responsible for "servicing" a loan—that is, collecting the interest and principal on a loan from the borrower. Why would someone want to service a loan? Because you can make money doing it. Let's say a homeowner takes out a home loan from ABC Bank and begins paying $1,000 per month. Unbeknownst to the borrower, a certain portion of that $1,000 payment is given to the servicer who keeps tabs on that loan. A mortgage servicer's job is to make sure the homeowner pays the loan on time and then pass on the principal, interest, and tax payments to the proper parties. In a nutshell, the servicer is the bill collector on that loan.

On a monthly mortgage payment, the servicer might receive anywhere from .28 percent to .57 percent of the interest charge to service that loan. This is peanuts, you might think, but when you're handling thousands of loans per month—even hundreds of thousands of loans per month—it becomes a tidy little business. (The mortgage servicing business in the United States is a multibillion-dollar-per-year business. Just think of all the mortgages out there: homes, condos, coops, apartment buildings, shopping centers, and warehouses, to name a few. The larger the dollar amount of the loan, the larger the servicing fee. However, the servicing cost of a $100,000 loan is the same as for a $500,000 loan.)

S&Ls, banks, and mortgage banking firms (mortgage banking companies make only mortgages but unlike banks and S&Ls do not accept deposits) regularly service mortgages. For some it's the only way they can make any money. Servicing rights are bought and sold like any financial commodity and the RTC and FDIC have billions of dollars' worth of mortgage servicing rights to sell. Mortgage servicing rights available from the government can be bought at steep discounts. Small investors should ignore this business unless they have extensive mortgage servicing experience and a good computer operation to keep track of the loans.

However, investors with money—doctors, lawyers, and other professionals—have banded together to form partnerships to buy the expertise and hire professionals who service loans for a living. Even foreign investors from Europe and Hong Kong have grouped together to buy servicing rights from the RTC and FDIC. Buying servicing rights can be one of the best "silver linings" of the S&L and banking messes.

KAMIKAZE INVESTING

INVESTING IN UNSECURED LOANS

Besides the loans we have already discussed, the RTC also has scores of "signature" loans available. A signature loan is secured by just that—the borrower's signature and little more. It's a plain old-fashioned personal loan where a borrower walked into an S&L, filled out a loan form, and strolled away with the money—no down payment, no equity, no nothing. During the "wild and crazy" 1980s—and thanks to S&L deregulation—these loans sprouted like weeds after a spring shower. Every S&L owner had friends who they believed were "as good as their signature"—but weren't.

By their very nature, unsecured signature loans are *highly* speculative. They can also yield large returns—as long as the buyer knows what he or she is doing. The key to collecting on a signature loan is the borrower's financial condition. By purchasing at steep discounts, an experienced collection agency that specializes in collecting unpaid debts from deadbeats can make a killing buying signature loans from the government. As one RTC official told us, "You put your money down and take your chances. This kind of loan is not for the amateur."

JUNK BONDS

Junk bonds. Just hearing these two words can turn many a stomach. When people think of junk bonds they think of convicted Wall Street felon Michael Milken and his "den of thieves" at Drexel Burnham Lambert.

Technically, a junk bond is a high-yield, high-risk debt issued by a corporation. Think of it as a very risky loan. Companies that issue junk bonds include upstarts, firms with bad or poor credit, or businesses that don't like the loan terms being offered by commercial banks. Junk bonds can be broken down into $1,000 denominations and sold on a retail basis to small investors. Savings and loans bought more than $14 billion in junk bonds, a healthy portion of which is now in the hands of the RTC. (By law banks were never allowed to invest in junk bonds. Only S&Ls had—but no longer have—this authority.)

Normally the RTC does not offer these bonds to the little guy. The agency sells junk bonds in bulk to Wall Street firms such as Merrill Lynch, Salomon Brothers, and First Boston, which in turn offer them to institutional investors and wealthy individuals. If you have money to burn and feel lucky, start with Wall Street. All the major investment banking houses—Bear Stearns, Donaldson Lufkin & Jenrette, Merrill, Morgan Stanley, Smith Barney, to name a few—sell junk bonds. A word of warning, though: Most of the better-quality S&L junk bonds have already been scooped up by savvy Wall Street investors. What's left can be best termed "toxic waste." If you're a real bottom fisher and know the junk bond market, you can still find bargains here. And the RTC will be glad to hear from you.

REAL ESTATE INVESTMENT TRUSTS (REITs)

Small investors who don't want to mess with collecting on delinquent loans can invest in an REIT, or Real Estate Investment Trust, sponsored by the RTC. Investing in a REIT is a lot like investing in a stock or bond. Depending on how the REIT is structured, it's akin to a mutual fund. But instead of investing in companies, you invest in delinquent loans collateralized by real estate. RTC REITs invest in what the agency calls sub- or nonperforming loans.

In the real world REITs—in general—are collateralized by real estate—hence the name "real estate investment trust." Some REITs invest in certain types of projects such as nursing homes or apartments, while others invest in a wide array of properties. Sold in denominations of $1,000 or more, REITs often are marketed to middle-class and upper-middle-class investors.

Beginning in late 1992 the RTC began to offer REITs to the general public for the first time, in an effort to dispose more quickly of its nonperforming loan portfolio. Under its new Multiple Investor Fund program (MIF) the RTC lumps nonperforming loans into large pools, divides the pool into affordable slices, and offers these slices to the general public. The pool is then managed by professional loan workout specialists, and if the pool performs better than expected the investors pocket the profits. Under the RTC's MIF program, the general public, rather than institutional investors, will get first crack at each REIT pool.

The RTC offers these REITs through "sponsors." Instead of the government, you'll be working with investment firms like Merrill Lynch. Phone your consolidated office and you will be told which brokerage firm near you is handling its REIT sales. If the RTC REIT program takes off, expect the FDIC to follow suit with its nonperforming real estate.

REITs are not without risk. RTC REITs are, after all, collateralized by pools of nonperforming loans it could not otherwise market. If an

REIT is not managed properly, your investment could head south. On the other hand, if it's well managed, investors can do well. The key is the REIT's manager, so ask about the sponsor or management team the RTC has selected for the REIT you are interested in investing in.

These REIT pools are a nice way to take a chance on the RTC's nonperforming loans without having to actually get your hands dirty. You just put your money down and let the REIT managers deal with the defaulted borrowers and foreclosures and resales. If they do well—you do well.

BUYING LOANS FROM THE FDIC

As far as selling loans and real estate is concerned, the RTC and FDIC— as already explained—are sister organizations. The FDIC handles bank assets; the RTC, S&L assets. Their sales methods are similar but not identical. As with the RTC, investors looking to buy loans from the FDIC should first approach the consolidated office nearest them. (Again, check our Yellow Pages.)

As the RTC's caseload of assets begins to shrink in 1995, the FDIC's inventory of available products will be increasing and may not peak until some time in 1997 or a bit later. In 1992, for example, the FDIC had available for purchase $2.1 billion in performing loans and $9.1 billion in nonperforming loans. Those numbers could double each year, depending on the depth of the nation's banking crisis.

There are two major differences when it comes to purchasing loans from the FDIC. First, the FDIC doesn't rely as heavily on "open-cry" auctions. That means if you want to buy loans from the FDIC you'll be doing so through the sealed-bid process. As with the RTC, you will have three to four weeks to review the loan file before making a bid. More times than not an auction house will not be involved in the process. You will deal directly with FDIC account executives who take your sealed bid along with all the others.

Another key difference is that unlike the RTC, the FDIC's consolidated office does not require a good faith or earnest money deposit. This is a plus for bidders who don't want to hassle with the formality of obtaining a cashier's check. However, if you win a sealed-bid auction for loans you have twenty-four hours to post a down payment (usually 10 percent). You then have ten business days to close the deal.

Most FDIC sealed-bid loan auctions involve large pools of loans. If you want just a few loans you'll have a tougher time of it. Still, FDIC account executives in charge of selling loans are more than happy to talk to you about buying small loans with balances of $20,000 or less. Like the RTC, the FDIC wants to get rid of the "small stuff" as soon as possible. Tell the FDIC account executive what you want. With a little luck you might be able to work out a deal without going through an auction process.

MORE CAVEATS

DUE DILIGENCE

The most important piece of advice to keep in mind when buying nonperforming loans is that it takes hard work and due diligence. Sure, you can acquire some loans for five or ten cents on the dollar—but will you know how to collect on those loans to make it worth your while? More so than buying real estate, acquiring delinquent loans takes a great deal of time and research. With real estate you size up the building. With a loan investors need to analyze the underlying property *plus* the entire loan file.

Purchasing loans from the government can be a profitable business. But go over the loan files with a fine-tooth comb. Get to know the collateral. Bargains abound, but so do black holes. "If you run a tight ship and watch the overhead you can make this business work for you," says Roland Russell, vice president of National Asset Management Corporation in Dallas, a specialist in nonperforming loans. The key word here is "work." Doctors and lawyers looking for a killing—listen up. You may be cash-rich but more than likely you don't have the expertise to buy delinquent loans. If that's the case, hire someone who does and factor the cost into your anticipated yield. Cash-rich doctors tend to be some of the worst investors we've ever met.

BANKRUPTCY

Another concern to loan investors is the bankruptcy court. With a simple wave of the pen, any citizen who has more debts than liquid assets can file a petition in the nearest federal courthouse, declaring him- or herself bankrupt and asking for court protection from creditors. By filing for bankruptcy, individual citizens, companies, or partnerships can obtain temporary relief from paying their bills—including loans.

For loan investors, bankruptcy filings can turn into major headaches, driving up legal bills. If you're functioning as your own lawyer, this won't be as great a concern, but it can delay resolution of the loan. The RTC or FDIC loan file should tell you whether the borrower is operating under bankruptcy protection. If a delinquent borrower has filed for bankruptcy, the court will prevent creditors (you, the loan investor) from foreclosing until a judge can better analyze the debtor's financial situation. In time a trustee is appointed by the court to oversee the estate or holdings of the person or company filing for bankruptcy protection.

Investors in delinquent loans can sometimes be broadsided by a bankruptcy filing. After reviewing a loan file you may think: "No way this guy's going to file for bankruptcy. He has too many assets." Then a couple of days after you buy the loan and send the debtor his first warning notice—lo and behold, he files for bankruptcy. However, just because a debtor has filed for bankruptcy, it doesn't mean a deal can't be worked out. If the loan is secured by something tangible, such as a car or house, you're considered a "secured" lender, and you still might make out. If you bought a delinquent unsecured personal line of credit or student loan, you're likely to have a tougher time of it.

Types of Bankruptcy Filings

There are a number of different types of bankruptcy filings: Chapter 7, Chapter 11, and Chapter 13.

Most individuals file for Chapter 13, which is for people with small amounts of debt. Chapter 13 cases often move quickly and can be resolved within a relatively short period of time. If someone has $100,000 or less in liquid assets he or she can file for Chapter 13. If the debtor has more, he or she has to file Chapter 11 (reorganization) or Chapter 7 (liquidation).

Chapter 11 is commonly used by struggling companies that for one reason or another are having severe problems paying their bills. Chapter 11 means the company is going to reorganize its operations by cutting staff and by trying to get you, the creditor, to accept less for the note you hold. Depending on what type of loan you hold—and how much you paid for it—this might not be so bad. Again, if the loan is collateralized by real estate, the debtor might just hand the property over and be rid of the headache. Then again, he may want to reduce the amount of money he's paying you every month—which isn't so good.

Chapter 7 means the debtor's problems are so bad that the debtor is going to sell everything (liquidate) and give whatever proceeds are raised to all the people to whom he or she owes money. Again, this isn't good news to an investor who has just bought a loan from the RTC or FDIC. Still, if the loan is secured by real estate your chances of collecting are better than if there's no collateral backing the loan.

As in all bankruptcy cases, you can always work out a deal to foreclose on the loan with the trustee, creditor, or the creditor's lawyer.

The Dreaded Cramdown

Cramdowns or pushdowns occur most frequently in cases where individuals and companies have filed for bankruptcy and have tried to get the mortgage amount they owe reduced by petitioning the court. Debtors ask the court to reduce the size of their outstanding mortgage by arguing that land prices have decreased so much that they, the debtor, have no chance of emerging from bankruptcy unless the court allows their mortgage to be legally reduced.

In other words, they're trying to reduce, or "cramdown," the debt they owe to the mortgage holder. This is a serious concern when it comes to large commercial mortgages on hotels, shopping centers, and raw land but less of a concern when it comes to residential and other types of mortgages. (Very few individuals filing for personal bankruptcy bother going this route.)

However, on a positive note, the courts have ruled against cramdowns. In fact, in early 1992, the Supreme Court ruled that companies and individuals liquidating their assets in bankruptcy court cannot reduce their mortgage debt just because the market value of their property has fallen. This is good news for lenders and investors in delinquent loans. Still, it remains a volatile issue that may not go away. It also is a highly technical issue. Any loan investor who gets entangled in a cramdown case should consult a lawyer and read very carefully the Supreme Court ruling (Dewsnup *v.* Timon, January 1992).

IN SUMMARY

Buying loans from the RTC or FDIC, though not for everybody, can be quite rewarding financially. But as we've said, it's not a sure thing—no free lunch here. As with buying real estate, it's essential that you do your homework and look before leaping. Sometimes you can make a killing; other times—watch out. If you don't have the expertise, either get it or hire it. If you don't have enough money to buy the type of loans you want, form a pool with other investors.

Carefully review the loan files. Employed debtors with steady incomes are safer bets than someone teetering on the edge of bankruptcy. The deeper the discount offered by the RTC or FDIC, the less the likelihood of repayment. If you're a novice, stick to buying delinquent loans collateralized by something tangible and within close physical proximity to where you live or work. You'll want to keep an eye on your investment.

If you're a small investor with not much to play with, contact an RTC or FDIC account executive in the consolidated office nearest you and tell him or her you're only interested in small loans of $20,000 or less (or whatever your range is). Performing loans are available to small investors—but again you'll have to approach the FDIC and RTC and ask for them by name. Both agencies like to get rid of the small stuff first and tend to package them in pools.

When it comes to performing loans, be prepared to pay close to par. Deep discounts won't be as plentiful as with delinquent loans.

If you want to avoid dealing with auctions and regulators, your best bet might be to approach an ailing bank before the FDIC or RTC moves in. Ask it about its bad loans. By purchasing bad loans before the government moves in, you can avoid competitive bidding and save thousands of dollars—millions even, depending on what type of investor you are.

Chapter 9

··

The Flea Market of the Century

*Buying Non-Real Estate Property from
the RTC and FDIC*

The RTC and FDIC call the stuff "FF&E" short for "furniture, fixtures, and equipment." But don't let these three narrow categories fool you. Besides selling billions of dollars' worth of real estate and loans, the government has millions of dollars' worth of "hard" assets to sell: artwork, adding machines, cars, computers, couches, microwaves, stereos, and the list goes on and on. It's a virtual treasure trove, a bargain hunter's ultimate dream—it's the flea market to end all flea markets.

FF&E property is taken right out of the corporate offices of the nation's failed banks and S&Ls. Once the government seizes an insolvent institution, it compiles an inventory of all property at all the branches of every failed financial institution. Its goal? To sell anything that isn't nailed down. Everything must go and almost any offer will be considered, because the longer the government has to maintain this stuff the more it costs the taxpayers.

WHERE DID ALL THIS STUFF COME FROM?

When S&Ls were deregulated by the government in 1982 some bankers read it as a sign to buy now (using the S&L's money) and worry about paying later. Having the combination to the vault transformed some bankers into world-class shoppers. Miami S&L owner David L. Paul (indicted in 1992) used CenTrust Savings's money to purchase a $12 million oil painting by Flemish artist Peter Paul Rubens and then took the painting home to hang over his fireplace. Paul claimed the humidity in the office would harm the artwork.

Other high-flying thrift owners used their institutions' federally insured deposits to buy yachts, planes, fleets of expensive cars, crystal, silverware, sculptures, antiques—all in the name of doing good business. The booty now belongs to Uncle Sam, who must sell it through auction.

Every few weeks, anywhere in America, the RTC or FDIC holds an FF&E auction. The goal is to sell everything, even the tables the merchandise sits on. Nearly every auction has at least a few truly unique items. Try these on for size: a mechanical gorilla, a magic museum, a racehorse—just a few actual items sold at RTC auctions in recent months. However, much of this FF&E inventory is banking-related office furniture and equipment. For anyone setting up a new business or expanding an old one, an RTC or FDIC auction is a great opportunity to get equipped on the cheap. You need copy machines? Uncle Sam has them. A PBX phone system? Yep. Need a forest of filing cabinets? A sea of desks? A fireplace for the corporate office? Some Western art? How about some power tools for the maintenance department? RTC and FDIC auctions have all this and much, much more.

At a single FDIC auction in early 1992 the auctioneer sold the remnants of eight failed northeastern banks. In all they sold 1,493 "lots"— items or groups of items. This included: thirty-one Olympia electric typewriters that went out the door for $5 apiece; a Karex Lektreiver for $200; a Micro Design microfiche reader for just $75; a $15,000 safe for $1,600. A Canon 450 FAX machine went for $400 and a complete Epson IBM-compatible desktop computer system sold for just $475. A professional bank electronic security system, which had cost its former owner several thousand dollars, went for just $75. As the auctioneer's gavel slammed down on each item an FDIC observer sat grim-faced, shaking his head in glum resignation as one item after another went for next to nothing—such as the multiplex telephone system with twelve extensions that sold for just $650. The FDIC official just shrugged his shoulders. With more than 150 people attending, everything sold that day, even the old teller cages that the auctioneer claimed were worth at least $15,000. In the end, though, he accepted $1,575 for them.[1]

WHEN THE RTC GOES TO AUCTION

The RTC requires its consolidated offices to use the auction process to dispose of FF&E property when:

- a wide variety of assets are available for sale. By combining FF&E into a single auction, the government strives to create buyer "frenzy," which it hopes will increase prices. From what we've found, this is not always the case.
- "difficult to sell" assets do not sell. When this happens, the RTC combines these assets (for example, the mechanical gorilla) with other more desirable assets (such as office computers), hoping that someone will want the computers enough to take the gorilla as well.
- all other attempts to sell FF&E have failed. On occasion the RTC may try to offer FF&E to a wholesaler before going to auction. Side deals can be worked out—as long as you have cash. If FF&E can't be sold to a wholesaler (like a used office equipment retailer), then it's time to hold an auction.
- holding assets begins costing the conservatorship or receivership a lot of money through maintenance and upkeep. This happens with cars, cattle, produce, and so on.

TYPES OF AUCTIONS

When selling FF&E the RTC utilizes two auction methods: absolute and reserve price. Absolute auctions are also known as "everything must go" auctions. FF&E is auctioned and sold without regard to any mini-

[1] Alan Wade, "Bidding for the Bones." *United States Banker*, January 1992, 11.

mum price. This is where you can pick up a used microwave oven for $5. At reserve price auctions, the RTC sets a minimum sales price for certain FF&E items (a car, for instance) and refuses to go below that minimum. Usually found in the classified section of your local newspaper, the posted auction notice will specify that the RTC or FDIC *reserves the right to accept or reject any bid* that is less than its minimum reserve price for that item. If a reserve price is established the auctioneer will advise buyers prior to the start of bidding.

Depending on circumstances, it's possible that the RTC and FDIC might use both absolute and reserve prices in the same real estate auction. If that's the case the assets will be clearly marked accordingly. However, with commercial real estate and bare land values still in flux, anticipate that many upcoming auctions will involve absolute sales. Also, it is more likely that absolute bids will be used when selling single-family residences and condos, as opposed to office buildings and shopping malls.

GETTING PLUGGED IN: FINDING OUT ABOUT AUCTIONS

Investors have a few different ways to get plugged into the RTC auction circuit. The quickest way is to telephone the RTC asset hotline (1-800-RTC-3006) and use the voice mail system. One of the choices listed is for the RTC's "Auction Calendar," which posts every auction event for that particular month. (Subscribers to RTCNET on the Business Information Network can also learn about auction dates and locations by accessing the agency's on-line computer data base. You'll need a personal computer to do so. See Chapter 2.) Using the toll-free number is the easiest way to get information quickly without having to explain yourself to a real human being. However, the asset hotline requires a touch-tone telephone. As already noted, a rotary won't work.

If you have a rotary telephone or don't want to talk to a machine, you can call the RTC Auction Center or the RTC National Sales Center in Washington, D.C. Both will supply you with the necessary information—dates, places, times, and the telephone number of the auction house in charge of the sale. In general, telephone operators and sales executives in Washington are knowledgeable, helpful, and polite. Both offices are particularly useful if you are looking for something unique, such as fine art or antiques.

If you want detailed information on what exactly is being offered, you have to call the auction house hired by the RTC. All FF&E is sold through private auction contractors who specialize in squeezing the most out of auction items. Free of charge, auction companies will mail you a list of *everything that is being offered* that day. If you have a FAX machine, most will fax you a list. (The ones we contacted did.)

KEY INFORMATION. *The RTC and FDIC do not auction FF&E themselves. However, if you're looking to buy office equipment in bulk, you can approach the consolidated office and make a bid for equipment, desks, or filing cabinets (whatever) without going through the auction process. RTC regulators allow the agency to sell FF&E to anybody at any time as long as they pay "fair market value." RTC personnel are in charge of determining fair market value.*

Middendorf & Co., a Washington, D.C. investment banking firm operated by former Navy secretary and ambassador J. William Middendorf, approached the RTC in March 1992 about buying office furniture for a new business. The firm walked away with dozens of desks, chairs, and a conference table, all for $3,780. This may sound like a lot of money until you learn that the original cost of the conference table alone was $7,000.

What other gems does the government have to offer? When we called the Regenhold Auction Consultants, Inc., in Clearwater, Florida, they immediately faxed us a list of items appearing in its next RTC auction:

- Sony color televisions
- Compaq and IBM computers
- IBM electronic typewriters
- Filing and storage cabinets
- Casio and Sharp desk calculators
- Microwave ovens
- Refrigerators and freezers
- Conference tables

- Secretarial chairs, armchairs, and couches
- Bruning blueprint machine
- Drafting tables
- Modular workstations
- Desks
- Credenzas
- Lamps
- Paper cutters
- Clocks
- Paymaster checks
- Coffeemakers
- Paper shredders

FF&E offered by the RTC and FDIC tend to be similar. Because S&L crooks were more colorful than bank looters, the RTC is the best place to shop if you're looking for something that might sell at Abercrombie and Fitch rather than Office Furniture USA.

Both the RTC and FDIC regularly advertise FF&E auctions at least two to four weeks ahead of time. Most of the ads appear in the classified section of your local daily newspaper (see Exhibit 10). But it is best not to leave things to chance. You may or may not spot an auction ad. Your best bet remains calling the RTC hotline and getting a schedule of auction events on a regular basis.

HOW THE GOVERNMENT APPRAISES FF&E

As with valuing real estate, the RTC has a system to evaluate the worth of FF&E. If an S&L has FF&E thought to be worth $5,000 or more, the RTC must get an independent appraisal on all items that will be sold. If the failed institution's FF&E is believed to be worth $250,000 or more, two appraisals are required.

If the S&L has a certain valuable item (e.g., a Ming Dynasty vase), the RTC will request that the auctioneer set it aside and offer it later in the auction, setting a "floor" or "reserve" price. If the floor isn't met the fixture will be taken back, reappraised, and offered again at a later date.

PREVIEWING THE MERCHANDISE

A few days before an auction occurs, the private auction house allows bidders to preview all the merchandise that will be offered. The viewing period usually lasts for only a few hours. If the merchandise you are interested in buying is mechanical, the auction house will allow bidders to check it out within certain limits. If it's an electrical appliance they will supply electrical hookups so you can see if the appliance operates. If it's a car or truck, chances are they'll let you run the engine, but they probably won't allow you to take it for a spin.

EXHIBIT 10. A typical advertisement for an RTC auction.

Generally the auction company will hand you an asset list with a box next to each asset up for bid. Each FF&E item is assigned a lot number. Bring a pencil and a notebook. Write down the lot numbers you're interested in bidding on. If it's a copy machine you want, plug it in and test it out. At some of the auctions we attended the copiers ranged in quality from poor to excellent. Usually there are plenty of copiers to choose from.

At the preview, take as much time as they allow. Take notes on everything. If you don't get one item, you might get the next. Once an auction gets rolling the bidding becomes fast and furious. One trip to the restroom and you can miss half a dozen items. If the S&L had a sea of filing cabinets the auction house might sell them all in one lot. As many as twenty cabinets might make up that lot. The auction house will first try to sell the lot as a "whole." If it doesn't sell, then they will begin spinning individual items out of the lot for bid.

We cannot emphasize enough: Take special care to inspect every item you're bidding on. Why? Because nothing you buy from the government can be returned. All sales are FINAL. Also, if it's broken or won't work right, guess what? It's your problem after that gavel drops on your winning bid. Before auction the RTC and FDIC will hand out fliers. Read them carefully. This is what you'll see:

NOTICE

THE PROPERTY IS BEING SOLD "AS IS," "WHERE IS," AND "WITH ALL FAULTS," WITHOUT ANY REPRESENTATION OR WARRANTY WHATSOEVER AS TO ITS CONDITION, FITNESS FOR ANY PARTICULAR PURPOSE, MERCHANTABILITY OR ANY OTHER WARRANTY, EXPRESS OR IMPLIED. SELLER HAS ONLY LIMITED KNOWLEDGE OF ITS CONDITION. BUYER WILL PURCHASE THE PROPERTY BASED SOLELY ON ITS OWN INDEPENDENT INVESTIGATION AND INSPECTION OF THE PROPERTY AND NOT IN RELIANCE ON ANY INFORMATION PROVIDED BY SELLER, ITS AGENTS, OR CONTRACTORS. SELLER WILL NOT REPAIR OR IMPROVE THE PROPERTY PRIOR TO SALE. THE PROPERTY WILL BE SOLD SUBJECT TO RENTAL AGREEMENTS -OR OTHER CONDITIONS, IF ANY. THE PROPERTY MAY BE WITHDRAWN WITHOUT NOTICE AT ANY TIME PRIOR TO SALE.

BIDDING AT AUCTION AND HOW TO BID

Most auction houses function by the same house rules. Before being allowed to bid you will have to post a deposit, usually $50 to $100. (It's refundable if you don't buy. If you do buy, it's applied to the purchase price.) Registration takes place early that morning or the day before. We advise that you go the day before and beat the crush.

When you arrive the day of the auction, an auction company employee will assign you a bidder's number, which is usually printed on a wooden ping-pong-like paddle. When you want to make a bid you hold up your paddle. Do not keep your paddle in the air for longer than it takes to gain the auctioneer's attention. The auctioneer will keep rattling off a new, higher asking price, and if your arm remains in the air he will interpret that as a sign that you want to bid even more. If this occurs you might top your own bid. We saw this happen at an RTC auction in Alexandria, Virginia. A young man kept his paddle in the air and wound up paying $400 more for a truck than he had intended.

Instead of using paddles, some auction houses use strips of cardboard with a number printed on the end. Others use nothing, but request that you raise your hand and shout out your bid registration number. If you don't want to bid, don't say a word and don't raise your arm. This is known as "sitting on your paddle."

Most auctions occur in the auctioneer's warehouse. But others are held right at the former S&L's headquarters or in a hotel ballroom—whichever can hold the most merchandise and is conveniently located to parking. Most auctions occur on a Saturday and begin at 9:00 or 10:00 in the morning. In general, one auctioneer does all the selling, aided by one or two assistants. Each company has "criers" (or spotters) who prowl through the audience watching for bids. When a bid is made a spotter will point to the bidder and issue forth a hearty—though often undiscernable—shout. At the more aggressive auction houses spotters will also prod bidders to bid, pointing at them as if to say, "Was that the thought of a bid I just saw cross your mind?" This is all part of the show and meant in good humor, so don't let yourself be bullied into a bid.

Before the auction actually starts, the auctioneer will take about twenty minutes to once again explain the rules. Then all the bidders gather around the item for sale (or it is placed on a stage in front of bidders seated in bleachers). The auctioneer starts the bidding, sells the item, and moves to the next item.

If you've never been to an oral outcry auction, treat yourself and go, even if you're not going to purchase anything. Auctioneers are a lot like politicians: real hams who like to put on a show. A good auctioneer knows how to stimulate bidding. By the expression on your face he knows if you're going to bid or not. Investors who frequent auctions learn early how to maintain a poker face. But don't be surprised if the auctioneer or one of his criers decides to confront you—"Well, ya gonna just sit on that paddle all day long or you gonna bid?" Don't be taken aback or embarrassed. Part of the show, it's all done with a sense of humor. (And no, you don't have to bid if you don't want to.)

Every auctioneer has a different style—from the "big city" auctioneer with his dignified ways to the "country bumpkin" who likes to regale the audience with stories about how he just sold a new Mercedes to his "rich uncle who just got out of the poorhouse." Some auctioneers still use the old-fashioned rolling fast-talk, which newcomers find colorful but impossible to understand. If you're not sure what he's saying, don't bid. When in doubt, ask one of his assistants to translate.

KEY INFORMATION. *Before bidding, keep in mind that you will be charged a 10 percent auction fee—in addition to the purchase price. If you buy a copier for $100 the final price will be $110. Then add in that state's sales tax. If it's Florida, for example, the final price on the copier is $117 (based on Florida's state sales tax of 7 percent).*

PAYMENT: CASH AND CARRY

If you win the bid, a spotter puts your registration number on the item and forwards the information to the bookkeeper. You have until the end of the auction to settle with the bookkeeper. At day's end you must pay up. Auction companies often require a certified check and tend to be annoyed with anything less. Other forms of acceptable payment include cash, cashier's check, travelers check, or a money order. Company or personal checks are accepted only when accompanied by a letter from your bank guaranteeing payment. Checks are made payable to the auction company, which then forwards the proceeds to the RTC or FDIC.

> KEY INFORMATION. *Once you've settled it's up to you, not the auction company, to cart the item away. If you purchase a large conference table, make sure you have the means to carry it away. Unless it's a Van Gogh, the government never wants to see this stuff again.*

SEALED BID AUCTIONS

On occasion the RTC or FDIC will hold its own sealed-bid auction for certain specialty FF&E items—usually artwork. During its first year of operation the RTC lumped artwork in with its regular FF&E auctions. This led to allegations by art experts that the government was selling "fine art" at "decorative art" prices.

Where did this fine art come from? From S&L owners who used the thrift's money to buy whatever they wanted. These guys had plenty of money, but were a bit short on taste. Sometimes S&L owners bought pure schlock, other times they did not—like David Paul of failed Cen-Trust Savings of Miami. Through Sotheby's Paul paid $12 million for Rubens's original *Portrait of a Man as Mars*, painted in the seventeenth century.

When the RTC seized Columbia Savings and Gibraltar Savings, both of California, it sold most of their artwork on a sealed-bid basis. The RTC produced glossy full-color catalogs, highlighting each piece. Art experts agreed that most of the paintings had little value, *but* a dozen were found to be "significant" contemporary works. By attending sealed-bid auctions, or getting a look at the catalog, investors who "know art when they see it" may find a few diamonds tucked away beneath the sofas and Xerox copiers.

In Phoenix in early 1992 the RTC sold 600 pieces of Western art acquired from failed thrifts. The works ranged from $10 prints to a $35,000 oil painting by Olaf Wieghorst. The agency said the auction was "just the beginning" of its sealed-bid sales effort, noting that it has hundreds of other pieces of artwork stored, but yet to be cataloged.

Under the category of "artwork" the RTC includes paintings,

antiques, photographs, prints, and sculpture. All items are appraised for the agency by art dealers, consultants, and other experts. Once an art-work is appraised and identified by a dealer as "fine art," the RTC establishes a minimum "reserve price" or "minimum acceptable bid" price of 70 percent of the appraised value. This applies to all fine art appraised at $5,000 or more. The RTC says it will not sell for less than that, and it will remove the item from the auction if bids come up short. Whether it sticks to its threat is another story. But if you see a piece you really want, bid anyway. After all, even at the reserve price of 70 percent you've just gotten a 30 percent discount. If you're speculating and don't care if you get the piece or not, go ahead and lowball your bid. See what happens. Desperate sellers can be unpredictable.

The RTC follows a set of predetermined guidelines for establishing reserve prices on FF&E artwork:

- If the item is worth $1,000 or less the agency does not have to establish a reserve price.
- If the item is appraised at $1,000 to $5,000, the reserve price cannot be less than 50 percent of that value.
- If the piece is worth $5,000 or more the reserve price can be no less than 70 percent of that value.

DIRECT SALE OF FF&E

As we noted earlier, the two agencies can avoid the FF&E auction process and sell directly to any buyer. These buyers might include a professional wholesaler or a business looking to buy in bulk (such as in the case of Middendorf & Co.). When this happens it's called a "direct sale."

When a direct sale occurs the inventory is sold directly from a failed thrift or bank. How can an investor determine whether the FDIC or RTC is willing to make a direct sale? The answer is simple: Just ask. If a failed bank or thrift was large and had many different branches and corporate headquarters, chances are better that the agencies will try to sell much of the FF&E on site through direct sales. But they will not advertise the fact. It's up to the aggressive buyer to inquire. Do so as soon as the agency places a bank or thrift into either a conservatorship or receivership. That fact, at least, will be in the local papers. Call the closest RTC or FDIC consolidated office and ask what plans it has for the FF&E. If you're told it's too soon to say, leave your name and number. But don't count on the RTC or FDIC calling you. Check on a weekly basis.

IN SUMMARY

When regulators close a bank or savings and loan and take it over, they inherit everything not human. If you can imagine it, the FDIC and RTC have either sold it or eventually will. It's easy to become an auction junkie the same way some people get hooked on garage sales. Once you get plugged into the FDIC and RTC auction circuit your biggest problem is going to be explaining to your spouse why a bank vault, a complete PBX phone system, or a crate containing two desktop computers and eighty staplers was a "great buy."

The whole trick to bidding at auction is to first inspect the merchandise. Kick the tires, open the hood, whatever. Don't get caught up in the feeding frenzy and overbid. Everything from cars to fireplaces, copiers to desks, is available from both the RTC and FDIC. This garage sale will be going on for at least the next couple of years. Call the closest consolidated office or check your local newspaper. Remember it's cash and carry and they don't deliver—so bring a pickup truck.

Chapter 10

....

Help Wanted—Inquire Within

Contracting and Employment Opportunities with the RTC and FDIC

One of the least-known benefits of the banking and S&L debacles is the job opportunities created by these scandals. If you're not looking to invest in real estate or loans, getting a government-related job or management contract is yet another way to profit from this financial meltdown. However, we do warn that the employment picture has changed dramatically since this book was first published in early 1993. There are jobs available at the RTC and FDIC—but the pickings are very slim. Also, the RTC eventually will be merged into the FDIC, probably by the end of 1995, maybe sooner. Keep in mind that many job openings at both agencies will be "term" appointments, meaning you could be laid off with little notice and few benefits. One other warning: The Clinton administration has promised to streamline government, and the FDIC and RTC could be prime targets. Your best bet is to find work as an outside contractor to the government.

WHAT'S AVAILABLE?

The amount of money up for grabs here is truly phenomenal. J.E. Robert Co., a real estate management and sales firm based in Alexandria,

Virginia, is expected to make *$55 million* in fees by working for the RTC over the next few years. Its task? To manage, auction, and sell for the government $3.1 billion worth of assets—mostly real estate and loans.[1] IBM, the computer conglomerate, is expected to make $51 million from the RTC for developing and maintaining the agency's computer network. Northcorp Realty Advisers, Dallas—which is classified as a "woman owned business" (WOB)—will earn $30 million in fees from the RTC by managing and selling real estate and loans.

J.E. Robert, IBM, and Northcorp are all RTC "contractors"—private-sector companies that have been contracted to do certain tasks for the RTC. Although it issued each of these firms a multimillion-dollar contract, the RTC—and FDIC—has thousands of other, smaller tasks that cannot be done "in-house" and must be assigned to private-sector firms. There's plenty of room here for the "little guy," especially small-town real estate brokers and appraisers.

The majority of the FDIC and RTC's contracts are to manage and sell real estate and loans. These contracts are called Standard Asset Management and Disposition Agreements, or SAMDA contracts. SAMDA contractors generally receive a negotiated fee to manage property and then are given a disposition fee once that property is sold. Real estate brokers that list and sell houses for the government are SAMDA contractors. The agency also assigns Standard Asset Management Agreement contracts, or SAMAs, where an asset manager receives management fees for overseeing and managing a property, but does not receive a disposition fee once that asset is sold.

If you're looking for work there are two ways to go here: Either become an RTC contractor or hire on with a firm that is already an RTC contractor. The RTC and FDIC need the following services:

- accountants
- appraisers—real estate, loans, securities, FF&E, and artwork
- attorneys and paralegals
- auction companies—for real estate, loans, and FF&E
- computer management, hardware, and software companies

---

[1] The J.E. Robert contract estimate is based on public contracting data issued by the RTC in early 1992.

- construction and demolition—to finish or destroy selected real estate projects
- investment banking firms (brokerage houses)—to manage and sell mortgage-backed securities and junk bonds
- marketing and advertising firms
- mortgage loan servicers
- private investigators
- printing companies
- real estate managers and realtors
- real estate and loan appraisers
- security companies—to guard half-finished real estate projects and other valuable items
- title companies and services

As of 1992 the RTC had already awarded 15,000 contracts with estimated fees totaling more than *$1 billion*.[2]

BECOMING A GOVERNMENT CONTRACTOR: GETTING STARTED

Like most government contracting work you must bid competitively against other companies or individuals. And before you can even bid you must register with the government so it can determine whether you're an eligible bidder.

As with most RTC and FDIC business, the best way to start is at an agency consolidated office. If you're based in Dallas but you want to bid on job contracts offered by the RTC's Newport Beach office in California, telephone Newport Beach, not the Dallas consolidated office. Upon request any consolidated office will mail you a contractor registration packet. Packets also are available by calling the RTC National Sales Center in Washington. It should take five to seven working days to get one. (The one we requested took four days to get to us.)

The contractor registration packet is 27 pages long, including instruc-

[2] *Source*: RTC Office of Inspector General semiannual report, released December 1991.

tions. Among the questions asked are the standard name and address questions. You will be asked what kind of work you're interested in. Some of the choices offered include:

- Leasing
- Security services
- Evictions
- Property maintenance
- Property management
- Real estate brokerage
- Broker's opinion
- Marketing/sales
- Marketing/promotion
- Securities (portfolio analysis)
- Loans (the form asks what loan size you want to manage)
- Construction
- Environmental consulting
- Tax consulting

And the list goes on for several more pages. Each category includes several employment subcategories. Almost every type of real estate and banking job is represented—and there's even a few you might not expect. Try these subcategories:

- Armored vehicle services
- Boat and airplane maintenance
- Expert witness (for RTC and FDIC civil lawsuits against alleged banking wrongdoers)
- Industrial hygiene survey
- Soils engineering

Your completed form should be mailed to the RTC's Contract Registration Department in Washington. Each of the consolidated offices will keep their own master list of "registered" contractors. To bid with different offices you will have to get on each office's master list. Each consolidated office relies on its own registered contractor or "source" lists to pick winning contractors. It costs nothing to register with the

SECTION VII

FITNESS AND INTEGRITY CERTIFICATIONS

QUALIFICATIONS OF CONTRACTOR (Sections 1606.4 & 1606.5)

Information and certifications required on this form will be used in determining contractor's fitness and integrity for entering into contracts with RTC as provided by Part 1606 of RTC's Rules and Regulations—Regarding Qualification of, Ethical Standards of Conduct for, and Restrictions on the Use of Confidential Information By Independent Contractors. **Please refer to those regulations for policies and procedures to be followed by both Contractors and RTC. The definitions of the terms used in this form are contained on page 20.**

If the answer to any of the questions in Parts B and C is "Yes," please provide RTC with a statement describing the past history of the situation and the matter's present disposition. RTC retains the right, in its sole discretion, to qualify or disqualify a Contractor.

PART A: Each of the following questions must be answered. If the answer to any of these questions is "YES," RTC is prohibited from hiring you.	YES	NO
1. Is the Contractor an individual who has been convicted of a felony?		
2. Has the Contractor been removed from, or prohibited from participating in the affairs of, any insured depository institution pursuant to any final enforcement action taken by any federal banking agency?		
3. Is the Contractor in default on two or more obligations to pay principal or interest to insured depository institutions in an aggregate amount in excess of $50,000 (which is defined in the regulation as constituting a pattern or practice of defalcation)?		
4. Has the Contractor caused a substantial loss to any federal deposit insurance fund?		
5. Is the Contractor currently in default on an obligation to FDIC, FSLIC or RTC?		

PART B: Each of the following questions must be answered. If the answer to any of these questions is "YES," RTC may decide, in its sole discretion, to qualify or disqualify a Contractor.	YES	NO
1. Has the Contractor (if not an individual) or any of the Contractor's related entities been convicted of a felony?		
2. Has any related entity been removed from, or prohibited from, participating in the affairs of any insured depository institution pursuant to any final enforcement action taken by any federal banking agency?		
3. Is any related entity in default on two or more obligations to pay principal or interest to insured depository institutions in an aggregate amount in excess of $50,000 (which is defined in the regulation as constituting a pattern or practice of defalcation)?		
4. Has any related entity caused a substantial loss to any federal deposit insurance fund?		
5. Have any of the following failed to pay an obligation to pay principal or interest at its full value owed to any federal deposit insurance fund, FSLIC, or RTC: (a) The Contractor or any related entity of the Contractor.		
(b) An entity that, during the past five years was a related entity of the Contractor.		
(c) An entity that, during the past five years, was a related entity of any individual or entity that now controls the Contractor.		
6. Is any related entity currently in default on an obligation to FDIC, FSLIC, or RTC?		

EXHIBIT 11.   Two-page RTC Contractor fitness and integrity questionnaire.

RESOLUTION TRUST CORPORATION

FITNESS AND INTEGRITY CERTIFICATIONS

QUALIFICATIONS OF CONTRACTOR (Sections 1606.4 & 1606.5) (Continued:)

PART C: The following questions relate to the Contractor and its related entities. If the answer to any of these questions is "YES," RTC may decide at its sole discretion, to qualify or disqualify a Contractor.	YES	NO
1. Is the Contractor or any related entity a party to an administrative or judicial proceeding in which any of them is alleged to have engaged in fraudulent activity or has been charged with the commission of a felony or which seeks a remedy that would prevent or materially interfere with its ability to perform on the contract?		
2. Is the Contractor or any related entity subject, to their knowledge, to an administrative or criminal investigation relating to fraudulent activity or the commission of a felony?		
3. Has the Contractor or any related entity, during the past 5 years been held liable for fraud, dishonesty, misrepresentation, or breach of fiduciary duty?		
4. Is either the Contractor or any related entity currently excluded from federal procurement or nonprocurement programs?		
5. Is the Contractor or any related entity subject to an unsatisfied final judgment in favor of FDIC, FSLIC or RTC?		
6. Is the Contractor or any related entity a party to a lawsuit in which the FDIC, FSLIC or RTC is seeking recovery in excess of $50,000 from the Contractor or its related entities?		

PART D: Does the Contractor agree that he/she will not employ any individual or subcontractor to directly perform work on the contract who:	YES	NO
(a) has been convicted of a felony?		
(b) has been removed from, or prohibited from participating in the affairs of, any insured depository institution pursuant to any final enforcement action by any federal banking agency?		
(c) has demonstrated a pattern or practice of defalcation?		
(d) has caused a substantial loss to federal deposit insurance funds? or		
(e) is currently in default on any obligation to FDIC, FSLIC, an insured depository institution or RTC?		

NOTICE: An individual who acts on behalf of RTC pursuant to a contract or any other agreement is deemed a public official, therefore is subject to federal bribery and graft rules as set forth in Title 18 U.S.C.

CERTIFICATION

In signing this certification I represent and warrant that I have the authority to execute this certification on behalf of the firm represented. I further certify that the above answers are true and correct and that all attached information provided to RTC is true and correct.

Signature of Principal Officer	Name and Title of Principal or Officer (Please print or type)
Firm's Name (Please print or type)	Date Signed

19

221

RTC or FDIC. It is anticipated that the contracting process will be streamlined in the coming year or two, making it even easier for individuals and firms to get work with these agencies.

A key part of the registration package you will complete is a Fitness and Integrity Certification form (see Exhibit 11). Among the questions asked:

- Are you a convicted felon?
- Are you in default on loans exceeding $50,000 at any insured S&L, bank, or credit union?
- Have you caused any type of loss to the Federal Deposit Insurance Corporation fund (which insures bank and S&L deposits)?
- Have you been banned by the government from working at a bank or S&L?

A "yes" response to any of these questions will automatically eliminate you from ever working for the RTC or FDIC. This also applies to *any* of your employees.

A note here: The government relies solely on your responses to these questions. After filing a contract registration form you will not be investigated. However, once you bid on a contract and become a finalist then the government will actually investigate the veracity of your answers. If you lie on the registration form, the RTC will boot you automatically. Just ask the Ralph Edgar Group Inc., in Lake Geneva, Wisconsin. A real estate manager, REGI had been an RTC contractor for about six months. When the RTC inspector general's (IG) office began auditing the firm it discovered that REGI had allegedly caused an $80,000 loss at a failed S&L. This alleged indiscretion was not listed on the company's registration form and REGI was shown the door.

In another case in 1992 the giant real estate management firm of Cushman & Wakefield was barred for six months from doing any work for the RTC after it was learned that one of its contract appraisers had once had a brush with a failed thrift. Everyone agreed that the use of the appraiser was an oversight and that otherwise Cushman & Wakefield had an unblemished record with the RTC. Nevertheless, the sentence was carried out—no new RTC contracts for six months.

Slow to get started, the RTC's Office of Inspector General (IG) is now up and running. Its goal is to audit and investigate as many RTC contractors as possible. So take the disclosure process seriously. The RTC sure does.

Question: What if I fill out the contract registration form honestly, win a contract, and then later on I discover one of my employees was responsible for a bad loan at a failed S&L?

Answer: In the RTC's eyes ignorance is not an excuse. If you're thinking of contracting with either agency, screen all your employees for their ties to any failed S&Ls or banks. Remember Cushman & Wakefield.

The only way to please the RTC when it discovers that one of your employees is an alleged S&L wrongdoer is to dismiss that person immediately. Then and only then can you apply for reinstatement as a contractor.

BIDDING ON CONTRACTS

When an RTC consolidated office needs a job done that it cannot accomplish with its own staff it sends out a Solicitation of Service (SOS) to every contractor on its regional contractor source list (see Exhibits 12–18). If you have not registered with that particular consolidated office or did not check off the box for that particular job category, you will not receive an SOS. (Previously the RTC had a national contractor data base but it was scrapped in favor of having each consolidated office keep its own local list.)

By law the RTC must use competitive bidding when selecting contractors. To date there has been little evidence of favoritism in the contracting process. There have been lots of cases of sour grapes when someone loses a bid but little in the way of proof that someone's brother-in-law was awarded a sweetheart contract. When sending out an SOS the RTC must solicit at least ten qualified contractors for bids. Many SOS's will also appear in the *Wall Street Journal* classifieds.

What to Bid? How Much Can I Make?

There is no easy answer to the question: How much can I make? The RTC does not reveal how much it's willing to pay for you to manage, say,

RESOLUTION TRUST CORPORATION

SOLICITATION OF SERVICES NO. _____

[Date]

Attention:_____
_____
_____

Re: Solicitation of Services for
      Asset Management and Disposition

Dear Prospective Offeror:

        Resolution Trust Corporation ("RTC") is seeking proposals from
qualified respondents to assist in the management and disposition of certain
assets owned by RTC. Your firm has been selected among others to submit a
proposal in a competitive format, as outlined in the enclosed Solicitation of
Services. The Solicitation is non-transferable.

        If your firm wishes to participate in this Solicitation, please
execute and return the enclosed Confidentiality Agreement on or before
_____ to:

        Resolution Trust Corporation
        A t t e n t i o n :   _
        _____
        _____
        _____

If RTC receives your executed Confidentiality Agreement on or before that
date, it will send you confidential materials describing the Initial Pool of
Assets in the portfolio as to which services are requested.   Proposals
responsive to this Solicitation must be received by Noon, Eastern Standard
Time, _____.

                            RESOLUTION TRUST CORPORATION

                            By: '_____
                            Title:_____

Enclosures

EXHIBIT 12.   Sample Asset Management Application Form.

224

RESOLUTION TRUST CORPORATION

SOLICITATION OF SERVICES
TO ASSIST IN
ASSET MANAGEMENT AND DISPOSITION

I.   INTRODUCTION

    A.   Overview. Resolution Trust Corporation ("RTC") is
soliciting proposals from qualified respondents to assist in the
management and disposition of certain assets owned by RTC. The
services RTC requires are described in RTC's Asset Management and
Disposition Agreement (the "Agreement"), which is attached as
Exhibit 1 to this Solicitation. If you submit a proposal, you
must accept the Agreement in its entirety, without modification,
and the terms of your proposal will be incorporated by reference
in the Agreement. By submitting a proposal, you agree to perform
the Agreement according to its terms if RTC accepts your offer
during the Acceptance Period defined below.

    B.   Amendments to Solicitation. You should
acknowledge receipt of any amendments to this Solicitation by (a)
signing and returning a copy of the amendment to the RTC office
publishing this Solicitation; or (b) by acknowledging receipt of
the amendment by letter or telegram. RTC must receive the
acknowledgement of any amendment by the time specified for
receipt of proposals.

    C.   Offerors Conference. This Solicitation provides
you with sufficient information to prepare a proposal. In order
to provide a forum for questions and to ensure equal opportunity
and knowledge for all offerors, RTC will hold an Offerors
Conference at _____
on _____, 199_ at ____.m. ("Conference").   You and other
offerors are limited to two attendees per firm at the Conference.
If you wish to attend the Conference, please submit the names of
the attendees from your firm to _____
by _____, 1990.

    RTC will respond to questions or requests for
clarification regarding the engagement only at the Conference.
Please submit any questions or clarifications you wish to have
addressed at the Conference in writing to _____ at the
above address by _____, 199_. RTC will respond to additional
questions at the Conference.

    You should be aware that an RTC Specialist familiar
with the Assets subject to the Agreement will attend the
Conference to explain the bases for the Estimated Recovery Values
established for Assets in the Initial Pool of Assets. If you
elect not to attend the Conference, you will be deemed to have
waived any objection based on your not having had access to
information provided at the Conference.

225

TO:

FROM:

DATE:

RE: Conflict of Interest Guidance for SOS No._____

In the interest of maintaining complete objectivity in this evaluation proceeding, I need to be sure that you do not have interests which might conflict with your duties in connection therewith.

You should keep in mind that a conflict of interest situation may exist where your private interests (including previous employment) conflict or raise a reasonable question of conflict with your duties and responsibilities. The potential conflict is of concern whether it is real or apparent.

The purpose of this memorandum is to request that you review on a continuing basis your situation and if you identify any financial and/or employment interest related to yourself, your spouse, minor child or dependent(s) which may create a conflict of interest or the appearance thereof in the context of your duties and responsibilities as a member or advisor to this panel, you should notify the chairperson immediately. In reviewing your situation, you should ask yourself the following questions:

1.   Have I, or my spouse, minor children, or dependent(s) (hereinafter "family"), been connected as an employee, officer, owner, director, member, trustee, partner, advisor, or consultant to any of the organizations to be solicited or those who submit proposals, or do I, or my family, have any continuing financial interests through a pension or retirement plan, shared income, or other arrangement as a result of any current or prior employment or business or professional association?

2.   Am I or my family now negotiating or do I or my family have any arrangement concerning prospective employment with any proposer?

3.   Do I or my family have any financial interest through the ownership of stock, stock options, bonds, securities, or other arrangements including trust, in any proposer?

EXHIBIT 13.   Sample Conflict of Interest Memorandum.

4. The undersigned as a member of the Technical Proposal
    Evaluation Committee, hereby acknowledges the notification
    that he/she is subject to Federal statutes relating to
    conflicts of interest and the regulations promulgated
    thereunder, as more particularly set out at Part 336, FDIC
    Circular 2410.2, entitled "Employees Responsibilities and
    Conduct" and 18 U.S.C. 201-209.

If you believe that no present conflict of interest exists, please
complete the attached agreement and return it to the chairperson
promptly.

SUMMARY RATING SHEET FOR SOS NO._____

ENTITLED

_____

Proposer:_____ Evaluator:_____ Date:_____

Evaluation Criteria: Element Weight x Numerical Rating = Points Rating

A. <u>Technical Performance of the Process</u> (30%)

    1. Adequacy of management personnel to
       effectively supervise the professional
       staff.   10% x _____ = _____

    2. Adequacy of professional staff to perform. 7% x _____ = _____

    3. Adequacy of support personnel to effectively
       perform the required work.   6% x _____ = _____

    4. Adequacy of clerical staff to support
       technical and management personnel.   3% x _____ = _____

    5. Acceptability of proposed management system
       to timely resolve problems.   2% x _____ = _____

    6. Adequacy of supporting equipment to perform
       over the entire duration of the contract. 2% x _____ = _____

B. <u>Soundness, Completeness, and Thoroughness of the
Proposal in Complying with the Major Tasks of the
Statement of Work</u> (20%)

    Project planning, engineering and design,
    procurement placement, installation and shakedown,
    test plan formulation, test plan implementation/
    process operation, process evaluation, and
    equipment and process removal.   20% x _____ = _____

EXHIBIT 14.   Sample Evaluation Form. From time to time management contractors will be evaluated by the RTC. This form helps the agency determine the quality of the work being performed by contractors.

C. <u>Key Personnel, Project Management, Corporate</u>
    <u>Resources, and Related Corporate Experience</u>
    <u>as They Pertain to This Project</u> (50%)

    1. Qualifications and experience of key personnel
        to be assigned to the project and the
        effectiveness of the proposed project
        management system.   25% x _____ = _____

    2. Corporate resources and related corporate
        experience of the proposing organization
        in related projects.   25% x _____ = _____

    TOTAL   100% x _____ = _____

D. Bonus Points for M/WOB   _____ = _____

    SEE SCORING PLAN FOR EXPLANATION OF NUMERICAL RATINGS.

229

TO: Technical Evaluation Panel Members

FROM:

DATE:

RE: Confidentiality Agreement - Proposal Evaluation for
             SOS No._____

In order to ensure the confidentiality of financial and technical
data which may be submitted by proposers under the subject
solicitation, you are requested to sign the following agreement and
promptly return this memorandum to the chairperson of your panel.

AGREEMENT

In anticipation of my participation as a member of, or advisor to,
the panel formed to evaluate proposals submitted in response to
SOS, I agree that I will not disclose any information during the
proceeding of the evaluation concerning the evaluation to anyone
who is not also participating in the same proceedings and then only
to the extent that such information is required in connection with
such proceedings. Subsequent to the conclusion of the panel's
activities, I further agree not to disclose any information in
connection with said proceedings except as authorized and/or
permitted by RTC concerning this action on the panel's composition
and activities direct to me from any source outside the panel.

_____   _____
Date   Name/Title

EXHIBIT 15. Sample Confidentiality Agreement. Before you can bid on a government contract the RTC or FDIC will ask that you sign a confidentiality statement.
The statement helps the government maintain the integrity of the contracting
process and protect the asset(s) you might manage.

AGREEMENT

This is to advise that to the best of my knowledge and belief, I have no current conflict of interest which may interfere with my assignment and I agree to report promptly any such conflict of which I become aware.

_____   _____
Date   Name/Title

```
XYZ Management
Attention_____
Address
City, State, Zip Code

     Re:  Proposal for Property Management Services
          (Receivership)/(Property Name)
          RTC Asset No. _____

Dear _____:

RTC appreciates the time you have taken to prepare and submit your recent
proposal to provide property management services for the referenced asset.
After reviewing all the proposals submitted, a decision was made to select
another contractor.

Although RTC attempts to include as many firms in its contractor selection
process, obviously, only one contractor can be selected.  If you want to
discuss the basis of our selection, please send a written letter to my
attention within three business days upon receipt of this letter.  Upon
receipt of your written request, we will schedule a conference to review your
proposal and our selection process.

Since our firm remains on our contractor data base as a potential contractor,
you may receive solicitations of services on other properties.  Your future
participation will very much be appreciated.

Thank you for your interest in working with RTC.

Sincerely,

RESOLUTION TRUST CORPORATION


By: _____
    Regional Contract Specialist

cc:  RTC Representative
```

EXHIBIT 16. Sample Letter for Unsuccessful Proposals. If you are rejected after bidding on an RTC contract the agency will send you a rejection notice. The notice is merely a formality. After being rejected you can bid again on other contracts.

PURPOSE

The Resolution Trust Corporation's (RTC) Contractor Selection and Engagement policy and procedures are intended to provide every contractor with a fair and equal opportunity to provide contract services relating to RTC assets. One important aspect of the policy is that contract awards are made on the basis of competitive proposals solicited from several interested contractors, spreading the proposal opportunities among as many different qualified contractors as possible. Because each asset is uniquely different, the expertise and qualifications required for a specific assignment may vary greatly. Our experience, however, shows that most contractors while promoting themselves as a full service firm, have limited areas of true expertise. Many of the contractors interested in providing services to RTC are unfamiliar with the federal procurement process or with the selection process used by RTC. Because of their unfamiliarity, many of these contractors believing they are the most qualified for the engagement, assume the selection was made on grounds other than expertise and qualifications. So that these contractors do not become frustrated or disgruntled with RTC, it is important that they fully understand the process used to evaluate their proposal. For such contractors, a debriefing conference is the best is the best way to explain this selection process and offer comments and suggestions for improving future contracting opportunities.

GUIDELINES

Once a final decision is made as to who is to be awarded the contract, all other contractors submitting unsuccessful proposals should be given written notice of the contract award. The written notice should thank them for their interest in offering their services to RTC and for their time and effort in preparing their proposal. If desired, the notice can specify the contractor selected. The notice should also offer the contractor an opportunity to review, in person or by telephone, the RTC Contractor Selection Process and possible reasons why their proposal was unsuccessful. This is best accomplished by giving the contractor a set time period (within 3 days of their receipt of the notice) within which to send written notice to the RTC Regional Contract Specialist of their desire for a debriefing conference. The debriefing can then be set up to fit his or her schedule and that of the appropriate RTC Representative.

These guidelines merely establish a general frame work for a debriefing conference. There are many items which can and should be discussed with the contractor. At the same time, there are many items which clearly should not be discussed during the debriefing conference. A suggested agenda for the conference is set forth below:

EXHIBIT 17. Guidelines for debriefing unsuccessful contractors.

233

<u>INSTRUCTIONS FOR COMPLETING THE PROPOSAL EVALUATION WORKSHEET</u>

<u>SAMPLE PROPOSAL EVALUATION WORKSHEET</u>
<u>(ATTACHMENT 3 TO COMPETITIVE BID MEMORANDUM)</u>

WORKSHEET FOR

<u>OFFICIAL USE ONLY</u>

EVALUATOR:____John Doe_____

FIRM: ABC Corporation

DATE:_____

EVALUATION CRITERA: A: Technical
                        Performance of the
                        Process (30)

EVALUATION SCORE:

(10,8,5,2,0):____300_____

Strengths: (1) Excellent upper management;

                (2) Demonstrated understanding of the statement of work;

                (3) Unique methodology

Weaknesses: (1) Workflow monitoring not indicated;

                (2) No discussion of emergency handling;

                (3) Minor training deficiencies of key personnel.

Correctable Weaknesses: (1) Request work flow chart;

                (2) How will emergency situations be processed?;

                (3) Schedule training for key personnel.

Uncorrectable Weaknesses: None

Desired Clarification or Substantiation: (1) Provide detailed work flow
     with names and responsibilities;

  (2) Provide written procedures for emergencies along with alternates who
       are responsible;

  (3) Provide details of training; i.e., inhouse, outside source, when,
       course description, etc.

EXHIBIT 18.   RTC personnel are asked to use this form as guidance in evaluating contract bids.

234

a hotel or a portfolio of loans. The agency generally asks for a flat fee bid, or on smaller jobs, a time and materials bid. If your bid is the lowest it doesn't necessarily mean you win the SAMDA contract. The RTC awards contracts based on cost, but it also analyzes a registrant's experience and technical skills. Supposedly, both are weighted equally. (Prior RTC experience is not a prerequisite for bidding.)

What you eventually bid on a contract depends on your assessment of your hourly costs and other overhead. During the RTC's first two years some contractors walked away with fat contracts that allowed them huge profit margins. With the agency's IG office watching every penny now and Congress just waiting for news that someone got rich off the RTC, pork barrel contracts are becoming rare. But there is plenty of honest work out there and the RTC is prepared to pay an honest wage.

There are a number of ways to make these contracts work for you or your company. Some SAMDA contractors decide to break even on the management part of the contract and to make their profit on the disposition fee when the property is sold, since they can receive fees for *both* management and disposition functions. Ideally you should be able to make a profit on both. It all depends on who you are bidding against and what their bidding strategy is. Don't underbid. You could wind up losing money, or at best breaking even. Remember, SAMA contractors do not get a disposition fee. All their money is made on management fees. If you are only bidding to manage RTC properties, bid accordingly. You will not make any disposition income to compensate for management losses.

The amount of money you can make depends on the size and type of the asset. Here's a sampling of contractors, the fees they make, and the book value of assets under management. (Book value is what an asset is listed for on the balance sheet of an insolvent institution. Market value is often significantly *lower*.)

Company	Fees	Book Value of Asset
J.E. Robert	$55 million	$3.12 billion
Coopers & Lybrand	$32 million	$753 million
Northcorp Realty	$30 million	$1.285 billion
FGB Realty	$16 million	$1.091 billion

Many contractors that work for the government are privately held and are not listed on any public stock exchanges. Therefore it is impossible to tell you how much of a profit they are making off their RTC contracts because neither they nor the RTC will disclose that information. Still, the estimated contractor fees available from the RTC in the agency's public reading room in Washington, D.C., reveal that as of the beginning of 1992, of more than one hundred major RTC contractors reviewed each was making $3 million or more in fees from the government.

It is assumed that the larger a contract the greater the economy of scale involved. Companies that manage and service loans know that it takes the same number of computers and personnel to manage one thousand loans as it does five thousand loans. Realtors that list properties for the RTC can receive up to a 5 percent commission on one- to four-family residences. On large commercial properties for which the sales price runs into the millions, sales commissions as a percentage of the sales price are scaled back as the price goes up.

A rare glimpse of how much a contractor can make comes from a Government Accounting Office (GAO)[3] audit done on the RTC's Denver office. In 1991 the RTC hired the Financial Management Task Force (FMTF), a Denver consulting firm specializing in audits of financial institutions, to audit the assets of ninety-two failed S&Ls. The RTC paid FMTF $51 per hour to audit the financial records and books of the ninety-two institutions. In turn FMTF paid its ninety-eight employees hourly rates of $14 to $45. According to the GAO, ninety-three of the ninety-eight (95 percent) employees were paid hourly rates of $25 or less.

FMTF's total take on the contract? More than $20 million. Its gross profit, according to GAO, was almost 30 percent. GAO wasn't crazy about this and neither was Congress, but FMTF certainly was. Are more great deals like this available? Here and there, perhaps, but the RTC has tightened up its cost accounting and contracting procedures and "killings" like this are now few and far between. But contractors we talked to said you can still make a healthy profit from the RTC. The key is watching your costs and not underbidding.

In case you're wondering, the RTC will reimburse contractors for all

---

[3] GAO is the auditing arm of the Congress of the United States.

travel and travel-related expenses tied to the job. Have receipts available and be prepared to prove that such travel is related to your contract with the government. On one RTC contract a New York accounting firm billed the government $662,000 for travel. Another firm, based in South Bend, Indiana, billed the agency $690,000. The bills were paid, but were later scrutinized by the IG's office.

When the RTC puts out a call for help with an SOS the process starts with the RTC consolidated office. When a given RTC consolidated office needs something done it calls RTC headquarters in Washington. Washington then sends out a notice to all available contractors that a contract is available and describes the work. Qualifying contractors are invited to make a bid for the job.

Most of the time the winning bidder is chosen by the consolidated office that "let" the contract. Each contract's guidelines can differ, but at last check, if a contract's dollar value is $100,000 or less the consolidated office can approve it without referring the matter to Washington. Larger winning contract bids are sent to Washington for approval. Most multimillion-dollar contracts will wind up on the desk of the Chair of the RTC.

It should take a maximum of ninety days to approve a contract. If you win a contract your paycheck will come directly from the RTC in Washington even though the work is being done for one of the consolidated offices.

WHAT'S AN MWOB AND WHY SHOULD YOU CARE?

MWOB stands for Minority or Woman Owned Business and offers such businesses a leg up on the competition. The Financial Institutions Reform, Recovery and Enforcement Act of 1989 (FIRREA), which bailed out the S&L industry, mandated that the agency be more progressive in giving women and minorities a chance to compete with the J.E. Roberts and IBMs of the world, akin to affirmative action hiring. So far no one has raised a big stink about the MWOB program. And it became the law of the land when President Bush signed FIRREA into law.

MWOBs are automatically awarded extra points that count toward the RTC's decision to hire a contractor when several bids are close. As noted, all contracts are determined by cost and technical skill of the firms bidding. But right from the start an MWOB firm receives 5 additional points on the RTC's cost evaluation and ten additional points on the technical evaluation. All contracts are awarded on a point system in which points are given based on experience and bid cost. The more points a company gains, the greater its chance of winning a contract.

To achieve MWOB status a firm must be at least 51 percent owned by a minority or a woman. If you fake it or lie and get caught by the IG's office you lose your contract instantly. It has already happened once to a firm "controlled" by the wife of its true owner.

CONTRACTOR TIP. *MWOBs that don't have all the skills needed to contract with the government can form a joint venture with a non-MWOB firm and bid on work together. The RTC awards joint ventures extra points toward contract consideration as long as the MWOB partner manages 25 percent of the joint venture's business.*

Who in the RTC's eyes is a minority? According to its own regulations any American who is of African, American Indian, Asian, Hispanic, Alaskan Native, or Pacific Islander descent is a minority for MWOB purposes. When in doubt, ask the consolidated office. Gays are not considered minorities. Keep in mind that under the liberal-minded Clinton administration more contracts will be steered to MWOBs.

THE FDIC AND CONTRACTING

The FDIC's contracting office functions in a similar manner but so far hasn't had the kind of need for contractors as the RTC. This too is changing as more banks fail. If you find RTC contracting too competitive you might consider trying the FDIC. Your chances of winning and obtaining a better deal could be greater.

Currently the FDIC awards most of its contracts through its headquarters in Washington. But the agency is trying to decentralize and by the time you read this many of its smaller contracts will be awarded by its regional and consolidated offices. (Remember, under the FDIC's structure the regional offices oversee the consolidated offices.)[4]

When the FDIC needs a contractor it sends out a nationwide Request for Proposal, or RFP. The RFP is akin to the RTC's solicitation of services request. The FDIC has a central source list of contractors it draws on to send RFPs. On occasion it coordinates with the RTC's contracting office on projects. But for the most part you must reregister with the FDIC to bid on its contracts. Just because you're an RTC-approved contractor doesn't mean your name automatically goes into the FDIC's data base. It's a pain, but if you want its business, register.

FIRST, WE HIRE ALL THE LAWYERS

Shakespeare may not have liked lawyers very much, but the government apparently loves them. The S&L and banking bailouts may be the best thing to happen to the legal profession since the invention of the United States judicial system. The S&L bailout bill, FIRREA, is often mockingly referred to as the "Lawyers Relief Act of 1989" because of all the job opportunities it created for the legal community. In 1990 and 1991 the RTC and FDIC paid private law firms more than $1.5 billion (yes, *billion*) in fees to handle a variety of chores. About thirty different law firms made $2.5 million dollars or more in fees from the two agencies in 1991 alone. What are these law firms doing for the government? Everything from foreclosures and asset seizures to investigations and civil complaints. The biggest profit center, though, is clearly in the area of civil litigation.

When an S&L or bank fails the RTC or FDIC hires a private law firm to see if it can sue any of the S&L's former officers or directors for negligence, fraud, dereliction of duties, and so on. Since 1985 the government has filed hundreds of lawsuits against alleged S&L and bank wrongdoers for contributing to the failure of a financial institution. Thou-

---

[4] Real estate brokers trying to get listings from the FDIC should approach the agency's consolidated offices. The commission paid is negotiable but should be similar to what the RTC is paying. (As we noted in an earlier chapter, HUD pays real estate brokers up to a 6 percent commission on single-family homes.)

sands of former S&L managers, and even real estate developers, have been targeted for damages by private law firms working for the RTC and FDIC.[5]

HOW MUCH CAN I MAKE AS A CONTRACT LAWYER?

The most profitable area for contract lawyers is in civil litigation. As a rule the RTC and FDIC hire entire law firms, rather than individual attorneys. Litigation cases are labor-intensive and take up hundreds, even thousands, of work hours. However, one lawyer working as a litigation specialist can find work with either agency working on fairly narrow cases or cases involving very small institutions, chasing down deadbeats, or unscrambling contract disputes.

The RTC and FDIC will pay hourly rates of anywhere from $100 to $400 to bring deadbeats and wrongdoers to the bargaining table—or to justice—whichever comes first. The New York law firm of Cravath Swaine and Moore made $12 million in one year pressing the RTC and FDIC's civil case against former Drexel Burnham Lambert junk bond king Michael Milken. (Cravath's regular hourly rate is $600, but the FDIC reportedly negotiated the price down to $450 per hour, offering the firm incentive clauses on the amount of money the government recovered in the case.)

Currently both agencies cap the annual fees a law firm can charge the government at $2.5 million. Waivers are frequently granted, especially if your firm is handling a large damage claim as in the government's case against Milken or former Lincoln Savings owner Charles Keating, Jr.

If you're a lawyer and civil litigation is your forte, the RTC and FDIC can keep you gainfully employed for the next decade. Although 90 percent or so of all civil defendants settle out of court with the government, cases must be investigated and lawsuits must be filed. (The

---

[5] The government has promised to leave no stone unturned in the S&L and banking debacles. Even Neil Bush, the son of President Bush, and Arizona Governor Fife Symington—both former S&L directors—have been sued for their alleged roles in savings and loan failures. Lincoln Savings former owner Charles Keating is being sued for over $1 billion by the law firm of Morrison & Hecker, which is working for the FDIC.

government has to sue before it can settle.) Most RTC and FDIC cases last anywhere from two to five years, some even longer, depending on the complexity of the charges.

Private investigators that work for law firms can do quite well by latching on to FDIC and RTC work. Who do you think does all the dirty work for lawyers? You think well-dressed lawyers sit in a car staking out a subject's recoverable assets? No way. That's "PI" work—short for private investigator. Ditto goes for paralegals. Lawyers don't do the grunt work. Paralegals, also known as legal assistants, are the ones with the dirt under their nails.

To become a contract lawyer you must first be approved by the agencies' Washington offices. Most of the usual contracting and conflict of interest rules that apply to other contractors apply to lawyers as well—even more so. If your law firm or any of its partners or associates have been sued by the government for contributing to an S&L or bank failure, close the book right here. You are disqualified. Besides former officers and directors, the government is going out of its way to sue law firms and accountants that aided and abetted S&L and bank criminals.

All civil litigation work is approved by the RTC or FDIC in Washington. The consolidated offices do not play much of a role in overseeing civil litigation. Lawyers who specialize in real estate foreclosure matters and the seizing of assets will be subject to a certain degree of oversight from the closest consolidated office.

A note to minorities and women: If your law firm is 51 percent owned by a woman or minority, the RTC offers extra points toward qualifying you for government legal work. The RTC program for lawyers is called MWOLF, meaning your shop is a Minority or Woman Owned Law Firm. Most of the rules that apply to the MWOB program apply here.

CAN I GET A "STAFF" JOB WITH THE RTC OR FDIC IN MY AREA?

The news here isn't promising. Staff jobs working directly for the RTC or FDIC are becoming impossible to get. As part of its effort to cut down on bureaucratic red tape, the RTC is trying to use as many private-sector firms as possible to manage and sell assets, eliminating the need for staff employees. Ditto for the FDIC.

If you're looking for S&L and bank cleanup related employment your best bet is to latch onto a firm that is already doing contract work for the government. Some government-approved contractors subcontract certain chores such as security jobs or construction. You can also form your own company and register with the RTC and FDIC to find work that way. (The irony of working for the RTC and FDIC in liquidations is that the better the job you do the quicker you'll be out of work.)

In March 1992 the RTC decided to cut more government red tape and announced plans to eliminate many of its twenty or so regional offices. By the beginning of this year (1994) the RTC will have just six regional offices. The FDIC hopes to eliminate many of its regional offices by 1996. Stripping away another level of bureaucracy is good news for buyers of government-owned real estate and loans but not such good news for those looking for staff jobs. It's good news for SAMDA contractors, though, because stripping away another level of government increases the likelihood that more contractors will be used. (Choose your silver lining.)

In the name of fiscal conservatism, the President and Congress do not want the RTC and FDIC staff to grow any more than it has to. Using more and more private contractors is the wave of the future.

A word of warning: Congress hates the RTC with a passion. Because Congress—along with Presidents Bush and Reagan—created the S&L mess by deregulating the industry, it now wants nothing to do with the agency except to grandstand when it finds something wrong with it. (The last thing in the world you will see is a member of Congress saying what a great job the RTC is doing.)

Still, if you can land one, staff positions at both agencies pay well. Here's a sampling of job openings with the agencies in 1992:

Job Title	Agency	Salary Range
Associate Director of Resolutions (Washington, D.C.)	FDIC	$88,000 to $99,000
Site Sales Coordinator (Somerset, N.J.)	RTC	$77,000 to $88,000
Freedom of Information Act Specialist (Atlanta)	RTC	$41,000 to $53,000

Both agencies hire Government Grade (GG) and Liquidation Grade (LG) employees. If you have a choice—and you probably won't—try to get a job as a GG employee. In five years both agencies will be downsizing, the RTC more than the FDIC. LGs (those more directly involved with liquidations) will be laid off first. GGs are less likely to be fired and are considered career employees who have the option of retiring with the agency if they so choose.

A lawyer likely can make more money in financial-institution-related work in the private sector, but the RTC and FDIC offer decent pay and excellent benefits, including paid medical and dental. A child care program is being considered as well. This is, after all, a government job.

REAL ESTATE AGENTS

The RTC already employs thousands of real estate agents across the country. These agents are given listings of RTC properties in their area to expose these properties to the open market. Realtors are paid a 5 percent sales commission if the property sells during the listing period.

To get on the RTC's list of approved real estate agents you must first fill out the RTC registration form and mail it back to Washington. After that is done you should call the consolidated office near you and make personal contact to let them know you are registered and eager to do a good job for them.

The RTC also uses real estate brokers when they need an independent assessment of value for a property. These "opinions of value" are issued by realtors rather than licensed appraisers, and the RTC will pay you for writing up such an opinion of value.

APPRAISERS

If you've read much of this book, you already know that the RTC's rules require it to perform *a lot* of appraising. To get all these appraisals done in a timely manner the RTC needs to hire private-sector appraisers. The government now requires appraisers doing work for federally insured financial institutions and federal agencies to be certified in the state in which they work. If you have not gotten your certification yet don't even apply to the RTC. Do that first, then fill out the RTC registration form and send it to Washington along with a copy of your state certification. Also contact your nearest consolidated office and make personal contact.

CERTIFIED PUBLIC ACCOUNTANTS

The RTC and FDIC use outside accountants to help analyze bids submitted in sealed-bid offerings. Accountants are hired to do net present value analysis of each bid and compare the results with other similar bids in order to advise the RTC and FDIC on which of similar bids offers the agency the most cash value.

LICENSED CONTRACTORS

Not all the properties the RTC and FDIC end up with are ready for the market. Some are projects that have either fallen into serious disrepair or were never completed to begin with. In such cases the RTC may decide it is in its best interest to complete the project before trying to market it and will hire a contractor to do the work. In other cases contractors are hired to simply maintain large projects while they are being marketed.

LAW ENFORCEMENT

The S&L scandal has created job opportunities for law enforcement officials. Approved by Congress and signed by President Reagan in 1982, S&L deregulation[6] legislation led to the white-collar looting of many of the nation's S&Ls. Real estate and loan scams that occurred as far back as five years ago are just now being investigated by the Federal Bureau of Investigation and Justice Department. The statute of limitation on these cases runs for ten years.

Currently there are more than nine thousand open cases of S&L and bank fraud being pursued by the FBI and a backlog of some twenty-eight

[6] The S&L industry was deregulated by passage of the Garn–Germain Act of 1982. The landmark legislation allowed S&Ls to go outside their traditional turf of home mortgage lending. Many of the new powers granted facilitated risky and fraudulent lending.

thousand criminal referrals yet to be investigated. If you're an accountant and don't want to work for the RTC or FDIC, try the FBI. Congress has allocated millions of extra dollars per year to prosecute S&L and bank wrongdoers. The FBI is literally drowning in bank fraud cases. If there was ever a career opportunity, this is it. Congress has allotted an additional $70 million to the FBI specifically targeted at bank fraud investigations. The agency is actively recruiting accountants and lawyers to follow paper trails and question suspects. The maximum age of applicants is thirty-five because the agency has a mandatory retirement age of fifty-five.

Special bank fraud task forces have already been formed in Boston, Dallas, Los Angeles, and Tampa. New task forces in other cities will be formed during the next two years. In particular New England, Southern California, and Washington, D.C., are expected to be "hot spots" for FBI hiring.

Conclusion

• •

Now you know more than you ever thought you'd care to know about buying assets from failed banks, S&Ls, and HUD. The purpose of this book is to demystify the process and to unlock this opportunity for every size investor—from the average citizen with little to invest up to the wealthy entrepreneur or portfolio manager. After all, each of us is paying the tab for the disaster; we should all have an equal crack at profiting from it as well.

Of course the old adage "Those who got, am those who get" will continue to function despite this book. The rich will get richer off the bank and S&L mess—which, ironically, some of those very tycoons helped create. But never mind, life has never been fair and it's not getting any better. But the fat cats are not interested in the small properties that clutter the RTC and FDIC's portfolio. They will continue to gobble up the multimillion-dollar resorts, golf courses, hotels, apartment complexes, and shopping centers. That will leave the individual homes, building lots, small farms, small shops, duplexes, fourplexes, sixplexes, and so on for you. And since the big investors aren't buying these properties, the RTC, FDIC, and HUD have little choice but to deal with you.

These two giant bureaucracies—the FDIC and RTC—are forever reshuffling their organizational cards, so things will change from time to time. The FDIC will inevitably become more and more like the RTC as time goes on. If you call a number in our Yellow Pages only to find the number disconnected, call the main toll-free number and select the asset specific line. When the human being comes on the line tell him or her what you want and you'll be told what consolidated office to call. This isn't the purpose of the asset specific line, but it's the quickest way to get an answer. If that doesn't work you'll have to make a toll call to the RTC in Washington—Main Office, Public Affairs—202-416-7566.

And one last time—though this book may help you "get rich quick," we make no such claim. The deals are there, but you will work and work hard to get your hands on them. Those individuals we met who have bought several pieces of property from these agencies have dedicated nearly full time to the task, had ten disappointments for every success, and have almost thrown in the towel more than once. But they didn't. They kept calling, kept looking, and kept making bids, and eventually the law of averages worked in their favor. So think of this book as a tool chest—not a treasure chest.

Now it's up to you. You can sit around and complain about the mess politicians made of the economy, particularly the banks and thrifts, or get out there and take advantage of that mess. It's your choice—the cloud or the silver lining. Which will it be?

Good hunting and good luck!

Glossary of Terms

. . . .

(RTC and FDIC related terms in *BOLD.)

ACCELERATION CLAUSE: A clause in a loan document that allows the lender to call the note, requesting payment in full based on certain predefined guidelines.

ACCOMMODATION PARTY: A person who cosigns a loan but has no ownership rights.

ACKNOWLEDGMENT: A formal declaration made before a notary public or attorney by a person signing a document. The acknowledgment certifies that the person signing the document is indeed the person indicated as the signator. Acknowledgments are required on nearly all recorded documents.

AD VALOREM TAX: A tax levied by state and local governments on real estate. The tax is a factor of the value placed on the property by the taxing entity.

ADJUSTED COST BASIS: For tax purposes, adjusted cost basis is calculated by adding the amount paid for a property, plus the amount spent on improvements, less total depreciation taken against the property.

ADJUSTABLE RATE MORTGAGE (ARM): A mortgage on

which the interest rate varies based on a certain, predetermined index such as the Treasury yield.

*AFFORDABLE HOUSING PROGRAM: A special program in which the RTC must first offer all houses appraised at $67,500 or lower to low- and moderate-income home buyers. The FDIC has a similar program but has the discretion to raise the cap according to local housing prices. A low- to moderate-income home buyer makes 115 percent or less of an area's median income.

ALL-INCLUSIVE DEED OF TRUST: Also known as an all-inclusive mortgage, it "wraps" two or more mortgages against a property into one larger loan. See *Wrap-around Mortgage*.

ALTA TITLE INSURANCE POLICY: A comprehensive title insurance policy that protects the lender from unknown defects in title, such as mechanics' liens. ALTA is an abbreviation for American Land Title Association. Lenders generally require the borrower to pay the one-time cost for this coverage.

AMENITIES: Features that make a home or property desirable. A brick fireplace, a large backyard, good location, and a swimming pool all are amenities.

AMORTIZATION: A loan is considered amortizing if its payment schedule results in repayment of the loan, interest, and principal in equal installments over a set period of time.

ANNUAL PERCENTAGE RATE (APR): The true interest expense to the borrower per year. Federal law requires interest charged on loans to be disclosed as an annual percentage rate.

ANNUITY: A sum of money paid or received annually or at other fixed periods.

APPRAISAL: The estimate of a property's current market value. Also an estimate of value at a specified time or under specified circumstances.

*APPRAISED VALUE: As used by the RTC and FDIC, appraised value represents the most current value of an asset as reflected on a failed institution's balance sheet. In ordinary real estate terms the appraised value of a property is the value placed on it by a professional appraiser.

ASSESSED VALUE: Not to be confused with appraised value. The assessed value of a property is determined by a local tax assessor. It never equals the market value figure. Market value is almost always much greater than the assessed value. Buyers are forewarned that most assessors immediately reassess a property following its sale, raising the assessed value based on the new sales price. This results in increased property taxes.

*ASSET ACQUISITION DATE: Found on RTC and FDIC asset forms, it indicates the date the agency took the asset over from a failed institution.

*ASSET CODE: A three-digit number used by the FDIC and RTC to identify property taxes. The codes are used to choose the appropriate contractor or vendor to dispose of the property.

*ASSET LOCATION: The specific address of an asset (usually real estate), which is cataloged by the RTC by separate "fields" for street, city, county, state, and zip code. RTC asset searches on a personal computer can narrow a search by selecting any combination of these fields.

*ASSET NUMBER: Every individual asset acquired by the RTC is assigned its own asset number. Referring to an asset by its specific number assures that you and the RTC are talking about the same property.

*ASSET OWNERSHIP: On its asset forms the RTC breaks down ownership into several different types: 100 percent owned by the agency; sub-owned by a failed institution's affiliate; J/V-owned, meaning it was held by a joint venture in which the institution had a share; or other, for complex types of mixed ownership.

APPURTENANCE: Anything located on or belonging to the land: a building or road, for example.

ASSESSMENT: Fees placed on real property by local and county governments to pay for sewer, sidewalks, street lighting, roads, and other services. Some assessments are permanent, while others are one-time only charges called "special assessments."

ASSETS: Personal and real property owned.

ASSIGN: To transfer ownership or title in an asset to another party. When a person signs over his or her rights to a note, loan, or property, he or she "assigns" those rights to another.

ASSIGNEE: The person to whom title or ownership is transferred.

ASSIGNOR: The person transferring (giving up) the title or ownership.

ASSIGNMENT OF RENTS: Future rents from a piece of property can be assigned to a lender as additional security for a loan. Assignments are often added to the property's deed for security in the event of a default.

ASSUME: When a buyer accepts the loan obligations of the seller. When a buyer agrees to this he or she signs an assumption agreement with the lender acknowledging responsibility for the loan.

ATTORNEY IN FACT: Anyone legally authorized to conduct certain business in another's name.

*AVAIL: Abbreviation used on RTC and FDIC asset forms indicating that a property is still available.

*AUCT: Indicates that an RTC asset will be sold at auction.

BALANCE SHEET: A financial statement listing a person or company's assets and liabilities and showing net worth.

BALLOON PAYMENT: A short-term loan—usually five or seven years—on which the principal amount owed is due in one lump sum. Most payments on a balloon loan are interest only, with no principal paid.

BENEFICIARY: The person legally entitled to certain benefits. On a trust deed or note the beneficiary is a creditor (usually the lender) who is secured by the property.

BILL OF SALE: A document that transfers ownership or title of personal property in the same manner that a deed transfers title to real estate.

BLANKET MORTGAGE: A loan secured by more than one piece of property. Blanket mortgages or blanket loans often are used in subdivisions or when a certain property of a borrower is inadequate to secure a loan.

BOND: Both the government and corporations issue bonds. When a municipality issues a bond to pay for streets or other infrastructure costs, residents pay for the bonds through (usually) higher taxes.

*BOOK VALUE: The value of an asset as carried on the books of a financial institution. Book value may not equal market value, which may be higher. When the RTC and FDIC use this term they employ a narrow definition: "Gross value as of three months prior to the semiannual report date as stated on the trial balance sheet of the (failed) institution." (Go figure.)

BROKER: A person licensed by the state to sell real estate. Loan brokers offer mortgages to home buyers. Real estate brokers sell real estate.

*BULK: Indicates that the RTC has decided to include a particular asset in a bulk sale with other assets. Loans are often sold in this manner.

BUSINESS OPPORTUNITY: A legal term describing a business that is for sale. A business opportunity may or may not include real property. A business opportunity without real estate is appraised according to its income potential.

CALL: To declare a loan due and payable in full.

CAPITAL: Also called "net worth." A person or company's capital or net worth is calculated by adding all assets and subtracting all liabilities. The resulting figure is capital.

CAPITAL GAIN: The profit received after selling an asset (real estate, for example) after subtracting cost and improvements from the sales price.

CAPITALIZATION: A technique used to appraise income property by multiplying the estimated net income by an "x factor" representing the desired rate of return.

CASH FLOW: The difference between a property's total income and its total expenses, including mortgage payments. When the result is negative this is known as "negative cash flow."

CEASE AND DESIST ORDER: A legal order issued by the government ordering a property or business owner to cease an activity—such as polluting ground water. C&Ds, as they are known, are sometimes used when a property owner has violated zoning restrictions.

CERTIFICATE OF DISCHARGE: A written document signed by the lender discharging the security when the debt (loan or note) is satisfied. Also known as a release of mortgage.

CERTIFICATE OF SALE: A document issued to a buyer of property purchased at a court-ordered execution sale or judicial foreclosure. The holder can redeem it for a deed in the property if the owner of the property fails to redeem it within one year.

CHATTEL MORTGAGE: A mortgage on personal property (rather than real estate). Today the chattel mortgage has been largely replaced by security agreements.

CLOSING STATEMENT: A statement given to both buyer and seller by an attorney or escrow agent accounting for all monies involved in the sale, including fees, charges, cash down payments, and loans.

COLLATERAL: Any kind of property used to secure a loan.

*COMMERCIAL ASSET DESCRIPTION: RTC and FDIC data elements listed for commercial asset listings. This includes year built, land size, zoning, parking information, present rental or lease status, number of units, floors, elevators, and a short narrative description.

COMMITMENT: A promise by a lender to make a loan on a property. Commitments come in many forms: a firm commitment, a standby commitment, and a conditional commitment. A conditional commitment is a promise to make a loan if specified guidelines are met. A standby loan commitment is a written commitment made by a lender to fund a loan up to a certain limit if the borrower should need such a loan for a specified reason or property during a specified time period at predetermined terms.

COMMUNITY PROPERTY: Property jointly owned by a husband and wife. Community property does not belong to one or the other but to both.

COMPOUND INTEREST: Interest calculated on the outstanding principal and interest already accumulated.

CONDEMNATION: The government has the power to condemn private property under a variety of circumstances. This is called the "power of eminent domain." When the government condemns a property it takes it for some public purpose, such as the construction of a highway.

CONDITIONAL SALE CONTRACT: A contract in which the seller retains title to the property until the full purchase price is paid.

CONDOMINIUM: Ownership in a single unit or apartment with shared ownership in common areas, such as swimming pool, lawns, and parking areas.

*CONSERVATORSHIP: An S&L or bank that has been taken over by the government but remains open to the public. Conservatorships are considered "wards" of the government. Even though it is insolvent, a conservatorship still makes loans and takes deposits. Conservatorships are run by government-appointed managers.

CONSIDERATION: In real estate, consideration is another term for money or something else of value given to induce another to enter into a contract.

*CONSOLIDATED OFFICE: A localized office of the RTC or FDIC. One consolidated office covers many states. The RTC's mid-Atlantic consolidated office, for instance, sells assets in Georgia, Maryland, North Carolina, South Carolina, Tennessee, Virginia, West Virginia, and Washington, D.C.

CONSTRUCTION LOAN: A construction loan is a short-term loan that generally lasts for a year or so. Once the building is complete, the lender, or another party, replaces the construction loan with long-term financing, called a "take out loan."

CONTINGENCY: Any condition placed on a contract. Contingencies must be met before a contract becomes binding.

CONVENTIONAL LOAN: A loan made without government insurance or government guarantees.

CONVEYANCE: A document that transfers title or some other interest in property.

COOPERATIVE APARTMENT: A "co-op" is an investment in which the buyer owns a share in an apartment house and the right to occupy, rent, or resell a specific apartment unit or units.

COSIGNER: A person, not the borrower, who also signs on a note, thereby accepting joint responsibility for its repayment. A cosigner is used when the borrower's income or assets are not enough to qualify or secure the desired loan.

COST APPROACH: An appraisal technique that uses the cost of replacement to determine the value of a property.

COVENANT: A promise in a contract. Covenants and conditions

are often also part of a subdivision approval and bind future owners.

CREATIVE FINANCING: When a property cannot be sold through conventional means the buyer and seller often find creative ways to close the deal—such as having the seller carry the loan and then selling the loan to an investor later. The permutations are endless. If you resort to creative financing to buy or sell a property you may want to consult an attorney.

CREDITOR: The person to whom a debt is owed.

*CULTURAL VALUE: Some RTC properties are considered to have special cultural value. To attain this classification a property must have been built before 1941 and have some special significance to U.S. history, architecture, archeology, engineering, or culture.

*DATE OF CONSTRUCTION: The RTC and FDIC include approximate dates or construction on all their improved property asset forms.

DEBENTURES: Bonds not secured by mortgages or liens.

DEBT SERVICE: The amount of money the buyer will need each month to make interest or interest and principal payments on a loan.

DEBTOR: The person who owes a debt.

DEED: That instrument that transfers title in property from one person to another.

DEED OF RECONVEYANCE: A deed of trust that releases a lien once the loan is paid in full, conveying full title.

DEED OF TRUST: Transfers title in a property to a trustee who holds it until the loan is paid in full.

DEFAULT: Failure to repay an obligation or perform as agreed.

DEFERRED MAINTENANCE: Maintenance and repairs on a

property that are required but not completed. A lot of RTC properties suffer from some degree of deferred maintenance.

DEFICIENCY JUDGMENT: A court-ordered judgment for obligations not fully covered by the sale of the underlying security.

DEPARTMENT OF HOUSING AND URBAN DEVELOPMENT (HUD): A federal agency created to promote affordable housing. HUD also oversees the Federal Housing Administration, which insures mortgages for low- and moderate-income home buyers. HUD forecloses on delinquent FHA loans and sells the underlying collateral—a house.

DEPOSIT RECEIPT: A document used by real estate agents that functions as a temporary contract for the purchase and sale of real estate.

DEPRECIATION: The loss of value in an asset for any reason. Depreciation is a concern to income property owners who use it as a tax reduction tool.

DISCOUNT: Buying a note for less than its current unpaid balance is called buying a note at discount. Doing so can greatly increase the note's effective rate of return for the buyer.

DISCOUNT POINTS: Points or fees are charged by lenders to either offset a low interest rate or to boost the loan's effective yield. One point represents one percent of the principal amount of the loan.

DISCOUNT RATE: The interest rate charged by the Federal Reserve Bank for money borrowed by its members (banks). When the discount rate decreases it allows banks to lower rates for home loans and other consumer credit.

DUE-ON-SALE CLAUSE: A clause in a loan contract that allows the lender to require that a loan be paid in full when the property collateralizing it is sold.

*DUE DILIGENCE PACKAGE: A package of documents distributed by the RTC or its asset managers that gives bidders detailed information about a loan or piece of real estate.

EASEMENT: An interest one piece of property has in another property for a specified use. For example, a parcel may require a road or "right of way" through an adjoining parcel.

ECONOMIC LIFE: The period of time over which a property will yield a return on an investment.

ECONOMIC OBSOLESCENCE: When certain properties, particularly commercial and industrial properties, lose value over time due to decreased desirability or usefulness.

EFFECTIVE AGE: A judgment of age determined by the condition of a property rather than its chronological age. A poorly built "young" building can have a higher effective age than a well-built older structure.

EFFECTIVE INTEREST RATE: The actual interest rate paid by a borrower.

*ELIGIBLE SINGLE-FAMILY PROPERTY: A home that is a one- to four-family property. Five or more units connotes multi-family status.

EMINENT DOMAIN: See *Condemnation*.

ENCUMBER: To place obligations (encumbrances) against a piece of property.

ENCUMBRANCE: Anything that limits the ownership in a property. This includes loans secured by the property, liens, easements, or any kind of restriction that runs (remains with) the property.

ENDORSEMENT: The signature on the back of a note or check that transfers ownership.

EQUITABLE TITLE: A state of ownership the buyer possesses

after he or she has contracted to buy a property but before legal title has been conveyed.

EQUITY PARTICIPATION: When a lender takes partial ownership in a project on which it lends.

EQUITY: The value of the owner's interest in excess of all debt against a property.

ESCALATION CLAUSE: A clause in a loan that calls for the interest to increase over a period of time.

ESCROW: Payments and fees on a piece of property that are temporarily held until certain conditions are met—such as the sale of a piece of property. In the past attorneys acted as "escrow agents" in real estate transactions. Today this service is mostly performed by escrow and title companies.

EXTENSION AGREEMENT: An agreement to extend the original terms of a contract. For example, an extension may be granted by a lender extending the term of a loan. A seller may extend a sales contract, extending the time allowed for the deal to close.

*FEDERAL DEPOSIT INSURANCE CORPORATION (FDIC): The regulatory agency and insurance fund that oversees the nation's banks. The FDIC administers the Bank Insurance Fund (BIF) and Savings Association Insurance Fund (SAIF), which insure deposits at banks and S&Ls up to $100,000 per account.

FEDERAL HOME LOAN MORTGAGE CORPORATION (FHLMC): Also known as Freddie Mac. Chartered by Congress, the publicly owned company buys mortgages in the "secondary" market from banks, mortgage bankers, and S&Ls. An extremely profitable company, it occasionally sells foreclosed homes.

FEDERAL HOUSING ADMINISTRATION (FHA): A government agency charged with insuring loans for low- and moderate-income home buyers.

FEDERAL NATIONAL MORTGAGE ASSOCIATION: Also

known as Fannie Mae. Like Freddie Mac, Fannie Mae buys loans from banks, S&Ls, and mortgage bankers. It too is quite profitable but occasionally forecloses on homes and sells them.

*FF&E: "Furniture, Fixtures & Equipment"—property seized from failed banks and S&Ls and auctioned to the highest bidder.

FIDUCIARY: A person in a position of trust. An attorney has a fiduciary responsibility to the client, for example.

FINANCE CHARGE: Points, interest, and other fees paid in connection with a loan. Truth-in-lending laws require that lenders inform all borrowers in advance about all charges associated with a mortgage.

FINANCIAL STATEMENT: A complete accounting of a person's assets and liabilities. A financial statement is reflective of a person's financial condition.

FINANCING STATEMENT: A document filed with a county recorder or secretary of state giving notice that a security interest exists on a specified property.

FINDER'S FEE: A fee paid to someone who locates for another a desired property or who brings a buyer to a seller. The fee is generally a percentage of the sales price and is paid upon consummation of the sale.

FIXTURE: When a building is sold it is sold with fixtures. Fixtures are anything attached to the building. Unattached items are considered personal property.

FORECLOSURE: When a lender takes control of a property through a legal action. The RTC and FDIC often foreclose on delinquent loans to secure the underlying collateral—usually real estate.

FORECLOSURE SALE: When the trustee for the lender sells a foreclosed property at auction. The lender can bid on the outstanding balance in order to seize control of the property.

FORFEITURE: The loss of a right or interest because of default.

FREE AND CLEAR: To owe nothing on a property is to own it free and clear.

GOVERNMENT NATIONAL MORTGAGE ASSOCIATION (GNMA): A government agency that buys from lenders loans insured by the VA and FHA.

GRANT: To transfer real property. See *Grant Deed*.

GRANT DEED: Deed which transfers ownership in Real Estate.

GRANTEE: The person to whom property is granted.

GRANTOR: The person granting or conveying a property.

GROSS INCOME: Total income before expenses.

GROSS RENT MULTIPLIER: A rule-of-thumb method to determine the approximate value of a rental property. Ask a local realtor for the current gross multiplier and then multiply gross rents by that number. The resulting figure should approximate the value of the property.

GROUND LEASE: A long-term lease on vacant land. Ground leases are made with the understanding that the tenant will build on the site.

GROUND RENT: Rent charged on a ground lease.

HARD MONEY: Cash loaned, as opposed to credit extended, which is called soft money.

HAZARD INSURANCE: Insurance covering a property against damage. A lender always requires the borrower to carry insurance for at least the amount owed.

HOLDER IN DUE COURSE: A person who takes possession of a negotiable instrument, such as a note in good faith.

HYPOTHECATION: Putting up property, real or personal, as security for a loan without giving up possession.

IMPOUND ACCOUNT: An account set up as a trust account by the lender to collect monies needed to pay taxes and insurance on a property.

*INAC: An RTC abbreviation, it indicates that a property is currently inactive or not available for sale at this time.

INCOME APPROACH: A way to appraise income properties by capitalizing their income.

INCOME RATIO: A ratio of the borrower's income and housing expense. Used by lenders to determine eligibility.

INSTALLMENT NOTE: A note that is paid off in regular installments.

INSTALLMENT SALE: A method of selling property by spreading out the gain or profit over many years for income tax purposes.

INSTITUTIONAL LENDER: A lender that originates loans. Banks, savings and loans, and credit unions are all institutional lenders.

JOINT NOTE: A note that has two or more signatories who share liability.

JOINT VENTURE: When two or more people join together in a single project for profit. Unlike a partnership, a joint venture is created for investment in a single project only.

JUDGMENT: A decision made by a court. Usually the term applies to monies payable from one party to another.

JUNIOR LIEN: A loan secured by a property that already has a loan against it. The new loan is then referred to as a "second mortgage." A junior lien is subordinate to the senior, or first, mortgage.

LAND CONTRACT: A contract between a buyer and seller. The buyer contracts to pay the purchase price in regular installments. The seller contracts to sign over legal title of the property when the full purchase price has been paid.

LATE CHARGE: A penalty fee charged a borrower when the monthly payment is late.

LEASEHOLD: A property interest created by a lease agreement.

LEGAL DESCRIPTION: A description of a given property as it appears in county records.

LESSEE: The tenant under a lease agreement.

LESSOR: The landlord under a lease agreement.

LEVERAGE: A method of investing whereby the investor uses money borrowed at rates lower than the effective income a property can produce.

LIEN: An unpaid obligation against a property. Liens can be filed against a property by unpaid contractors or others with a valid claim. A court judgment is a lien.

LIEN RELEASE: A document signed by a lienholder releasing the property from the lien.

LIMITED PARTNERSHIP: A legal partnership consisting of different investors and managed by one "general" partner. Limited partnerships often are formed to invest in real estate or other businesses.

LIQUIDATION: The complete sale of a business or asset during which everything connected to that asset is sold. Insolvent S&Ls are often liquidated by the government.

*LIST PRICE: The asking price in U.S. dollars of an RTC or FDIC asset. If the RTC or FDIC has not completed its appraisal, "TBD" (to be determined) will be typed next to "Listing Price."

LOAN BROKER: Brokers who find lenders for borrowers and receive a fee for the service.

LOAN COMMITTEE: A committee at an institutional lender that reviews and approves loan applications.

LOAN CORRESPONDENT: A loan broker or agent used by a non-local lender to originate loans in a certain area.

LOAN PACKAGE: The file of documents created by, and required in, the loan approval process. Documents include the loan application, the appraisal, financial statements, and employment verifications.

LOAN-TO-VALUE RATIO: The value of the loan as a percentage of a property's price. On new loans the down payment is subtracted from the purchase price to achieve a loan-to-value ratio. When a buyer makes a 20 percent down payment the loan-to-value is said to be 80 percent. Most lenders prefer 20 percent down but will accept less if a borrower takes out a private mortgage insurance policy.

LOCK-IN CLAUSE: A clause in a mortgage that prohibits the early repayment of a loan.

*LOW- AND MODERATE-INCOME HOME BUYERS: Home buyers who earn 115 percent or less of an area's median income, the median being the point where half the people earn more and half earn less. Low- and moderate-income buyers are eligible to purchase homes from the RTC and FDIC's Affordable Housing Programs.

MAI: A professional designation for appraisers. The letters stand for Member American Institute.

MARKET PRICE: The price paid for a property on the open market by a buyer without regard to motives, market pressures, or sophistication.

MECHANIC'S LIEN: A judgment filed by a contractor to encumber a property. Mechanics' liens are filed to ensure that a contractor is paid in full. If a lien is on a house, then that home cannot be sold. When the contractor is paid, the lien is removed.

*MEDIAN HOME PRICE: The middle point where half the homes cost more and half less.

*MEDIAN INCOME: The middle point where half the people make more and half make less.

*MINORITY OR WOMAN OWNED BUSINESS (MWOB): Companies that are 51 percent minority or woman owned. MWOBs receive special consideration when bidding on RTC contracts.

*MINORITY OR WOMAN OWNED LAW FIRM (MWOLF): Same as above but for law firms.

MORTGAGE: A lien or note secured by real property—a home or office building, for example.

MORTGAGE BANKER/MORTGAGE COMPANY: A person or company that originates mortgages but does not take deposits. A mortgage company is usually "funded" by a bank or a group of investors and then immediately sells the loans into the secondary mortgage market.

MORTGAGE POOL: More than one mortgage. A series of mortgages make up a mortgage pool. Also known as a loan pool.

MORTGAGEE: The person (lender) to whom the mortgage is given.

MORTGAGOR: The borrower or person who executes the mortgage.

*MULTIFAMILY PROPERTY (MFH): FDIC and RTC-speak for an apartment building with five or more units.

NARRATIVE APPRAISAL: A descriptive appraisal that divulges details about a property, its amenities, and the reasoning behind those values.

*NATURAL VALUE: Properties considered by the RTC to have natural values or environmental or cultural significance. These include natural landmarks, wilderness areas, wildlife refuges, and wetlands, among others.

NEGOTIABLE INSTRUMENT: A check is a negotiable instrument. So is a note. Negotiable instruments can be transferred (sold) to others who then obtain their benefits.

NET SPENDABLE INCOME: That which is left from gross income after operating expenses, loan payments, and taxes are deducted.

NET WORTH: The financial worth of an individual after liabilities are deducted from gross assets.

NOMINAL INTEREST RATE: The interest rate that appears on the note or loan documents. Not to be confused with an "effective" or "true" interest rate, it does not include fees and points and other actual costs charged to the borrower.

NONJUDICIAL FORECLOSURE: A foreclosure that is effected without recourse to the courts. A foreclosure under a trust deed, which is carried out by the trustee, is a nonjudicial foreclosure.

NONPERFORMING LOAN: A mortgage that is not current—the borrower is behind in payments. Also known as a delinquent loan.

NOTARY PUBLIC: A public official who is empowered to witness signatures and administer oaths. Most recorded documents need to be signed before a notary.

NOTE: A promise to repay a loan. In a note the borrower promises to pay the beneficiary a set amount of money over a set period of time.

NOTICE OF DEFAULT: A notice filed by a lender, declaring a loan in default. Before a lender can foreclose and sell the property the notice must be published in a general circulation and the borrower informed.

OBLIGEE: The person to whom a legal obligation is owed.

OBLIGOR: The person who owes another person a legal obligation.

OFFEREE: The person to whom an offer is made.

OFFEROR: The person making an offer.

ORIGINATION FEE: A fee paid by a borrower to the lender to obtain a mortgage.

OWNER-OCCUPIED UNIT: A home or condo unit in which the mortgagor actually lives (as opposed to renting it out.)

PARTIAL RECONVEYANCE: A reconveyance that releases part of a property or subdivision as security for a loan.

PARTICIPATION: Certificates that sell like securities. Each certificate represents an interest (a participation) in a loan or venture.

PAYEE: The person to whom a note is payable.

PAYOR: The person who agrees to pay on a note. (Also known as the "maker.")

*PARTICIPATION STATUS: Often banks and S&Ls sell part of large commercial loans to other institutions in order to spread out the risk. These parts are called participations. Sometimes participations are sold in large joint venture projects. The RTC and FDIC indicate the participation status of an asset as "LD" for lead participation or "JR" for junior participation.

*PEND: Indicates that there is a pending sale on a specific asset. A pending sale is not a sale. Many pending sales fall apart before they can close. So if you are interested in a particular property that is listed as "pend," keep in touch with the RTC or FDIC until the sale closes.

PERFORMANCE BOND: A bond posted by a contractor that guarantees completion of a project according to pre-agreed-upon conditions.

PERSONAL PROPERTY: Property that is not real property. Personal property is movable and is also called "chattel."

*PITA LOANS: Pain-in-the-ass loans—usually small or odd loans that are difficult for the RTC or FDIC to service. The government wants to get rid of these as soon as possible.

PMI: Private Mortgage Insurance.

POINT: One percent of the principal amount of a loan charged by the lender to increase the effective interest rate of the loan. Points are charged when a loan is made or renewed.

POWER OF ATTORNEY: A document authorizing one person to act for another.

POWER-OF-SALE CLAUSE: The clause in a trust deed mortgage that gives the trustee authority to sell a property that is security for a loan in the event of default.

PRELIMINARY TITLE REPORT: A report, generally required by lenders, that shows the condition of a property's title, including all liens.

PREPAYMENT CLAUSE: A clause in a mortgage that allows the borrower to pay the loan off before its due date without penalty.

PREPAYMENT PENALTY: A clause in a mortgage that charges the borrower a penalty for paying a loan off early.

PRIVATE MORTGAGE INSURANCE: An insurance policy taken out by a borrower to insure that he or she will not default on a high loan-to-value ratio mortgage.

PROGRESSION: An appraisal concept that says a building of lower value can be increased in value by its proximity to a higher-quality building.

PROMISSORY NOTE: A promise to pay back a specified loan amount on specified terms at a specified time. This note may be secured or unsecured. If secured by real estate it will be secured by a trust deed.

*PROPERTY CONDITION: The FDIC and RTC describe on their asset lists a property's physical condition. The condition is listed as P for poor, F for fair, G for good, and E for excellent. On newly acquired assets this information may not be available. In such cases the agencies may default to a simple n/a rating.

PRORATION: If you buy a property three months into a tax year the property taxes will be "prorated" to reflect this. The seller will pay for the three months of the year it owned the property and you will pay for the remaining nine months. This is how prorating works. It applies to many period costs associated with a property. Not only taxes can be prorated, but loan payments, insurance, annual condo maintenance fees, and so on.

PURCHASE MONEY DEED OF TRUST: This is a mortgage. In some states, such as California, the law protects a borrower from "deficiency judgments" when money is borrowed under a purchase money deed of trust to buy real estate.

QUIET TITLE ACTION: For many reasons a property's chain of title may have a "cloud" over it. This means that somewhere along the line of ownership somebody either forgot to file a document clearing an old loan or easement or ownership. The people who need to sign to clear up such a defect may be long dead or otherwise unavailable. To clear up such a cloud on title you file a court action called a "quiet title action." You should require the seller to do this at his or her expense before you buy the property. Lenders will not loan on a property with a defective title.

REAL ESTATE SETTLEMENT PROCEDURES ACT: Professionals refer to this federal law simply as RESPA. The law requires a number of things and forbids others. For example, it forbids lenders paying realtors kickbacks for sending borrowers to them. It also requires lenders to provide borrowers with specific information about their loan.

REAL ESTATE INVESTMENT TRUST: An investment fund collateralized by real estate or loans. The RTC plans to offer REITs to investors beginning sometime in 1993.

REALTOR: Another name for a real estate broker.

RECAPTURE: The time it takes for an investor to "recapture" an initial investment in income property.

*RECEIVERSHIP: An RTC receivership consists solely of all assets from a failed S&L or bank that have been slated for liquidation. Receiverships are closed to the public and, unlike conservatorships, do not take deposits.

RECONVEYANCE DEED: When you pay off a note secured by a trust deed, the lender files a "deed of reconveyance." This reconveys the title in the property from the trustee to you and acknowledges to the public record that the loan has been paid in full.

RECORDATION: Any document recorded for the public record at the county recorder's office.

REDEMPTION: When a property is foreclosed on, the owner has a "redemption period"—a period of time during which he or she can bring the loan current, including penalties, and redeem the property.

REFINANCE: To take out a new mortgage on an existing property that you already own.

REGRESSION: The opposite of progression. If you build an expensive house in a neighborhood where other homes cost less, the other homes reduce the value of your home.

REINSTATEMENT: Curing a default under a deed of trust.

RELEASE CLAUSE: A clause in a deed of trust that allows for the release of portions of a property upon the meeting of specified conditions. Release clauses are often used in subdivisions.

RELEASE OF MORTGAGE: Also called a "certificate of discharge." It releases a lien or mortgage on a property.

REPLACEMENT COST: An estimate of what it would cost to reproduce an existing structure. Replacement cost is used as part of the appraisal process.

*REQUEST FOR PROPOSAL (RFP): A notice sent by the FDIC to registered thirty-party contractors when the agency solicits work that it cannot do in house. The RTC equivalent is an SOS, or solicitation of services.

REQUEST FOR RECONVEYANCE: A request made by a

trustee under a deed of trust for a reconveyance from the lender when a loan is repaid.

*RESOLUTION TRUST CORPORATION (RTC): The federal agency created by Congress in 1989 to resolve and sell the nation's insolvent S&Ls (thrifts). RTC assets are overseen and sold by its fourteen consolidated offices.

*RTC CONTRACTOR OR ASSET MANAGER: A third-party, nongovernment company that performs contract work for the RTC or FDIC—usually real estate or loan managers. Also known as a "contract agent."

*RTCNET: The RTC's on-line computer data base. Anyone with a personal computer can access information on available real estate and loans.

*SAMDA: Standard asset management and disposition agreement.

*SAMDA CONTRACTOR: Thirty-party contractors that manage and sell real estate and loans for the government are known as SAMDA contractors.

*SAMA: Standard asset management agreement.

*SAMA CONTRACTOR: SAMA contractors are paid only to manage, not sell, RTC assets.

SALE-LEASEBACK: When a property owner sells his or her property and then leases it back from the new owner.

SATISFACTION: When a party to a contract performs on all terms of the contract, the party is said to have "satisfied" his or her obligation.

*SCIENTIFIC VALUE: RTC properties of scientific significance or archeological importance.

SEASONED LOAN: A loan that is more than five years old is considered seasoned. Most have a steady payment history and are desirable to companies that service loans.

SECONDARY FINANCING: A junior loan, usually a second mortgage.

SECURITY: Collateral that is pledged to secure a loan.

SECURITY AGREEMENT: A document securing interest in personal, rather than real, property.

SECURITY DEPOSIT: A sum of money put up by a tenant to secure the condition of the property or terms of a lease.

SHORT-FORM APPRAISAL: An appraisal that uses a check-off sheet rather than a running commentary.

SIGNATURE LOAN: A loan secured only by a borrower's signature.

SIMPLE INTEREST: Interest paid only on the principal, not on accrued interest already paid or owed—as opposed to compound interest.

SOCIAL OBSOLESCENCE: Also known as "economic obsolescence." Refers to a structure that has outlived its social or economic usefulness. A blacksmith's shop would be a good example.

SOFT MONEY LOAN: When a portion of the loan is held by the seller to facilitate the sale of a property. If the seller provides cash it as known as a hard money loan.

*SOLICITATION OF SERVICES (SOS): A notice sent to registered third-party contractors when the RTC needs work done by a private management firm—usually for real estate or loan management services. (See Standard Asset Management Disposition Agreement and Request for Proposal.)

*SPEC: An RTC abbreviation on property listings that indicates that a particular asset has "special significance," meaning it could be environmentally sensitive or have some type of cultural or scientific value.

STRAIGHT NOTE: A note under which the principal amount is due in a lump sum at a specified time rather than in periodic payments.

SUBJECT TO: If you acquire a property with existing financing, then you are acquiring the property "subject to" existing obligations. A property may be subject to many forms of encumbrances, such as easements, besides financing.

SUBORDINATE: If you have a first loan on a property and agree to allow the buyer to bring a new first loan in front of your loan, you have agreed to "subordinate" your loan to the new one. Your loan will still be secured by the property but will be junior to the new first.

SUBSTITUTION: An appraisal term that says if you have two identical properties the one sporting the lowest price will receive the greatest demand. The buyer will "substitute" the cheaper one for the more expensive property.

SUBSTITUTION OF MORTGAGOR: Where a lender agrees to allow a buyer to assume an existing loan.

TAKE-OUT LOAN: Permanent financing for a property. A construction loan is a short-term loan. When a property is completed the owner then seeks long-term financing, called a take-out loan.

TAX-FREE EXCHANGE: If you sell a property at a profit you will be taxed on that profit as ordinary income. But if you swap the property for one of a "like kind" (an apartment house, for example), you will not be taxed on the exchange value.

TERM: The length of a loan, contract, or lease.

TERMINATION STATEMENT: A release of lien on personal property.

TIMESHARE: Instead of owning a property outright, timeshares allow you to own anywhere from two weeks to two months of a single unit—usually an apartment unit. These apply strictly to resort and vacation properties.

THRIFT INSTITUTION: Another name for an S&L.

TITLE INSURANCE: Protects the buyer and lender against unknown defects in title.

TRADING ON EQUITY: Borrowing against a property at rates lower than your anticipated net income from the property.

TRUSTEE: A person who holds title to real property until the loan is paid off.

TRUSTEE'S SALE: The sale of a property at foreclosure under a trust deed.

TRUSTOR: The person conveying property to a trustee.

UNLAWFUL DETAINER ACTION: A legal action taken to quickly recover possession of real property. It is used by landlords, for example, when a tenant fails to pay rent and refuses to leave.

VETERAN'S ADMINISTRATION LOAN: A loan backed by the Veteran's Administration. The government guarantee is reflected by a lower interest rate.

VARIABLE INTEREST RATE: Same as an Adjustable Rate Mortgage. The interest rate increases or decreases according to a predetermined index.

VESTING OF TITLE: Taking or receiving title to a property.

VOLUNTARY LIEN: A lien placed against a property intentionally by its owner to secure an obligation.

WAIVE: To give up something. To waive a right or privilege.

WRAP-AROUND LOAN: A loan in which two or more mortgages—usually a seasoned loan and a newer one—encumber a property and are wrapped into one. This is often done when a seller does not want to pay off a first mortgage because it may carry a big prepayment penalty. Instead the seller creates a new loan, leaving the old one intact. The seller continues to make payments on the first from payments he or she receives from the buyer on the new note.

YIELD: The interest rate earned by a lender on a mortgage. It also applies to the interest rate an investor receives on a note or investment.

Yellow Pages

. . . .

THE RESOLUTION TRUST CORPORATION

Resolution Trust Corporation, Washington, D.C. (Main headquarters)
801 17th St. N.W.
Washington, D.C. 20434

(202) 416-7600
(202) 416-7566 (public affairs)

REGIONAL OFFICES OF THE RTC (AS OF 1/94)

Western Region

Intermountain Consolidated Office
1515 Arapahoe St.
Tower 3, Suite 800
Denver, CO 80202

(303) 556-6500
(303) 556-6552 (FAX)

Territory: Utah, Colorado, New Mexico

Coastal Consolidated Office
400 MacArthur Blvd.
Newport Beach, CA 92660

(714) 852-7700
(714) 852-7775 (FAX)

Kansas City Consolidated Office
Board of Trade Building II
4900 Main Street
Kansas City, MO 64112

(816) 531-2212
(816) 531-3017 (FAX)

Northeast Consolidated Office
Valley Forge Corporate Center
1000 Adams Avenue
Valley Forge, PA 19482

(215) 650-8500
(215) 650-8550 (FAX)

Mid-Atlantic Consolidated Office
Colony Square
Building 100, Suite 2300
Atlanta, GA 30361

(404) 881-4840
(404) 881-4999 (FAX)

NATIONAL RTC AND REGIONAL SALES CENTERS

The RTC has centralized sales centers that provide investors with information and assistance on large commercial properties and loan sales and auctions.

National Sales Center
1133 21st Street, N.W.
Washington, D.C. 20036

(202) 416-4200

Additional Sales Center Locations

Dallas (Southwestern) Regional Sales Center
300 North Ervay
24th Floor
Dallas, TX 75201

(214) 953-4673

Denver (Western Regional) Sales Center
1225 17th St.
Suite 3200
Denver, CO 80202

(303) 291-5700
(303) 556-6500

RTC AFFORDABLE HOUSING CONTACTS

The following telephone numbers are for RTC affordable housing specialists who work out of the agency's regional and consolidated offices. These specialists will tell you what properties are being offered for sale and whether you qualify for any of the available units. They also can inform you about the different types of financing that are available.

Arizona
(602) 224-1776 (Phoenix)
(800) 937-7782

California
(714) 631-8600 (Costa Mesa)
(800) 283-9288

Colorado
(303) 556-6500 (Denver)
(800) 873-5815

Florida
(813) 870-7000 (Tampa)
(800) 283-1241

Georgia
(404) 225-5600 (Atlanta)
(800) 628-4362

Illinois
(708) 806-7750 (Elk Grove Village)
(800) 526-7521

Louisiana
(504) 339-1000 (Baton Rouge)
(800) 477-8790

Minnesota
(612) 683-4400 (Eagan)
(800) 873-5815

Missouri
(816) 531-2212 (Kansas City)
(800) 365-3342

New Jersey
(908) 805-4000 (Somerset)
(800) 431-0600

Oklahoma
(918) 587-7600 (Tulsa)
(800) 456-5382

Pennsylvania
(215) 650-8500 (Norristown)
(800) 782-6326

Texas
Dallas
(214) 443-2300
(800) 782-4674

Houston
(713) 888-2700
(800) 782-4221

San Antonio
(512) 524-4700
(800) 388-4254

Washington, D.C. (RTC Main Headquarters)
801 17th St.
6th Floor
Washington, D.C. 20434

(202) 416-6995
(202) 416-7219

"QUICK-DEX": COMMONLY CALLED RTC TELEPHONE NUMBERS

National Sales Center, Washington, D.C. (202) 416-4200

Real Estate Information Center and Orders for Asset Inventory
(800) 431-0600

Asset Specific Inquiry Service (800) 732-3006

Bulk Sales Information (800) 782-8806

Sales of Mortgage and Investment Securities (202) 416-7544

Office of Third Party Contracts (800) 541-1782

Contracting Information Packets (202) 416-6940

Office of Contractor Oversight (202) 416-7592

Contract Administration (202) 416-2192

Low Income and Affordable Housing Information (202) 416-7348

Public Affairs and Media (202) 416-7566

FEDERAL DEPOSIT INSURANCE CORPORATION

REGIONAL OFFICES OF THE FDIC

Chicago Regional Office (Alabama, Arkansas, Delaware, District of Columbia, Florida, Georgia, Illinois, Indiana, Iowa, Kansas, Kentucky, Louisiana, Maryland, Michigan, Minnesota, Mississippi, Missouri, Nebraska, North Carolina, North Dakota, Ohio, South Carolina, South Dakota, Tennessee, Virginia, West Virginia, Wisconsin)
30 South Wacher Drive
32nd Floor
Chicago, IL 60606

(312) 207-0200

Dallas Regional Office (Oklahoma, Texas)
1910 Pacific Ave. #1700
Dallas, TX 75201

(214) 754-0098

New York Regional Office (Connecticut, Maine, Massachusetts,
New Hampshire, New York, Pennsylvania, Rhode Island,
Vermont, Puerto Rico, Virgin Islands)
452 5th Avenue—21st Floor
New York, NY 10018

(212) 704-1200

San Francisco Regional Office (Alaska, Arizona, California,
Colorado, Guam, Hawaii, Idaho, Montana, Nevada, New Mexico,
Oregon, Utah, Washington, Wyoming)
25 Ecker St., Suite 1900
San Francisco, CA 94105

(415) 546-1810

CONSOLIDATED OFFICES OF THE **FDIC**

Consolidated Offices of the Chicago Regional Office

Atlanta Consolidated Office
285 Peachtree Center Avenue NE
Marquis Building Tower II, Suite 300
Atlanta, GA 30303

(404) 880-3000

O'Hare Consolidated Office
9525 West Bryn Mawr
Suite 300
Rosemont, IL 60018

(708) 671-8800

Orlando Consolidated Office
5778 South Semoran Blvd.
Orlando, FL 32822

(407) 273-2230

Consolidated Offices of the Dallas Regional Office

Addison Consolidated Office
14651 Dallas Parkway
Suite 200
Dallas, TX 752450

(214) 239-3317

Houston Consolidated Office
7324 Southwest Freeway
Suite 1600
Arena Tower #2
Houston, TX 77074

(713) 270-6565

Dallas Consolidated Office
5080 Spectrum Dr.
Suite 1000E
Dallas, TX 75248

(214) 701-2400

Midland Consolidated Office
N. Petroleum Building
303 Air Park Dr.
Midland, TX 79705

(915) 685-6400

San Antonio Consolidated Office
4440 Piedras Dr. South
San Antonio, TX 78228

(512) 731-2000

Consolidated Offices of the New York Region

South Brunswick Consolidated Office
Cornwall Rd.
Jersey Center Metroplex
Monmouth, NJ 08852

(201) 422-9000

Franklin Consolidated Office
124 Grove St.
Franklin, MA 02038

(508) 520-7250

Hartford Consolidated Office
111 Founders Place
East Hartford, CT 06108

(203) 244-4571

Consolidated Offices of the San Francisco Regional Office

Irvine Consolidated Office
3347 Michelson Dr.
Irvine, CA 92715

(714) 975-5400

Denver Consolidated Office
707 17th St.
Suite 3000
Denver, CO 80202

(303) 296-4703

Anchorage Consolidated Office
440 East 36 Avenue
Anchorage, AK 99503

(907) 261-7400

FDIC ORE (OWNED REAL ESTATE) SALES CENTERS

The FDIC has six regional sales centers that market and sell commercial real estate valued at $1 million or greater. They are located at the consolidated offices based in Atlanta; Franklin, Massachusetts; and Orlando for the Eastern U.S.; Dallas for the Southwestern part of the country; Denver for the Mountain states; and Irvine, California for the West Coast. These offices are similar in nature to the RTC national and regional sales centers.

FDIC AFFORDABLE HOUSING PROGRAM (AFH)

The FDIC AFH program is still in its infancy. Initial inquiries should be made to the FDIC headquarters in Washington at:

550 17th St. N.W.
Washington, D.C. 20429

(202) 393-8400

NATIONAL AUCTION COMPANIES THAT SELL LOANS AND REAL ESTATE FOR THE RTC AND FDIC

Hudson & Marshall
717 North Avenue
Macon, GA 31298

(912) 743-1511 (Macon)
(800) 842-9401 (Atlanta, toll free)

JBS Associates
200 North LaSalle St.
Chicago, IL 60601

(312) 701-0777

Ross-Dove & Co.
330 Hatch Drive
Foster City, CA 94404

(415) 571-4700

Yellow Pages note: All auction companies offer free brochures on real estate, loans, and furniture, fixtures, and equipment (FF&E) that is available to purchase. To get a listing, just pick up the telephone (most auction companies have toll-free telephone numbers) and ask. Auction companies are more than happy to supply you with listings.

REAL ESTATE

The listing below is alphabetical. Some companies, acting as "realtors" for the RTC, just sell properties; some companies just auction, while others do both. Many real estate and auction companies working for the RTC and FDIC offer properties on a national basis, meaning that a Virginia-based company can offer properties located in Southern California, Texas, Louisiana, or elsewhere.

There are thousands of realtors who sell properties for the RTC and FDIC. We decided to limit our listing to the large regional and national realtors and auction firms. We list only their corporate headquarters.

REAL ESTATE AND AUCTION COMPANIES

Atlanta Auctions Inc.
20 Park Ave.
Baltimore, MD 21201

(410) 752-5300 (Baltimore)
(800) 345-2628 (toll free)

Century 21
2601 East Main Street
Irvine, CA 92714

(714) 553-2100

Coldwell Banker
1953 Gallows Road
Suite 340
Vienna, VA 22182

(703) 556-6100

Cushman & Wakefield
300 South Grand
Suite 3750
Los Angeles, CA 90017

(800) 676-6798

Grubb & Ellis
One Montgomery St.
Ninth Floor
San Francisco, CA 94104

(415) 433-1050

J.E. Robert & Co., Inc.
11 Canal Center
Alexandria, VA 22314

(703) 739-4440

NRC Auctions
720 North Franklin St.
Suite 400
Chicago, IL 60610

(312) 642-7900

RE/MAX
5445 DTC Parkway
Suite 1200
Englewood, CO 80111

(303) 770-5531

Sheldon Good & Co.
333 West Wacker Dr.
Chicago, IL 60606

(312) 346-1500

DEPARTMENT OF HOUSING AND URBAN DEVELOPMENT (HUD)

HUD sells foreclosed homes, condos, co-ops, and apartment buildings through its 10 regional and 80 field offices. Most of the action is at the regional level.

REGIONAL OFFICES

Boston Regional Office
Thomas P. O'Neill Federal Bldg.
10 Causeway St., Room 375
Boston, MA 02222

(617) 565-5234

New York Regional Office
26 Federal Plaza
New York, NY 10278

(212) 264-8068

Philadelphia Regional Office
105 South Seventh St.
Philadelphia, PA 19106

(215) 597-2560

Atlanta Regional Office
Richard B. Russell Federal Building
75 Spring St. S.W.
Atlanta, GA 30303

(404) 331-5136

Chicago Regional Office
626 West Jackson Blvd.
Chicago, IL 60606

(312) 353-5680

Fort Worth Consolidated Office
1600 Throckmorton
P.O. Box 2905
Ft. Worth, TX 76113

(817) 885-5401

Kansas City Regional Office
Professional Building
1103 Grand Ave.
Kansas City, MO 64106

(816) 374-6432

Denver Regional Office
Executive Tower Bldg.
1405 Curtis St.
Denver, CO 80202

(303) 844-4513

San Francisco Regional Office
405 Golden Gate Ave.
P.O. Box 36003
San Francisco, CA 94102

(415) 556-4752

Seattle Regional Office
1321 Second St.
Seattle, WA 98101

(206) 442-5414

FEDERAL NATIONAL MORTGAGE ASSOCIATION—FANNIE MAE

FNMA—Fannie Mae as it is known—is a large, well-operated congressionally chartered company that buys mortgages from S&Ls and banks. Although it is quite profitable, it too gets stuck with millions of dollars worth of bad loans that it must foreclose on and sell. Anyone with cash or financing is eligible to buy real estate from Fannie Mae. The same holds true of the Federal Home Loan Mortgage Corporation (FHLMC), commonly referred to as Freddie Mac.

Main Headquarters
3900 Wisconsin Ave. N.W.
Washington, D.C. 20016

(202) 752-8400

Midwestern Regional Office
One South Wacker Dr.
Suite 3100
Chicago, IL 60606

(312) 368-6201

Northeastern Regional Office
510 Walnut Street
16th Floor
Philadelphia, PA 19106

(215) 575-1421

Southeastern Regional Office
950 East Paces Ferry Road
Atlanta, GA 30326

(404) 365-6079

Southwestern Regional Office
Two Galleria Tower
13455 Noel Road
Suite 600
Dallas, TX 75240

(214) 770-7663

Western Regional Office
135 North Los Robles Ave.
Suite 300
Pasadena, CA 91101

(818) 568-5170

FEDERAL HOME LOAN MORTGAGE CORPORATION—FREDDIE MAC

Main Headquarters
8200 Jones Branch Drive
McLean, VA 22102

(703) 903-2000

Northeast Regional Office
2231 Crystal Dr.
Suite 900
Arlington, VA 22202

(703) 685-4500

North Central Regional Office
333 West Wacker Drive
Suite 3100
Chicago, IL 60606

(312) 407-7400

Southeast/Southwest Regional Office
2839 Paces Ferry Rd. N.W.
Suite 700
Atlanta, GA 30339

(404) 438-3800

Western Regional Office
15303 Ventura Blvd.
Suite 200
Sherman Oaks, CA 91403

(818) 905-0070

FEDERAL HOME LOAN BANK SYSTEM

The FHLB system consists of 12 Federal Home Loan Banks. It was chartered by Congress during the Depression to provide liquidity to the savings and loans. Although it does not sell real estate, it provides financing to home buyers and investors who purchase affordable housing units from the RTC and FDIC.

PUBLICATIONS

A number of news organizations cover the RTC and FDIC on a regular basis. Some, including the *Bank Resolution Reporter, Resolution Trust Reporter*, and *Thrift Liquidation Alert* regularly list available properties and auction dates. Among the best ones:

SPECIFIC COVERAGE

Bank Resolution Reporter (26 issues per year)
Dorset Group Inc.
225 West 34th St.
Suite 918
New York, NY 10122

(212) 563-4405
(212) 564-8879 (Fax)

Price: $348 to $398 per year

Resolution Trust Reporter (26 issues per year)
The address, phone, and price are the same as above

Thrift Liquidation Alert (50 issues per year)
One Riverfront Plaza
Suite 1480
Newark, NJ 07102

(201) 596-1300
(201) 596-0148 (Fax)

Price: $629 per year

GENERAL AND OCCASIONAL COVERAGE

American Banker (daily newspaper, except weekends and holidays)
One State Street Plaza
New York, NY 10004

(212) 943-6700

National Mortgage News
212 W. 35th St.
Suite 1300
New York, NY 10001

(212) 563-4008

Wall Street Journal (daily newspaper except weekends and holidays)
200 Liberty Street
New York, NY 10281

(212) 416-2000

Index